CHICAGO 365

INTRIGUING EVENTS FROM EACH DAY OF THE YEAR

JOE SONDERMAN

STELLAR PRESS - ST. LOUIS, MISSOURI

Chicago 365
by Joe Sonderman

ISBN   1-932860-02-9

Printed in the United States of America

Published and distributed by:

Stellar Press
634 N. Grand Boulevard, Suite 10 C
St. Louis, Missouri 63103
877-572-8835 (toll-free)
www.StellarPress.com
e-mail: info@StellarPress.com

Dedication

For Lorraine, Cathy and Kim. For Kimberly, Cory & Mindy Powell.

Acknowledgements

Ken Christian and the staff at Stellar Press for their creativity. Everyone at KMOX, particularly Tom Langmyer, John Butler, Steve Moore and Kevin Killeen. John Pertzborn and Randi Naughton. The entire Gateway Guide team for their help and encouragement, Bo Sanders, Chris Teague, Jill Crocker, Tom Miller, Theresa Krenning.

Chicago 365
Intriguing Events from Each Day of the Year
Table of Contents

Introduction

This is a different kind of history book. Some of the greatest writers in the world have documented the history of this great city. But they tend to write for scholars and other historians. I wanted to put together a book for the average person. I do not claim to be a professional historian or even an average writer. I am someone who is interested in the stories that make Chicago what it is today. You won't find lengthy dissertations or social analysis inside these pages. You won't find a single footnote.

Of all the histories written about Chicago, none has taken a day-by-day approach. You can start out by seeing what happened on the day you were born and then go from there. This book won't be discussed in an expensive college, but I hope it will be used to settle arguments in bars. Or better yet, maybe some one will start an argument. We searched for more pop culture oriented items and events that we all will remember.

All of the familiar names are here. The same city that gave us Jane Addams also gave us Al Capone. This is the city that housed the world's most lavish brothel, and yet boasts one of the great symphonies. There are stories about the skyscrapers and the stockyards, the authors, the artists and the sports heroes. Of course, the politicians and the criminals could fill a book on their own. Our modern pop culture, movies, music, television and radio are a part of history too.

I confess that I am not from Chicago. I am from St. Louis. Chicago gives us an inferiority complex. We were once the bigger city, but our shortsighted leaders allowed Chicago to take over. When I started out writing books about St. Louis history, I saw how more than just Route 66 links us. Marquette and Joliet passed by the sites of both cities. Both of our World's Fairs are considered shining moments. Our mobsters schemed with yours and our architects dreamed with yours. Your airport is named after a St. Louisan. Both cities have contributed more than their share of great musicians and sports figures. And, of course, there is the best rivalry in baseball and the great home run race of 1998.

But the history of Chicago overwhelms St. Louis. We had one World's Fair. You had two. (Three if you count both years of the Century of Progress) You've had two baseball teams for over a century. We had just over 25 years of mediocre football with the Big Red and the Rams arrived just 10 years ago. Chicago boasts the most storied football franchise in history. Forget about basketball. I also found that disasters and joyous occasions happen on a bigger scale in Chicago. I was astonished at the horror of the Great Fire, the Iroquois Theater and the Eastland but thrilled by the story of those who reversed a river and built Millenium Park. And I have to admit; your politicians are certainly more colorful, the buildings are taller and the pizza is better.

Flipping through each day, you will learn about the names that made Chicagoland great, how communities were founded, and how the roads you drive everyday were named. In the interest of brevity, I have probably left some items out that a historian might find essential. There are probably some items that would give an English major night sweats. Local history can be hard to pin down. In the instances of multiple sources giving different dates, I tried to reconcile it with newspaper files. Any errors are entirely my fault. For me, writing this book was like a great treasure hunt. It was fascinating to turn up stories I had never heard before. I hope reading it will give you the same experience. If this book whets your appetite to learn more about your great city, then I've done my job.

- Joe Sonderman, 2004

January

January 1

1858   Chicago policemen were required to wear uniforms for the first time. Later in 1858, voters would elect John Haines as Mayor of Chicago. Haines owned part of a Michigan copper mine, and his opponents tagged him with the nickname "copper stock." His men became known as "coppers."

1869   The first vehicle tunnel beneath the Chicago River was completed at Washington Street. The tunnel was necessary because, as river traffic grew heavier, the bridges would remain raised for long periods of time and cause massive traffic jams. The first tunnel was 1,605 feet long and cost $517,000. It remained in use until 1953.

1890   Chicago officially became "The Second City." The results of the 1890 census showed a population of 1,099,850, a 119% increase from 1880. Chicago was now second only to New York. The city had just annexed a 120-square mile area, but most of the new arrivals were immigrants from Europe. They made up 40% of the city's population.

1951   Bushman the gorilla died. In June 1950, 120,000 thousand people had flocked to the Lincoln Park Zoo in a single day to see the largest gorilla in captivity when he first became ill. He recovered enough to escape from his cage in October 1950. Bushman wandered around for a bit before a garter snake scared him back to the cage.

January 2

1900   The waters of the Chicago River were reversed and began flowing west. It took eight years for thousands of men to dig the 28-mile long Sanitary and Ship Canal, the largest earth-moving project in the world at the time. The canal began carrying the polluted water to the Des Plaines River at Lockport and then to the Illinois River. St. Louis, fearing pollution of the Mississippi, lost a legal battle to halt construction.

1928   Daniel David Rostenkowski was born in Chicago. Rostenkowski served as U.S. Congressman from 1959 to 1995. As chairman of the Ways and Means Committee from 1980 to 1994, he was the most powerful man in Congress. In 1994, Rostenkowski was indicted on corruption charges. He lost his bid for re-election and served 17 months for mail fraud. President Clinton pardoned him in 2000.

1999 Chicago recorded its greatest single-day snowfall total as 18.6 inches fell. Traffic came to a halt as drifts piled up to four-feet high. A total of 21.3 inches fell across the Chicago Metro Area during the three-day storm, making it the biggest winter storm ever. Five deaths were blamed on the blizzard.

January 3

1929 William S. Paley, the 27-year-old son of a Chicago cigar merchant, became president of CBS. He bought the struggling company for $400,000 and quickly started turning a profit. Paley foresaw the impact of television, and CBS began network broadcasts in 1939.
Paley brought Lucille Ball, Ed Sullivan, Edward R. Murrow and Walter Cronkite to television.

1939 Bobby Hull was born in Point Anne, Ontario. The "Golden Jet" was the first NHL player to score more than 50 goals in one season. He did it five times. His 604 goals still stands as the most ever by a Blackhawks' player. Hull added another 304 goals while playing in the WHA. He was elected to the Hockey Hall of Fame in 1983.

1967 Jack Ruby, born Jacob Rubinstein in Chicago in 1911, died of a pulmonary embolism in prison. At the time of his death, Ruby was awaiting a retrial for killing Lee Harvey Oswald, the man accused of assassinating President John F. Kennedy. The Texas Supreme Court had ruled Ruby didn't receive a fair trial due to publicity in Dallas.

January 4

1896 Everett McKinley Dirksen was born in Pekin, Illinois. Dirksen was one of the most powerful senators of the 1950's and 60's. He served as Republican Whip and became Senate Minority Leader, helping secure passage of the Nuclear Test Ban Treaty and the 1964 Civil Rights Act. In 1967, his "Gallant Men" won a Grammy for best documentary recording. Dirksen died after surgery for lung cancer in 1969.

1967 Opera star Mary Garden died. She was the prima donna of Chicago opera for two decades. In 1910, her sensual portrayal of *Salome* caused the production to be cancelled after two sell-out performances. The Chief of Police said "Miss Garden wallowed around like a cat in a bed of catnip." Although he never saw the production, the head of the Law and Order League said the opera should be "suppressed along with houses in the red light district."

1977 Mary Shane became the first female play-by-play announcer in Major League history when she was hired to call the White Sox games on WSNS television. Shane struggled and didn't last very long.

January 5

1916 Charles Weegham, owner of the Chicago Whales of the defunct Federal League, purchased the Cubs from Charles P. Taft. Chewing gum magnate William Wrigley Junior bought $50,000 in stock. The Cubs moved to to Weegham Park, constructed in 1914 as the home of the Whales. The Wrigley family bought the team in 1920 and changed the name of the stadium to Cubs Field, then Wrigley Field in 1926.

1957 CBS broadcast the first network television hockey game and introduced the character "Peter Puck." The Rangers beat the Blackhawks 4-1. The broadcast was blacked out in Chicago. No local sponsors were interested in the rights to a game featuring the last place Hawks and owner Arthur Wirtz wasn't interested in his team appearing on television.

1960 Ada Everleigh died in Roanoke, Virginia. From 1900 to 1911, Ada and her sister Minna ran the most famous and elegant brothel in America. After Mayor Carter Harrison shut down the Everleigh Club, Ada and Minna left town with over $1 million and lived quiet lives in New York. Ada moved to Virginia when Minna died in 1948. The Hilliard Homes stands on the site of the Everleigh Club today.

January 6

1828 "The Father of Chicago" died at the age of 65. John Kinzie was the city's first permanent white settler, having arrived in 1804. Kinzie traded furs and caused trouble by selling booze to the Indians. He killed a business rival in a brawl but was acquitted. Kinzie was captured in the 1812 massacre near Fort Dearborn, but survived due to the intervention of Billy Caldwell, a half-breed also known as Chief Sauganash.

1878 Poet Carl Sandburg was born in Galesburg. The former hobo became nationally known in 1914, when his work was published in *Poetry* Magazine and his *Chicago Poems* was released in 1916. "Chicago" described the city as "Hog butcher for the world, tool maker, stacker of wheat, player with railroads and the nation's freight handler; stormy, husky, brawling, City of the Big Shoulders."

1879 Joseph Medill Patterson was born. The grandson of the founder of the *Chicago Tribune* invented the comic strip "Andy Gump" in 1917. He went on to found the *New York Daily News*. While head of the Tribune Syndicate, Patterson gave Dick Tracy his name, and changed the name of the character "Little Orphan Otto" to "Little Orphan Annie."

1917 A banner headline in the *Chicago Defender* read "Millions to Leave South." The nation's leading black newspaper described Chicago as "The Promised Land," where jobs were available for blacks longing to escape poverty and racism. The *Defender* launched the "Great Migration" that led to over 110,000 blacks moving to Chicago in just two years. A second wave followed the Great Depression and World War Two.

January 7

1927 A group of basketball players who started out as the Giles Post American Legion Team played their first game under a new name. Abe Saperstein founded the team, which consisted of Tommy Brookings, William Grant, Inman Jackson, Lester Johnson, Joe Lillard, Randolph Ramsey, Walter Wright and William Watson. Before a crowd of 300 in Hinckley, Illinois, they made their debut as the Harlem Globetrotters.

1946 Six-year-old Suzanne Degnan disappeared from her home. Her body parts were discovered in the sewers. When arrested in the Degnan case, William Heirens admitted he was also the "Lipstick Killer," who killed Frances Brown and Josephine Ross in 1945. The killer had scrawled "For heaven's sake, catch me before I kill more" in lipstick on Brown's wall. Many believe Chicago Police beat a confession out of Heirens.

Chicago 365

1949 The NBC owned and operated television station in Chicago began regular programming on Channel 5. "These Are My Children" was one of the first shows on WNBQ. Irna Phillips wrote the first daytime serial in the history of television. A few days later, WNBQ began beaming "Kukla, Fran and Ollie" to the NBC network. Also in 1949, Dave Garroway made his debut with "Garroway at Large."

1954 McKinley Morganfield welcomed studio bass player and composer Willie Dixon to a recording session at 2120 South Michigan Avenue. Morganfield was better known as "Muddy Waters," and his work with Dixon made Chess Records the most legendary blues label of all time. They would team up on classics such as "Hoochie Coochie Man," "I Just Want to Make Love to You" and "You Shook Me."

January 8

1923 The Village of Shermerville changed its name to Northbrook. The name comes from the West Fork of the North Branch of the Chicago River. Northbrook is famous for some fictional characters. It's the home of Shadowcat in the WB TV show "X-Men: Evolution" and Glenbrook High School served as a location for filming the movie *The Breakfast Club*.

1969 Robert S. Kelly was born in Chicago. He grew up poor, singing on the streets and trains for money. A record label representative discovered him singing at a friend's barbecue. As R. Kelly, he scored huge hits such as "I Believe I Can Fly." But he may be best known for his relationships with underage women. He married Aaliyah when she was just 15 and was indicted on child pornography charges in 2002.

1991 Ferguson Jenkins was elected to the Baseball Hall of Fame. He is one of only two men to be inducted into both the U.S. and Canadian halls. Jackie Robinson is the other. Jenkins pitched for the Cubs from 1966 to 1973, winning the NL Cy Young Award in 1971. He managed an impressive 3.34 lifetime ERA, despite spending much of his career in hitter's ball parks like Wrigley Field and Boston's Fenway Park.

1993 Five employees and the two owners were killed at the Brown's Chicken and Pasta Restaurant at Northwest Highway and Smith Road in Palatine. The crime was never solved, due to bickering between agencies in a regional task force. PR Stones Gang member Reynaldo Aviles confessed to the crime, but was found dead in his jail cell in May 1993. His death was ruled a suicide, despite evidence of murder.

January 9

1901 Murat Bernard Young was born in Chicago. He grew up in St. Louis, where the 1919 McKinley High School yearbook features his drawings under his nickname "Chicken." "Chic" Young's comic strip "Blondie" made its debut on September 8, 1930. Chic Young died in 1973. His son, Dean, still writes the strip.

1929 Gangster Patsy Lolordo, Al Capone's head of the Union Sicilione, drank a toast with three men at his home at 1921 North Avenue. The men then shot Lolordo eleven times and placed a pillow under his head as a token of respect. Joseph Aiello of the Moran Gang wanted to run the union and was one of the killers. Capone had him killed in October 1930. The other men involved died in the St. Valentine's Day Massacre.

1984 Mildred Lane, Elizabeth Shaw and an 82-year-old retired manicurist from Chicago shot a commercial for a struggling fast food chain. Clara Peller stared at a tiny hamburger on a massive bun and shouted, "Where's the beef?" The spot made her a millionaire and helped turn the Wendy's chain around. Wendy's dumped Peller in 1985 after she did a commercial for Prego Plus spaghetti sauce.

1989 The "Pat Sajak Show" premiered on CBS-TV. The former desk clerk at the Palmer House Hotel and alumni of Columbia College said the 18 months that he hosted the late-night talk show were the happiest of his career. Even though the talk show was short-lived, Pat continues to do well with his other gig, hosting the game show "Wheel of Fortune."

January 10

1850 Architect John Wellborn Root was born in Lumpkin, Georgia. Root and John Burnham established their influential architectural firm in Chicago in 1873. Burnham and Root designs include the Monadnock Building, one of the first to use steel beams along with traditional masonry load bearing walls. Root was a key planner of the 1893 Columbian Exposition, but did not live to see it completed.

Chicago 365

1964   The Chicago City Council unanimously voted to change the name of the Congress Expressway to the Dwight Eisenhower Expressway. Eisenhower created the Interstate Highway System. Ike didn't seem too impressed. He issued a brief statement; "I am highly complimented by the action of the City Council and the Mayor and express my appreciation to anyone connected with this thought."

1982   Bitterly cold weather held much of Illinois in its grip. The overnight lows dropped to 26 below in Chicago, breaking a 109-year-old record. The cold was blamed for 24 deaths in the area. Six days later, the temperature dipped to 25 below. On January 17, it fell to 23 below. There have only been ten days recorded in Chicago history where the low fell under 20 below.

January 11

1896   John "Paddy" Driscoll was born in Evanston, Illinois. Chicago Cardinals owner Chris O'Brien lured the sensational halfback to his team with an unheard offer of $300 per game. Driscoll was at his best when the Cardinals played the archrival Bears. He was traded to the Bears in 1926, and played for three more seasons. Driscoll was named to the Football Hall of Fame in 1965.

1976   Dorothy Hamill won the U.S. Female Figure Skating championship. Hamill was born in Chicago on July 26, 1956. She grew up in Riverside, Connecticut and began skating at age eight. On February 13, 1976, she won the gold medal at the Olympics in Innsbruck, Austria and caused a fashion sensation with her wedge style haircut.

1999   George Ryan was inaugurated as governor of Illinois. Democrat Jesse White was sworn in as the first African-American to serve as Illinois Secretary of State. Corinne Wood became the first female Lieutenant Governor. Ryan made headlines in 2003 when he commuted the sentences of all 167 death row inmates in Illinois. He was indicted on corruption charges in the licenses-for-bribes scandal after leaving office.

January 12

1925   Gunmen for Hymie Weiss riddled Al Capone's car with bullets at 55th and State. A police officer said, "They let it have everything but the

9

kitchen stove." But Capone was not in the car, and his men somehow survived. The attack rattled Capone, who bought the first of his famous armored cars. It was built on a Cadillac chassis, weighed seven tons, and cost about $20,000.

1926   Freeman Gosden and Charles Correll debuted their blackface comedy routines on WGN. The "Sam and Henry" characters traded in ethnic stereotypes and humor, but the show became so popular that WMAQ lured Gosden and Correll away with the offer of a spot on the NBC network. WGN retained the rights to "Sam and Henry," so the characters became "Amos 'n' Andy." The show came to television in 1951.

1931   The first television drama seen in Chicago aired on W9XAO. Irene Walker starred in "The Maker of Dreams." Using a mechanical (not electronic) transmission system, the video was broadcast on shortwave while the audio aired over WIBO-AM. In January of 1931, W9XAP and W9XAO teamed up for the first program made specifically for television, a musical comedy called "Their Television Honeymoon."

1960   The only film ever presented in "Smell-O-Vision" opened at the Cinestage Theater. One mile of piping was used to pump scents to the theater seats during the screening of Mike Todd Junior's *Scent of Mystery*. The crowd got a whiff of perfume, tobacco and even smelled wine during a scene when a man was crushed to death by casks. Henny Youngman later quipped, "I didn't understand the picture. I had a cold."

January 13

1919   Robert Stack was born Robert Langford Modini in Los Angeles. He will forever be linked with Chicago for his portrayal of Eliot Ness in the TV series, "The Untouchables." The show ran from 1959 to 1963 and Stack won a best actor Emmy for his role in 1960. He also played Ness in 1991 at the age of 77, appearing in the made for TV movie "The Return of Eliot Ness."

1939   Monty Stratton was listed again on the White Sox roster. Stratton won 30 games for the Sox in 1937 and 1938 before he lost his right leg in a hunting accident. He was determined to pitch again. Stratton would take the mound when the Sox and Cubs played a game for his benefit in 1939. He won 18 games in the minors in 1946. His life story became the basis for a movie starring Jimmy Stewart and June Allyson.

1979   Singer Donny Hathaway apparently jumped to his death from the 15th floor of the Essex House Hotel in New York City. Born in Chicago, Hathaway grew up in a St. Louis housing project. His biggest hits were duets with Roberta Flack, "Where is the Love" and "The Closer I Get To You."

1999   "This is a day that I hoped would never come," said Bulls chairman Jerry Reinsdorf as Michael Jordan announced his retirement. Jordan had retired in 1993 to pursue a baseball career. But he returned in 1995, and led the Bulls to three more titles. Jordan would come out of retirement again in 2001 to play for the Washington Wizards.

January 14

1896   John Dos Passos was born in Chicago. Dos Passos would rise to fame by mixing fact and fiction in his writing. The *U.S.A. Trilogy* is his most famous work. He wove biographies of the famous and typical people with snippets from pop songs, newspaper headlines and current events to tell the story of America from the turn of the century to the Great Depression.

1975   Police found the body of "The girl who died for *Playboy*" in the sleazy Maryland Hotel. U.S. Attorney Jim Thompson was pressuring Hugh Hefner's assistan, Bobby Arnstein to help bring Hefner down on a drug charge. Arnstein refused to betray her boss, but snapped and killed herself when Thompson said there was a contract on her life. A bitter Hefner was cleared of the drug charges, but left Chicago forever.

1979   The region began digging out from the "Blizzard of '79." The storm set a record at the time for the greatest snowfall here in a single day, some 16.5 inches. (The record was broken in 1999) The total from the storm of 18.8 inches also set a record at the time, but now ranks third in Chicago history.

2004   Lovie Smith became the first African-American head coach in

Chicago 365

Bears history. Smith was the former defensive coordinator for the Tampa Bay Buccaneers and for the St. Louis Rams and was given much of the credit for turning around St. Louis' porous defense after the team finished with a 10-6 record in 2001.

January 15

1848   The first telegram was received in Chicago, sent from Milwaukee. On April 6, a message was sent from New York by way of Detroit. Chicago residents were impressed that it took less than one day to arrive.

1909   Eugene Bertram Krupa was born in Chicago. His recordings with the "Austin High Gang" were the first to use a bass drum and defined the Chicago Jazz sound. Krupa formed his own orchestra after a stint with Benny Goodman. The "Chicago Flash" was the first drummer to perform flamboyant solos. In 1959, Sal Mineo portrayed him in *The Gene Krupa Story.*

1913   A couple was arrested at the Blackstone Hotel and accused of violating the law against public dancing in restaurants. The hotel owners went to court to fight the measure and the Illinois Supreme Court overturned it in 1916. Hotel attorney Levy Mayer said, "We contend that the right to dance is as sacred as the right to pray, and the City Council could no more prohibit one than the other."

1960   The *Sun-Times* broke the story of eight police officers from the North Side Summerdale District who were looting the businesses they were supposed to protect. Richard Morrison, "The Babbling Burglar," committed the crimes with the crooked cops and blew the whistle. The worst police scandal in Chicago history led to the resignation of Police Commissioner Timothy O'Connor and a drastic shakeup of the department.

1981   The television series "Hill Street Blues" premiered on NBC. Many of the exterior shots were filmed in Chicago, including the Maxwell Street Precinct House. Critics hailed the combination of multiple plot lines with a mix of comedy, drama, and gritty realism. The techniques used by producer Steven Bochco paved the way for shows such as "E.R.," "NYPD Blue" and "CSI."

Chicago 365

1836   The first railroad in Chicago was chartered. Businessmen fought William Ogden's plan for a line to the mines at Galena. They believed the future lay in Great Lakes shipping and the Illinois and Michigan Canal. But Ogden met with farmers all along the proposed route of the Galena and Chicago Union and convinced them to buy his stock.

1906   Marshall Field died in Chicago. On the day of his funeral, all the stores along State Street closed in his honor. Field was the first to offer a money back guarantee and free delivery. His motto was "Give the lady what she wants." He also donated money for the athletic field at the University of Chicago and gave $1 million to found the Field Museum of Natural History.

1967   A flame flickered to life in a booth at the National Housewares Manufacturers Association 46th Semi-Annual Exhibit at McCormick Place. There was no sprinkler system and hydrants were closed due to construction on the Stevenson Expressway. Over 500 firefighters and 94 pieces of equipment fought the blaze. A new McCormick Place designed by C.F. Murphy opened in January 1971, complete with a sprinkler system.

1995   Nineteen-year-old Violin prodigy Rachel Barton boarded a Metra train, carrying her 300-year-old Amati violin. She was dragged 366 feet after the train door closed on her violin case. Barton's left leg was amputated after the accident and she nearly lost her right leg. Barton sued the Chicago and Northwestern Railway/Union Pacific and Metra. A jury awarded her $29.6 million.

January 17

1899   Alphonse Capone was born in Brooklyn, New York. He fell in with mobster Johnny Torrio after dropping out of school. A brawl left him with the nickname "Scarface." Al followed Torrio to Chicago in 1919 and took over when Torrio retired after an assassination attempt in 1925.

1899   Educator Robert Maynard Hutchins was born in Brooklyn. He became president of the University of Chicago in 1929 and instituted a liberal arts approach. Students were not required to attend classes; they just had to pass extensive tests. He abolished football, calling it a handicap to education.   Hutchins also served as director of the *Encyclopedia Britannica* for 27 years. He was chancellor of Chicago University from 1945-1951.

1920   The most notorious era in city history began at 12:01 a.m., as the Volstead Act went into effect. Chicago was home to an estimated 20,000 speakeasies and at least 15 breweries. While Mayor Bill Thompson looked the other way, Al Capone spent over a million dollars each year buying off officials and earned $60 million annually on liquor sales alone.   Gang warfare probably killed as many as 800 before repeal.

1992   A series of natural gas explosions and fires devastated a 16-square block area in the West Town Neighborhood on the Near Northwest Side. Four people were killed, four injured and 18 buildings damaged or destroyed. State regulators said a supervisor for Peoples Gas Light and Coke accidentally caused a surge in pressure that sparked the blasts.

January 18

1887   The Village of Arlington Heights was incorporated.   The town was originally known as Dunton, in honor of William Dunton, the first settler.   After World War Two, a building boom transformed the quiet village into one of Chicago's largest suburbs.   The population exploded from 8,000 in 1950 to 64,000 in 1970.

1939   Phil Everly was born in Chicago. Beginning in 1957, Don and his brother Phil teamed with songwriters Felice and Boudleaux Bryant and scored huge hits such as "Wake Up Little Suzy," "Bye Bye Love" and "All I Have to do is Dream."   In 1986, the Everly Brothers were one of the first ten inductees into the Rock and Roll Hall of Fame.

1941   The first Chicago Housing Authority community developed for African Americans opened. The Ida Wells project originally covered 47 acres and was designed to house 1,662 low-income black families. The project is now being redeveloped as part of a 10-year, $1.5-billion transformation of the city's public housing.

1988 Colleen Moore died. In the late 1920's, flapper roles made Moore a top box office attraction.   But she may be better remembered for her

Chicago 365

"Fairy Castle" dollhouse. When it made its debut in 1934, the 8'7" x 8'2" x 7'7" palace complete with electricity, running water, and over 2,000 miniatures was valued at nearly $500,000. Colleen loaned it to the Museum of Science and Industry in 1949 and donated it permanently in 1976.

January 19

1935 In the midst of a blizzard, Coopers Incorporated introduced a new product in a display window at Marshall Field and Company. The store manager thought long johns should be on display instead, and ordered the extremely small men's underwear removed. But before workers could remove the display, the store had sold 600 pairs of the new underwear with the brand name of Jockey Shorts.

1977 President Gerald Ford pardoned "Tokyo Rose." Ikuko Toguri was a U.S. citizen stranded in Japan. At Radio Tokyo she helped POW's and never used "Tokyo Rose" on the air. G.I.s called all the women on Radio Tokyo by that name. Needing money after the war, Toguri told the press she was "Tokyo Rose." She served seven years for treason, and then settled in Chicago, where her family ran J. Toguri Mercantile.

1977 The Baseball Writers Association elected Ernie Banks to the Hall of Fame. "Mr. Cub" slugged 512 home runs in his career, and hit 40 or more in a season five times. He won the MVP awards in 1958 and 1959, the first time the National League named the same player as MVP two years in a row. Banks played for the Cubs from 1953 to 1971, and is probably the greatest player to never appear in the post-season.

1993 The Chicago Bears named former Dallas Cowboys defensive coordinator Dave Wannstedt as the 11th head coach in club history. Wannstedt would lead the Bears to a 41-57 record over the next six seasons. He was named as the NFC coach of the year in 1994, after guiding the Bears to the playoffs. Wannstedt was fired after the 1998 season.

January 20

1894 Harold Lincoln Gray was born in Kankakee, Illinois. He started as a cub reporter for *The Tribune* before developing his idea for an adventure comic strip featuring a young boy named Otto. But there were many strips featuring young boys, so he changed the character to a girl. "Little Orphan Annie" made her debut on August 24, 1924.

1909 Sixty men died when fire destroyed a water intake crib under construction off the Lake Michigan shore at Dunne and 68th Street. The men were living in the crib during the winter so construction work could continue. Many were forced to jump into the icy lake. The fire occurred during the morning shift change, when a larger than usual number of men were on the site.

1982 "Iron Mike" Ditka was named coach of the Chicago Bears. At the time, the Bears had managed only two winning seasons in the past 19 years. Ditka would guide the team to six Central Division titles, three NFC title games and the Super Bowl XX championship. Ditka is one of only two men to have won a Super Bowl as a player, assistant coach, and head coach.

1983 Millionaire insurance executive Allen M. Dorfman was shot to death outside the Hyatt Lincolnwood Hotel. Dorfman was a friend of Jimmy Hoffa and had been convicted of taking kickbacks to secure a loan for the Teamsters Pension Fund. Facing sentencing for bribery and conspiracy, Dorfman decided to help the government investigate mob ties to the fund. The killer was never caught.

1985 The temperature plunged to 27 below zero at O'Hare International Airport, the lowest reading ever recorded in Chicago. A record was also set for the lowest high temperature of four below zero.

January 21

1806 William Quarter was born in Killurin, Ireland. He became the first Bishop of Chicago in 1844. Quarter and his brothers were the only ordained priests in Illinois at the time. He purchased the property where Holy Name Cathedral now stands and established the University of St. Mary's of the Lake, the first in Illinois. He died in 1848 at age 42.

1867 Crosby's Opera House was the finest west of the Atlantic coast, but its builder was near bankruptcy. Uranus Crosby held a lottery for the building and valuable paintings inside. He sold 210,000 tickets at $5 each but kept 25,000 of them. The winner of the Opera House sold everything back for $200,000 and Crosby won the paintings! He used the "lottery" money to renovate the Opera House.

1921 Judge Kenesaw Mountain Landis was named as the first commissioner of baseball. In an effort to restore credibility to the game in the wake of the Black Sox Scandal, Landis was given virtually unlimited power. The former Chicago United States District Judge would ban eight of the disgraced White Sox players for life, even though they were acquitted in court.

1975 Dizzy Dean was elected to the Baseball Hall of Fame. The Cubs traded three players and $185,000 to the Cardinals for Dean on April 16, 1938. But Dean was never the same after being hit in the foot by a line drive off the bat of Earl Averill during the 1937 All-Star Game. He managed a 7-1 record while helping the Cubs to the pennant. But Dean would only appear in 30 games over the next three seasons.

January 22

1925 "Big Jim" O'Leary died. For 40 years Catherine O'Leary's son was the King of Chicago gambling. He openly ran a gaming and bookmaking empire from his saloon at 4183 South Halstead. The saloon was raided repeatedly, but somehow police never found anyone gambling! Big Jim always denounced the story of his mother's cow kicking over a lantern and starting the Great Fire as a "monumental fake."

1931 Sam Cooke was born in Mississippi. His father was a reverend who moved the family to Chicago in the 1930's. Sam sang with his siblings as the Soul Children and became lead singer for the Soul Stirrers gospel group in 1951. Sam's first pop records were released under a fake name to avoid offending gospel fans. "You Send Me" hit number one in 1957, and hits like "Cupid" and "Twistin' the Night Away" followed.

1957 The nude bodies of Barbara and Patricia Grimes were discovered in a culvert on German Church Road. They were last seen at the Brighton Theater on December 28, 1956. Joseph Loman, the Cook County Sheriff who botched the investigation into the 1955 murder of the Schuessler-

Chicago 365

Peterson boys, was involved in the inter-agency infighting that hampered the Grimes investigation as well. The case remains unsolved.

January 23

1837 Citizens met at the Saloon Building and approved a charter incorporating Chicago as a city. The charter became official on March 4, 1837. At the time, the population of Chicago stood at 4,170. On May 2, elections were held as provided by the charter. William B. Ogden was elected as mayor and Isaac N. Arnold became the first city clerk.

1891 Doctor Daniel Hale Williams founded Provident Hospital and Training School in a three story building at 29th and Dearborn. The nation's first interracial hospital contained 12 beds. The first class of nurses consisted of seven women, including Emma Reynolds. She inspired the founding of Provident when every nursing school in Chicago turned her down in 1889.

1913 Chicago architect Arthur Aldis and investors such as Cyrus McCormick formed a trust to build the first planned shopping center. Market Square in Lake Forest was designed for the automobile, since many in the wealthy community owned one. Howard Van Doren Shaw combined several types of European architecture for the complex of 28 stores, 12 office units and 30 apartments. The square opened in 1916.

1995 Demolition work started at the Washington Park extension public housing development. Washington Park was the first of several Chicago Housing Authority buildings to be demolished. Chicago Housing Authority Chairman Vincent Lane said, "If there's anything whose time has come, its demolition of those god-awful places. We can no longer isolate the poor in those high-rise prisons."

January 24

1916 Jack Brickhouse was born in Peoria. He began his career there at WMBD and came to WGN in 1940. Brickhouse called Cubs games from 1941-81 and White Sox games from 1948-67. He became the announcer on WGN-TV when the station signed on in 1948. For 24 years, he was also the voice of the Chicago Bears and called Bulls games in the 1960's. He was named to the Baseball Hall of Fame in 1983.

Chicago 365

1921 George Wellington "Captain" Streeter died. Streeter created 186 acres of landfill after his steamship ran aground in 1886, declared it the "District of Lake Michigan" and defended it with a shotgun. "Ma" Streeter sued for the land after his death, but a court ruled that "Pa" never divorced his first wife. Ma Streeter died broke, and the land is now home to the Hancock Building and Grant Park.

1925 Hymie Weiss and Bugs Moran of the O'Banion Gang shot Johnny Torrio several times outside his home at 7016 South Clyde. Vincent "The Schemer" Drucci waited inside the getaway car. Moran put a pistol to Torrio's head to finish the job, but he was out of bullets. Refusing to name his assailants, a shaken Torrio retired to New York and turned operations over to Al Capone. Capone vowed revenge on the Northsiders.

1947 Warren Zevon was born in Chicago. His witty lyrics brought him fame with the release of the LP *Excitable Boy* and the hit single "Werewolves of London" in 1978. A battle with alcohol kept him from sustained stardom. Diagnosed with terminal lung cancer, Zevon decided to release one more album. *The Wind* was released to critical acclaim in August 2003. Zevon died on September 7, 2003.

1949 John Belushi was born in Chicago. The son of an Albanian immigrant played football and was the homecoming king at Wheaton Central High School. The college dropout joined Second City in June 1971 and came to "Saturday Night Live" in 1975. Belushi's roles in the films *National Lampoon's Animal House* and the *Blues Brothers* in made him a legend, but he died of an overdose on March 5, 1982.

January 25

1947 Al Capone died at his home on Palm Island, Florida. Sentenced to 11 years in prison on tax charges in 1931, Capone began showing signs of syphilitic dementia while serving time on Alcatraz. In 1938, he was transferred to the Terminal Island Prison in Southern California. Capone continued to deteriorate following his release in November of 1939 and spent his final days as a recluse on Palm Island.

1993 Sears discontinued its "Big Book." The Sears Catalog dated back to 1888, when Richard Sears mailed out advertisements for watches and jewelry. After the introduction of rural free delivery in 1896, the catalog would give farmers access to everything from clothing to complete homes. (More than 100,000 Sears Catalog homes were sold from 1908 to 1940)

1995 The Illinois Supreme Court ordered the adoptive parents of four-year-old "Baby Richard" to turn the boy over to his biological father Otakar Kirchner. The child's mother gave Richard up for adoption while the couple was estranged, and told Kirchner the child had died. The Warburton family raised Richard. But Kirchner reconciled with the mother and they launched a legal fight to get the child back.

1996 The Blackhawks played their first game at the United Center, a 5-1 victory over the Edmonton Oilers before a crowd of 20,536. Joe Murphy scored the first goal in the new building.

January 26

1892 Bessie Coleman, the first licensed black pilot, was born in Atlanta, Texas. She moved to Chicago in 1915. Because Bessie was a black woman, she had to learn to fly in France. She died while practicing for a show in Florida on April 30, 1926. In 1990 Mayor Richard Daley renamed Old Mannheim Road at O'Hare Airport as Bessie Coleman Drive. The Postal Service honored her on a stamp in 1995.

1946 Eugene Kal Siskel was born in Chicago. He took over as movie critic for the *Tribune* in September 1969. In the fall of 1975, he was paired up with his archrival from the *Sun-Times*, Rogert Ebert, for a show called "Opening Soon…At a Theatre Near You" on WTTS. Their show went national in 1982. Siskel developed a brain tumor in 1998 and died on February 20, 1999.

1967 Just two days after an unseasonable high of 65 degrees, snow started falling about 5:00 a.m. When it finally ended, a record 23 inches was on the ground. Abandoned cars and 800 CTA buses littered the streets and expressways. Thousands of travelers were stranded at the airports. A 10-year-old girl died in crossfire between looters and police. She was one of 29 deaths related to the blizzard.

Chicago 365

1986   The Bears blasted the New England Patriots 46-10 in Super Bowl XX. The Bears won the first 15 games of the season, and scored a hit song with "The Superbowl Shuffle." QB Jim McMahon changed headbands constantly while 310 pound William "The Refrigerator" Perry scored three touchdowns during the season. Walter Payton rushed for 1,551 yards and Mike Singletary led the dominating defense.

January 27

1890   Mathias "Paddy" Bauler was born in Chicago. Bauler was the last of the old-fashioned brash saloon-owning aldermen, a tradition dating back to "Hinky Dink" Kenna and "Bathhouse" John Coughlin. First elected in 1933, Bauler is best known for saying "Chicago ain't ready for reform" when Mayor Daley was elected in 1955. He retired in 1977.

1894   The first basketball game involving a college team took place. The University of Chicago, led by Alonzo Stagg, defeated the Chicago YMCA Training School 19-11. The team took part in the first intercollegiate basketball game on January 18, 1896, defeating The University of Iowa 15-12.

1926   Newton Minnow was born in Milwaukee. President Kennedy appointed the Chicago lawyer as chairman of the FCC in 1961, and he went down in history for calling television a "Vast Wasteland." Minnow was instrumental in the growth of educational television. He had served as WHTT's Chairman of the Board prior to his appointment as FCC chair.

1972   Mahalia Jackson died in Evergreen Park at the age of 60. Her health had deteriorated since a heart attack in 1964. Jackson had made her professional signing debut in 1928 at Olivet Baptist Church. In 1947, the beauty shop owner and former maid's recording of "Move On Up A Little Higher" became the first gospel record to sell a million copies.

January 28

1851   Northwestern University was incorporated. John Evans was one of the founders. The railroad man, former alderman, and former head of the obstetrics department at Rush Medical College assumed the mortgage for the future campus site north of Chicago. Evans built a home in the drained swamp that the trustees named Evanston.

1904   The first college sports "letters" were awarded. The University of Chicago began the tradition when the school awarded blankets emblazoned with the letter "C" to all seniors who had played football in 1903.

1922   Chicago's football team was officially renamed the Bears. The team originally played in Decatur and was known as the Staleys, after the owner of a corn company. George Halas agreed to keep the name for one year after the team moved to Chicago in 1921. He chose the Bears in honor of the other tenant of Wrigley Field. The Bears moved their games to Comiskey Park later in 1922.

1961   Nine firefighters died during a fire in a six-story building at 614 West Hubbard Street. Several firefighters standing on the roof of a neighboring two-story building were trapped when an outer wall of the larger building fell. Several of their comrades rushed to help, and all were killed when the roof of the smaller building caved in.

January 29

1900   Charles Comiskey gained permission to move the St. Paul franchise of the Western League to Chicago to play in the newly formed American League. He named the team the White Stockings, in honor of the city's original National League team. Sportswriters quickly began shortening the name to White Sox when writing headlines.

1954   Oprah Winfrey was born in Kosciusko, Mississippi. Male relatives and her mother's friends sexually abused her before Oprah moved to live with her father in Nashville. She began her broadcasting career there. In January 1984, she became the host of "A.M. Chicago" on WLS-TV. The expanded program was re-named "The Oprah Winfrey Show" in 1985 and syndicated nationally on September 8, 1986.

1981   An ownership group led by Jerry Reinsdorf and Eddie Einhorn bought the White Sox from Bill Veeck's group. A few weeks later, the new owners signed free agent Carlton Fisk. Reinsdorf made a fortune in real estate and ran the multi-billion-dollar Balcor Corporation. In 1985, he would purchase controlling interest in the Bulls.

January 30

1945   Sixty-two men died when the heavy cruiser *USS Chicago* was torpedoed during the battle of Rennell Island. Four US Navy ships have been named for the city. The first was a protected steel cruiser launched in 1885 and active during World War One. A new heavy cruiser named the *Chicago* was launched in 1945. The fourth *Chicago* (SSN-721) is a nuclear attack submarine commissioned in 1986.

1976   Fire broke out at the Wincrest Nursing home, 6326 N. Winthrop. The damage was minor, but 23 patients died from smoke inhalation. A 21-year-old temporary housekeeper would be charged with murder for setting the fire. A special panel appointed by Mayor Daley following the disaster would recommend that fire sprinklers and building compartmentalization be used in all new and existing nursing homes.

1989   Daniel Barenboim was named as the ninth musical director of the Chicago Symphony Orchestra. He succeeded Sir Georg Solti. Barenboim's tenure has been marked by the opening of Chicago's new Symphony Center and 12 international tours. In 1992 the prolific recording artist also became General Music Director of the Deutsche Staatsoper Berlin.

January 31

1915   Speaking in Philadelphia, Billy Sunday condemned Chicago. He declared, "Chicago openly defies the law; there's just as much booze sold on Sundays as any other day. The Sabbath is just a rum-guzzling day for Chicago and nothing is done to stop it."

1931   "Mr. Cub" was born in Dallas. Ernie Banks starred in several sports in high school and signed with a black barnstorming team at age 17. Cool Papa Bell brought him to the Kansas City Monarchs and the Cubs signed him in 1953. The most popular Cubs player of all time is known for his love of the game, exemplified by his words "Let's Play Two." His number 14 was the first Cubs number to be retired.

1949   The first daytime TV soap opera premiered on WMAQ. "These are My Children" was a 15-minute show that aired live. Creator Irna Phillips wrote the first soap, "Painted Dreams," for WGN radio in 1930. She went on to create such shows as "The Guiding Light," "As The World Turns," and "Days of Our Lives." She was the first to use cliffhanger endings and address social issues on daytime dramas.

1976   Evel Kneivel crashed his motorcycle while practicing a jump over a tank of killer sharks at the Chicago Amphitheater. Kneivel suffered a concussion and two broken arms. A cameraman lost an eye as shrapnel flew through the air. It was Evel's last major jump. His son Robbie took over as the daredevil in the family.

2000   Governor George H. Ryan declared a moratorium on executions in Illinois. Ryan later commuted the sentences of all 167 inmates on death row. The governor pointed out that since the death penalty was reinstated in Illinois in 1977, 12 Death Row inmates had been executed while 13 had been exonerated.   In 2003, Ryan was nominated for the Nobel Prize for his work on the death penalty issue.

February

February I

1900 Minna and Ada Everleigh opened the most opulent brothel in the world in a 50-room mansion at 2131-33 South Dearborn Street. Guests were entertained in lavish themed parlors, including the Japanese Throne Room and "The Gold Room," complete with gold-rimmed fishbowls and a miniature gold piano. Mayor Carter Harrison Junior shut the club down on October 24, 1911.

1951 As the temperature hit eleven below zero, a drunken Dorothy Mae Stevens Anderson passed out in an alley. By the time she was discovered, her temperature had plummeted 64.4 degrees, and her blood had turned to slush. Mrs. Anderson lost both her legs and all but one finger, but "The Deep Freeze Woman" lived until 1974.

1974 The television series "Good Times" premiered on CBS. The series was set in Cabrini-Green and starred Esther Role as the wisecracking maid Florida Evans, a role she originally played on the series "Maude." John Amos starred as her husband Henry. A virtually unknown comic named Jimmie Walker played older brother JJ. He uttered the phrase "Dyn-o-mite!" in the second episode.

1990 The new 708 area code took effect. Phone company officials declared that new technology was generating a demand for new phone numbers. Few expected that millions more cell phones, fax machines, computer modems and pagers would require three more new area codes for the Chicago area within the next decade.

1994 Police found 19 children alone and living in squalor in a two bedroom apartment at 219 North Keystone Ave. Six mothers, five of whom were sisters, were collecting $4,500 monthly in welfare while the "Keystone Kids" lived amid roaches, rotting food and filth. "Not in Calcutta, in Chicago," President Bill Clinton said later. The parents were found guilty of child neglect on April 22.

Chicago 365

February 2

1895　George "Papa Bear" Halas was born in Chicago. Halas founded the team that became the Bears. He played for nine years, coached for 40 years and owned the team for 63 years. Halas was the first coach to hold daily practice, the first to use game film and was the first owner to allow games to be broadcast on the radio. He was elected to the Hall of Fame in 1963 and the NFC Championship trophy bears his name.

1925　The first Sears retail store opened in the Merchandise Building. Sears Vice President Robert E. Wood saw that since the advent of the automobile, rural buyers were no longer dependent on catalogs and were abandoning the farms to move to the city. By the late 1920's Sears was opening new retail stores at the rate of one every other day.

1954　The curtain rose on the Lyric Theater of Chicago's presentation of Mozart's *Don Giovanni* at the Civic Opera House. It was renamed the Lyric Opera of Chicago in 1956. Carol Fox served as general manager until 1980, ensuring that the Lyric would not end up bankrupt like all seven previous opera companies in Chicago. She founded the company along with Lawrence V. Kelly, and Nicola Rescigno.

1983　Pope John Paul II installed Archbishop Joseph Bernardin as a cardinal. The seventh Archbishop of Chicago was born in Columbia, South Carolina. In 1966 at age 38, he was appointed as Auxiliary Bishop of Atlanta, and became the youngest bishop in the nation. Bernardin served as Archbishop of Cincinnati from November 1972 until he was appointed to lead Chicago's 2.3 million Catholics on July 10, 1982.

February 3

1876　With capital of $800, pitching star A.G. Spalding and his brother opened a sporting goods emporium in Chicago. A ball Spalding developed helped him become the top pitcher of his day, winning 241 games between 1871 and 1875. He won 47 while leading the White Stockings to the first NL pennant in 1876. For the next 100 years, Spalding's company would manufacture the official Major League baseball.

1913　Chicago women registered to vote for the first time. They would

Chicago 365

be permitted to vote only in the state and local elections. Nearly 154,000 women would register, three times the number election officials were expecting.

1917   The Village of Mount Prospect was incorporated. The village got its name because a real estate man wanted potential buyers to know the site was on high ground, above the surrounding swamp. In the movie *The Blues Brothers,* Dan Akroyd and John Belushi drive an old Mount Prospect Police car. Akroyd said he chose Mount Prospect Police because the department had a reputation for toughness.

1975   Billy Herman was named to the Baseball Hall of Fame. He played in the Cubs infield from 1931 to 1947, batted over .300 eight times and played on three pennant winning teams. He was traded to Brooklyn in 1941, reportedly because Cubs manager Jimmy Wilson felt Herman wanted his job. He went on to serve as a coach and manager for several major league teams.

February 4

1869   Radical Socialist leader William "Big Bill" Haywood was born. He founded the International Workers of the World in Chicago in 1905. In 1918, a jury convicted him of sedition for organizing a strike during wartime. He fled to the Soviet Union where he died in 1928. Half of his ashes were buried at the Kremlin. The rest were sent to Chicago and buried near the monument to the Haymarket anarchists.

1928   A magnificient Spanish-baroque theater opened at 47th and South Parkway (now King) in the heart of Bronzeville. Nearly every great name in black entertainment would play the Regal Theater in the decades to come, including Duke Ellington, Louis Armstrong, Count Basie, Cab Calloway and Lena Horne. The theater was torn down in 1973. The 47th Street cultural center now stands on the site.

1977   A fully loaded Chicago Transit Authority Lake-Dan Ryan train hit a Ravenswood Line train stopped on a curve above Wabash and Lake. Although the Ryan train was traveling at just ten miles per hour, its first four cars plunged 20 feet to the ground. The crash killed 11 people, including two on the ground. About 260 people were hurt. A drug test showed the motorman had used marijuana.

February 5

1837 Dwight L. Moody was born in Massachusetts. He started out selling shoes in Chicago, but turned to evangelism. The Billy Graham of the 19th century founded the independent Moody's Church and the Moody Bible Institute. Both Presidents Lincoln and Grant attended his famous revivals. Over 130,000 people heard him preach in one day at the Columbian Exposition in 1893.

1900 Adlai Ewing Stevenson II was born in Los Angeles, California. The grandson of Grover Cleveland's Vice President, Stevenson earned his law degree at Northwestern University, edited the family newspaper, and became Governor of Illinois in 1948.
He ran unsuccessfully for president in 1952 and 1956. In 1960, he lost the Democratic nomination to John F. Kennedy. Kennedy appointed him minister to the U.N.

1923 The last horse drawn fire engine in Chicago made its final run. A crowd watched the horses pull out from Fire Engine 11, at 10 East Austin Avenue. While the horses made a run to alarm box 846 at State and Chicago Avenue, a new fire truck was backed into place at the station. The horses were sent to the House of Correction to be sold.

1931 Hack Wilson, who set an NL record with 56 home runs and 191 RBI's in 1930, became the highest paid National Leaguer ever. He signed a deal for $35,000 per season. In 1931, manager Rogers Hornsby would bench him for drinking and poor hitting.

February 6

1887 Albert Spalding met with White Stocking players and demanded that each pledge to abstain from alcohol. A few days later, star catcher King Kelly demanded a promised good behavior bonus, even though Spalding had fined him $225 for drinking in 1886. Spalding sold Kelly to Boston for $10,000, more than double the highest amount previously paid for a player.

Chicago 365

1911   Ronald W. Reagan was born in Tampico, Illinois. The Reagan family moved to Chicago when "Dutch" was two years old. His dad worked as a shoe salesman at Marshall Field's department store. They lived in a tiny flat at 832 East 57th Street, near the University of Chicago. The family moved less than two years later. Reagan returned to Chicago as a young man seeking a job in radio, but was unsuccessful.

1952   Republican Committeeman Charles Gross had tried to keep crooked politicians owned by the mob out of his 35th Ward. That night in front of the Scandinavian Evangelical Church, two men blasted him seven times with a shotgun. The murder spurred calls for something to be done about the West Side Bloc of corrupt officials. But a three-year inquiry failed to discover just who was behind the murder.

1956   The *Chicago Defender* became a daily paper. The black-owned paper had published weekly since John S. Abbott founded it in 1905. The newspaper became very influential among the black community in the south, with its editorials condemning lynching and urging blacks to come north to find jobs. Gwendolyn Brooks and Langston Hughes are among those who wrote for the *Defender.*

1980   The trial of John Wayne Gacy for the murder of 33 people began in Chicago. Gacy pleaded not guilty by reason of insanity. But a jury deliberated just two hours before finding him guilty and sentenced him to death on March 13th. Gacy said the jury had done "The same thing I have been trying to do for the last ten years: destroy myself."

February 7

1804   John Deere was born in Rutland, Vermont. He came to Illinois to work as a blacksmith in Grand Detour. Deere noticed that farmers had to scrape the thick prairie soil from their plows. He designed a new plow made of polished steel that solved the problem. He gave up the blacksmith business and moved to Moline in 1848 to begin mass-producing the plows. John Deere and Company was incorporated in 1868.

1857   The Village of Naperville incorporated. Captain Joseph Naper was the first resident. He settled along the DuPage River in 1831.

Chicago 365

Naperville served as the original DuPage County seat from 1839 until it was moved to Wheaton in 1868. The population of Naperville quadrupled during the 1980's and 90's to over 128,000.

1926   All traffic in the Loop came under control of new automatic "stop and go lights." The lights were installed at 49 intersections, making it the largest system in the world, and were operated from a control board at City Hall. John Hertz (of Yellow Cab and Hertz Rent-A-Car) convinced the city to invest in stoplights by using his own money to install them on Michigan Avenue between Randolph and 12th Streets.

February 8

1853   The village of Aurora was incorporated. The settlement was originally known as McCarthy's Mill, for Joseph and Samuel McCarthy. The brothers came from New York and built a sawmill. The community was renamed Aurora in 1837. Of course Aurora may be better known as the home of Wayne Campbell and Garth Alger, the characters portrayed in the *Wayne's World* movies by Mike Myers and Dana Carvey.

1869   The Illinois Legislature created Lincoln Park. The city began turning the cemetery site into a park back in 1860. Permission was obtained to remove all of the bodies, except for the Couch family mausoleum, which still stands. The park was expanded as more bodies were removed, including thousands of Confederate soldiers who died in a Chicago prison. A final 1950's expansion brought the park to its current 1,208 acres.

1910   William D. Boyce of Chicago incorporated the Boy Scouts of America. On a visit to London, Boyce asked a young lad for directions and was surprised when the boy refused a reward for his good deed. The boy told Boyce he was a Scout, a member of a movement organized by Sir Robert Baden-Powell. An inspired Boyce met with Baden-Powell and founded the U.S. Scouts upon his return home.

1977   The high temperature in Chicago struggled above the freezing mark for the first time in 43 days. The string of below freezing days was the longest ever. Chicago had three record low temperatures set during the cold snap.

Chicago 365

2000 Two small planes collided just north of the Waukegan Regional Airport. Three people were killed, including "Uncle Bob" Collins, WGN-AM radio personality. The top rated morning host was an accomplished pilot. He had been on the air in Chicago since 1974 and took over the morning slot on WGN from the legendary Wally Phillips in 1984. Collins had more than one million listeners each day.

February 9

1837 Elijah Peacock opened the first jewelry store in Chicago. Today, The House of Peacock is the oldest business in the city. The firm survived the Great Fire because the merchandise was locked in a fireproof vault. Eighteen years later, Elijah passed the mantle to his son Charles Daniel. In 1889, the name was changed to C.D. Peacock.

1898 The North Side "Sausage King" was sentenced to life in prison. On May 1, 1897, Adolph Luetgert killed his wife, boiled her body in acid and disposed of it in the smokestack at his factory at Hermitage and Diversey. Rumors swept the neighborhood that Louisa had been ground up into sausage and sausage sales slumped for a while. Luetgert was sent to Joliet, where he claimed his wife's spirit haunted him.

1914 Bill Veeck was born in Chicago, the son of the Cubs president. Veeck decided to plant ivy along the wall at Wrigley Field in September 1937. As an executive, he was responsible for such innovations as Bat Day, fireworks at the ballpark and names on the backs of uniforms. He once sent a midget to the plate in St. Louis and installed the exploding scoreboard at Comiskey Park.

1916 George Mundelein was installed as Archbishop of Chicago. In 1918, he purchased land in Area, Illinois for St. Mary of the Lake Seminary. The town was named Mundelein in his honor. Mundelein worked hard to Americanize the church and became a Cardinal on March 24, 1924. He made headlines for refusing to allow gangsters to be buried in consecrated ground.

1979 Just before the close of trading, DEA agents raided the Chicago Board Options Exchange. Eleven people were arrested for allegedly selling or distributing cocaine, near or on the floor of the exchange. Three of those arrested held seats on the exchange and two were brokers who did business on the exchange. The arrests were part of a year-long undercover investigation.

February 10

1916   Three people were dead and dozens were sick after being poisoned at a University Club dinner celebrating George Mundelein's elevation to Archbishop. Anarchist and atheist chef Nestor Dondoglio had poisoned the soup. But he used too much poison, which caused the guests to vomit and saved many of their lives. Mundelein passed up the soup because he was dieting. Dondoglio was never caught.

1926   Frank McErlane introduced the Thompson submachine gun to the bootlegging wars. McErlane led a machine gun attack on the saloon ran by Martin "Buff" Costello. Two men were wounded. The next day, Chicago detective Captain John Stege said he wanted some Thompsons for his "own boys." Al Capone was reportedly very impressed and quickly placed an order for the guns.

1993   Two very famous figures from the Chicago area drew massive ratings on a TV special. Over 90 million people tuned in to see "Michael Jackson Talks to Oprah Winfrey" on ABC. Jackson said that his skin color was changing due to a disorder known as vitiligo and claimed he only had two plastic surgery operations. The 90-minute interview was broadcast live from Jackson's Neverland Ranch.

February 11

1835   The legislature extended the area of the Town of Chicago to about 2 and 2/5 square miles. At the time, the population stood at 3,265. As late as November of 1834, it was reported that there were only two girls of marriageable age in the town.

1869   The first women's suffrage convention convened in Chicago. Mary Livermore served as chairperson. Elizabeth Cady Stanton and Susan B. Anthony traveled to Chicago to lend their support to the movement. The convention resolved to seek the right to vote for females and blacks at the Illinois Constitutional Convention. The effort failed.

Chicago 365

1917   Sidney Sheldon was born in Chicago. His screenplay for *The Bachelor and the Bobbysoxer* won an Oscar in 1937.   He made his directorial debut in 1953 with *Dream Wife.*   Sheldon also won four Tony awards for the Broadway musical *Redhead.* He went on to create the TV shows "I Dream of Jeannie" and "The Patty Duke Show." In 1974, *The Other Side of Midnight* became the first of his many best selling novels.

1993   George G. Stephens died at the age of 71. The sheet metal man wasn't happy with the type of pie-shaped barbeque grills that were popular in the 1950's. While working at the Weber Brothers Metal Works in 1951, he took one of the buoys made there, sawed it in half and put a vented cover on top, creating the Weber Grill. His company went on to produce millions of them, with the design little changed over the years.

February 12

1882   Oscar Wilde arrived in Chicago.   The flamboyant Irish poet and dramatist wasn't impressed. He said the city was dreary and called the water tower "a castellated monstrosity with pepperboxes stuck all over it."   The newspapers fired back. They blasted Wilde for wearing knee breeches and silk stockings.

1901   Famed saloon smasher Carrie Nation toured the saloons of the notorious Levee District. Warned by Mayor Carter Harrison Junior to leave her hatchet at home, she didn't smash up any bars. She did yank a cigar from a man's mouth and barked for a Dearborn Street bar keeper to cover a partially nude statue in his window. She said, "Oh, how I would like to do some smashing."

1917   Readers of the *Tribune* met Andy Gump and his family. Joseph Medill Patterson created the story of the inventor of the flowerpot and the man who introduced the polka dot tie. "The Gumps" was syndicated nationally two years later. Illustrator Sidney Smith drew the strip from 1917 until he died the crash of his new Rolls Royce in 1935. The last strip featuring the Gump family ran on October 17, 1959.

1955   An old man dropped his cigarette into the alcohol solution he was using to massage his legs at a skid row motel. The fire swept through the Barton Hotel on West Madison Street, killing 29 men. About 20 of the

33

residents, mostly transients, were able to escape. Many fled into the sub-zero cold wearing only their underwear.

February 13

1920   Members of the National American Women Suffrage Association met at the Congress Hotel to celebrate passage of the amendment granting women the right to vote. They would vote to disband and form a new group, the League of Women Voters. Carrie Chapman Catt first proposed the group to "finish the fight" against other forms of discrimination faced by women.

1923   Michael Anthony Bilandic was born in Chicago, the son of Croatian immigrants. The City Council appointed Bilandic as the 40th Mayor of the city following the death of Mayor Daley in 1976. He was elected in his own right in 1977. Jane Byrne upset Bilandic in the 1979 Democratic primary, but he went on to become Chief Justice of the Illinois Supreme Court.

1933   Marilyn Novak was born in Chicago. When the former dime store clerk signed with Columbia pictures, the studio wanted to change her name to Kit Marlowe. She agreed only to change her first name to Kim. Her 1950's roles in *Picnic, Pal Joey,* and *Vertigo* made her a star. In 1999, *Playboy* ranked her at number 18 on its list of "The 100 Sexiest Stars of the Century."

February 14

1894   Benjamin Kubelsky was born at Mercy Hospital in Chicago. He grew up on South Genesee Street in Waukegan and played violin at the Barrison Theater. He joined a vaudeville team and changed his name to Ben K. Benny after violinist Jan Kubelik complained. Then, violinist Ben Bernie complained and forced him to change again! Today, no one remembers those violinists, but we all remember Jack Benny.

1929   A fake police car pulled up to the SMC Cartage Company at 2122 Clark. Inside, five members of the George "Bugs" Moran Gang, a mechanic, and an optometrist who liked to hang around gangsters had gathered to wait for a truckload of stolen whiskey. It was a setup. Two of the five men who burst into the garage were dressed as police officers, so the Moran men offered no resistance. The other three men pulled shotguns and Thompson sub machine guns from beneath their trench coats. They opened fire, leaving six dead and one mortally wounded. Al Capone had ordered "Machine Gun" Jack McGurn to mastermind the murders. But his target, Bugs Moran, was not there. Moran had smelled a set up when he saw the fake cop car.

1992   The motion picture *Wayne's World* was released. Mike Myers and Dana Carvey starred as Wayne Campbell and Garth Algar, hosts of a local cable access show in Aurora. They took the AMC Pacer "Mirthmobile" to see the local bands at The Gasworks nightclub. Wayne and Garth loved to hang out at Stan Mikita's donut shop, a takeoff on the chain established by hockey great Tim Horton.

February 15

1809   Cyrus Hall McCormick was born in Rockbridge County, Virginia. His father had tried to perfect a mechanical reaper, and Cyrus did it in 1831. The reaper revolutionized farming, handling the work of dozens of men. In August 1837, McCormick came to Chicago, to build a factory closer to his customers. William Ogden was his first investor. By 1860, the factory was cranking out over 4,000 machines annually.

1933   The Mayor of Chicago lay mortally wounded as the car sped towards a Miami hospital. He turned to the uninjured man next to him and said, "I'm glad it was me instead of you." Anton Cermak was speaking to President Franklin D. Roosevelt. Italian immigrant Guiseppe Zangara shot at the president as Roosevelt stepped off a boat after a fishing trip. Four bystanders, including Cermak were hit. Cermak died of his injuries on March 6th. Zangara met the executioner on March 20.

1936   The mastermind of the St. Valentine's Day Massacre met his fate. "Machine Gun" Jack McGurn was gunned down at the Avenue Recreation Parlor and Bowling Alley. A few feet from the body, the cops found a valentine left behind by the gunmen. It read: "You've lost your job, You've lost your dough, your jewels and handsome houses, But things could be worse, you know, You haven't lost your trousers."

1964 Chris Farley was born in Madison, Wisconsin. "Saturday Night Live" producer Lorne Michaels discovered Farley performing at Second City. Motivational speaker Matt Foley, who lived "in a van down by the river" was Farley's best known "SNL" character. Farley also starred in movies such as *Tommy Boy* and *Black Sheep*. On December 18, 1997, he died of the effects of substance abuse, just like his hero John Belushi. Farley was just 33.

1964 Cubs second baseman Ken Hubbs died when the private plane he was piloting crashed near Provo, Utah en route to Colton, California. Hubbs won the National League Rookie of the Year honors in 1962, playing record 78 straight games without an error. His performance had tailed off quite a bit in 1963.

February 16

1903 Edgar Bergen was born in Chicago. The young ventriloquist asked woodcarver Theodore Mack to create a dummy based on a newsboy named Charlie who worked near Bergen's high school. Charlie McCarthy and Edgar Bergen made their radio debut on "Rudy Vallee's Royal Gelatin Hour" in 1936.

1911 Thomas Jennings was executed, the first felon convicted on fingerprint evidence. The Criminal Court of Cook County found him guilty of killing Clarence B. Hiller during a robbery on September 19, 1910. The prints were found on the freshly-painted stair rail of Hiller's home. The case would go all the way to the U.S. Supreme Court, which ruled that fingerprints were admissible evidence.

1953 James L. Kraft died in Chicago. Kraft started out with $65 and a horse named Paddy, selling cheese wholesale. In 1916, he developed pasteurized process cheese, which made it possible to ship the product over long distances. The U.S. government ordered six million tons during World War Two. Kraft introduced Miracle Whip in 1933 and the Kraft Macaroni and Cheese Dinner in 1936.

1978 The first computer bulletin board system to use a common home microcomputer was unveiled in Chicago. Ward Christensen and Randy Suess began working on the CBBS System while snowed in during a 1978 blizzard. It was the first system to post messages electronically.

Chicago 365

Christensen and Suess also developed the "X-modem," which allowed users to transfer files and data.

February 17

1844   Aaron Montgomery Ward was born in Chatham, New Jersey. Ward founded a mail-order house to offer rural customers a variety of items at prices lower than local merchants. The Great Fire wiped him out. But in August 1872, he launched his company with two employees and a list of 163 items shipped from a warehouse on North Clark Street.

1963   Michael Jordan was born in Brooklyn. He led North Carolina to a National Championship in 1982 before the Bulls picked him third in the 1984 draft. Jordan helped the Bulls win championships in 1991, 1992 and 1993, and then retired to play baseball. He returned to the Bulls 18 months later to help them win three more titles. Jordan retired again in 1999 but returned at age 38 to play for the Washington Wizards in 2001.

1977   The Brach Candy heiress checked out of the Mayo Clinic and was never seen again. In 1994, Richard Bailey, a member of the "Horse Mafia," was convicted of conspiring to have Helen Voorhees Brach murdered. Bailey romanced rich older women and sold them worthless horses. The Brach investigation solved a string of murders dating back to 1955 and uncovered a ring that killed horses to scam insurance companies.

2003   Twenty one people died in the crush as a panicked crowd tried to flee down a flight of stairs at the E2 nightclub, 2347 South Michigan. Hundreds rushed for the single narrow stairwell after a security guard sprayed pepper mace to break up a fight. The owner was under a court order not to re-open the second floor club because of code violations. City officials had been trying to shut the club down for seven months.

February 18

1950   John Hughes was born in Lansing Michigan. He grew up in the Chicago suburbs, where he would base many of his classic 80's films. Those include Sixteen Candles (1984), The Breakfast Club (1985) Pretty in Pink (1986) Weird Science (1986) Ferris Bueller's Day Off (1987) She's Having A Baby (1988- and the perfect "Link to Kevin Bacon" movie) and Uncle Buck (1989).

1967   "Kind of a Drag" by The Buckinghams hit number one. The group formed on the North Side and was originally known as The Pulsations. They made regular appearances on WGN-TV's "The All Time Hits Show," where someone suggested they find a name that sounded British. They scored big hits such as "Mercy, Mercy, Mercy" "Susan" and "Hey Baby They're Playing Our Song" before breaking up in 1968.

1970   The Chicago Seven trial ended with all defendants acquitted of conspiring to incite riots during the 1968 Democratic convention. Rennie Davis, David Dellinger, Tom Hayden, Abbie Hoffman, and Jerry Rubin were convicted of seeking to incite a riot individually. All seven, and their lawyers, William Kunstler and Leonard Weinglass, were cited for contempt. The convictions were reversed in November 1972.

1998   Cubs broadcaster Harry Caray died, four days after collapsing during a Valentine's Day dinner with his wife. Caray broadcast baseball for 53 years, including the last 16 with the Cubs. A crowd gathered at his restaurant and sang "Take Me Out to the Ball Game." Fans left flowers on the sidewalk outside Wrigley Field. The Cubs would dedicate the 1998 season to Caray and wear a patch honoring him on their sleeves.

February 19

1913   The first toys were placed inside a box of Cracker Jack. F.W. Rueckheim introduced the mixture of caramel coated popcorn and peanuts at the Columbian Exposition. His brother and partner discovered a way to keep the mixture from sticking together, a process that remains a secret to this day. Louis Ruckheim gave a sample to a salesman who said, "That's a Cracker Jack." It was a popular expression at the time.

1973   Seventh Circuit U.S. Court of Appeals Judge Otto Kerner was convicted on 17 counts of conspiracy, fraud, perjury, bribery and income tax evasion in connection with his dealings in race track stock while governor. He was the highest-ranking judge ever convicted of bribery. Kerner would be released early from federal prison when it was discovered he was suffering from terminal cancer. He died on May 9, 1976.

1994   Bonnie Blair of Champaign won the fourth gold medal of her career as she captured the 500-meter race in Lillehammer, Norway. Four days later, she won a fifth gold and the sixth medal of her career, winning the 1,000-meter. That win made her the most successful female athlete in US Olympic history.

February 20

1862   The first Confederate prisoners began arriving at Camp Douglas. The camp was located near what is now Cottage Grove and 35th Street on the former estate of Stephen Douglas. Camp Douglas had the highest mortality rate of any Civil War prison, including the notorious Andersonville. Over 18,000 prisoners would be housed there and over 6,000 may have died due to brutal treatment, exposure and disease.

1943   Cubs owner Phil Wrigley and Dodgers president Branch Rickey formed the All-American Girls Softball League in case baseball was shut down due to the war. It became the All-American Girls Baseball League early in the 1943 season. The first four teams were in Rockford, Racine, Kenosha and South Bend. The girls played with a pitching distance of 40 feet and bases 68 feet apart.

1999   Film critic Gene Siskel died following surgery for a brain tumor at the age of 53. Siskel joined the *Tribune* in 1969. In 1975, he teamed up with rival *Sun-Times* critic Roger Ebert for a monthly PBS program called "Opening Soon at a Theater Near You." That show grew into the syndicated "Siskel and Ebert," the longest running movie review show of all time.

February 21

1903   Advertising Executive Fairfax M. Cone was born in San Francisco. He formed the firm of Foote, Cone and Belding in Chicago 1942 and worked hard to make advertising a respectable profession. The firm produced such campaigns as "Does she or doesn't she?" for Clairol and "Aren't you glad you used Dial? Don't you wish everybody did?" for Dial Soap, and "The quality goes in before the name goes on" for Zenith.

1913   The Chicago Orchestra officially changed its name to the Chicago Symphony Orchestra. In 1889, businessman Norman Fay asked Theodore Thomas, the top conductor in America at the time, if he would come to Chicago if given a permanent orchestra. Thomas said, "I would go to hell if they would give me a permanent orchestra." The first concerts took place in October 1891.

1970   Bobby Hull scored his 500th career goal. It came in his 861st career game, a 4-2 win over the New York Rangers at Chicago Stadium. Bobby's son Brett would also score over 500 goals in his NHL career, making them the only father and son duo to accomplish that feat. Bobby's brother Dennis played for the Hawks for 13 years.

1970   The Jackson 5 made their debut on "American Bandstand" Jackie, Jermaine, Tito, Marlon and Michael were among nine children raised by Joe and Katherine Jackson in Gary. Michael was just five years old when their first gig at Mister Lucky's nightclub netted them $8. The boys often piled into a van to perform at the Regal Club in Chicago, where singer and producer Bobby Taylor heard the group and recommended them to Berry Gordy at Motown.

February 22

1854   The Chicago and Rock Island Railroad completed its line to the town of Rockford on the Mississippi River. Abraham Lincoln defended the railroad's right to build a bridge across the Mississippi. It was completed in 1856, and Chicago was on its way to becoming the railroad center of the nation.

1880   Dry goods and hotel magnate Potter Palmer bought the site of former frog pond for his castle. Palmer built a lavish mansion on what would become Lake Shore Drive at Banks Street. Soon, the most fashionable residents were moving to "The Gold Coast." The home cost over $1 million. It included an 80-foot tower, a three story great hall and the first elevator in a Chicago home. The Palmer Castle was leveled in 1950.

1896   John Alexander Dowie organized the Christian Catholic Church. The self-proclaimed faith healer formed his own community after being charged with manslaughter and neglect in Chicago. Dowie oversaw every aspect of life in his City of Zion. In 1901, Dowie was widely denounced after declaring he was Elijah the Restorer. His fiscal irresponsibility bankrupted the city and Dowie was deposed in 1906.

1907 Robert Young was born as George Young in Chicago. He trained at the Pasadena Playhouse and starred in several movies during the 1930's and 40's. In 1949, Young starred as Jim Anderson in the radio program, "Father Knows Best" Five years later, the show moved to television. The show ran until 1962 and is still seen in syndication today. From 1969 to 1976, Young starred in "Marcus Welby, M.D."

February 23

1905 Chicago lawyer Paul Percy Harris founded a new service club. Harris and businessmen Sylvester Schiele, Gustavus Loehr and Hiram Shorey decided to meet in rotation at each member's offices, so they named the group the Rotary Club. Today, there are 1.2 million Rotarians belonging to 31,000 chapters in 166 countries.

1875 Edgar Rice Burroughs was born in Chicago. Burroughs failed as a pencil sharpener salesman before writing for pulp magazines. His "Dejah Thoris, Princess of Mars" appeared in the February 1912 issue of *All Story* magazine. In May 1912, he finished *Tarzan of the Apes*. The book tells the story of young Lord Greystoke, John Carter, abandoned in the jungle and raised by apes.

1900 An election was held to incorporate a new village in rural Cook County. Residents had several choices for a name, Bellwood, Lovedale, Bottleville, Manure Park and Hogs Alley. (There was a big manure dump at 25th Avenue and Saint Charles Road) Fortunately, the majority voted to name the village Bellwood.

1988 The Board of Aldermen voted 7-2 to allow lights at Wrigley Field. But the measure called for no more than 18 night games each season. The Aldermen faced threats from The Tribune Company to move the Cubs to the suburbs and Major League Baseball declared there would be no post-season games played in the daytime. Manager Jim Frey said, "If we went by tradition, we would still be playing without gloves."

1995 Former Chicago stockbroker Steve Fossett became the first person to fly solo across the Pacific Ocean in a balloon, as he landed in

Chicago 365

Leader, Saskatchewan. Fossett soon turned his attention to making the first solo balloon flight around the world. It took six attempts, but Fossett made it in July 2002.

February 24

1843   The town of Blue Island was incorporated. The settlement was established as a rest stop for travelers on the Vincennes Trail. The Indians named the area after the bluish mist sometimes seen in the distance from atop the ridge. The arrival of the Rock Island Railroad in the 1870's transformed Blue Island into a trading hub.

1859   Wheaton was incorporated. Erastus Gary came to the area in 1837.   He returned to New England several times, and talked Jesse and Warren Wheaton into moving to Illinois. In 1848, they gave the railroad several miles of right-of-way, and the railroad named the depot Wheaton. The Wheaton brothers gave land free of charge to settlers who would build immediately in the new community.

1924   Johnny Weissmuller, set a new record for swimming in the 100-meter race. (57:2/5 seconds). In the 1924 Olympics at Paris, the former altar boy at St. Michael Church would win the 100-meter and the 400-meter freestyle. He would also capture a bronze in the 4 X 200 meter relay. Four years later, he won two more Olympic titles in Amsterdam. In 1935, Weissmuller would make the first of his 18 Tarzan films.

1991   George Gobel died.   He was a child star from Chicago who played the roles of all the children on the Tom Mix radio shows and made frequent appearances on the WLS "Barn Dance." The popular nightclub comedian hosted "The George Gobel Show" on CBS from 1954 to 1960. He may be best remembered for his appearances on "The Hollywood Squares."

February 25

1845   The City Council was authorized to collect "one mill on the dollar" for a school tax.   Free public schools had been established in November 1840 and the first public school house was built on Madison Street between Dearborn and State in 1844. A charter amendment in February 1857 would establish a school board.

Chicago 365

1940 Ron Santo was born in Seattle. As a Cubs rookie in 1960, he hid his diabetes, stashing Snickers and Cokes in the dugout. The fiery third baseman played 14 seasons with the Cubs and one with the White Sox. He took over as color commentator on WGN in 1990. In recent years, Ron faced a quadruple bypass and loss of a leg. The Cubs retired his uniform number on September 28, 2003.

1983 Ten-year-old Jeanine Nicarico of Naperville was raped and murdered. Rolando Cruz and Alejandro Hernandez spent over a decade in prison, much of that time on death row, for the murder. But Chicago lawyer and author Scott Turow became convinced the men were innocent. They were freed in 1995.

1994 "The Lip" was elected to the Baseball Hall of Fame. Leo Durocher managed the Cubs from 1966-1972, nearly leading them to a pennant in 1969. But he clashed with several players, particularly Ron Santo. In September 1971, Phil Wrigley took out an ad criticizing the players who wanted Durocher fired. Durocher insisted he wasn't forced out when he stepped down on July 25, 1972.

February 26

1845 Joliet was incorporated. Louis Joliet and Father Jacques Marquette camped on a mound in the Des Plaines River in 1673 while returning from their journey of discovery. The spot became known as Joliet Mound. James B. Campbell laid out the town in 1834 and named it Juliet, probably in honor of his daughter. President Martin Van Buren visited and suggested the town should be known as Joliet.

1859 Louise De Koven was born. Although born into a life of privilege, DeKoven became a tireless social reformer and advocate for children. She was instrumental in the establishment of the first juvenile court in the nation at Chicago. Louise De Koven Bowen took over Hull House after Jane Adams died and led the fight for women's suffrage. She was briefly considered as a candidate for mayor in 1923.

1914 William Grant Stratton was born in Ingleside, Illinois. Stratton served as Governor of Illinois from 1952 to 1960. He was instrumental in the construction of the Kennedy, Eisenhower, Stevenson, Edens and Dan

Ryan Expressways. Stratton was indicted for tax evasion after he left office, but was acquitted after Senator Edward Dirksen defended Stratton's use of campaign funds.

2004   A crowd gathered at Harry Caray's Restaurant on Kinzie Street to witness the destruction of the ball that many fans believe cost the Cubs the 2003 pennant. The restaurant paid $113,824.16 for the foul ball deflected away from Moises Alou by Steve Bartman. A Hollywood special effects artist used heat, pressure and explosives to destroy the ball. The remnants are on now display at three Harry Caray's Restaurants.

February 27

1904   Thomas Farrell was born in Chicago, one of 15 children. His grandmother raised him because his family could not afford another child. Farrell began writing at age 21, and based his work upon his experiences growing up in Washington Park among the lower-middle class Irish. He is best remembered for his trilogy featuring a tough Irish-American youth named Studs Lonigan.

1911   Chicago City Hall was dedicated. Architects Holabird & Roche designed the twin building that takes up the entire block bounded by Randolph, LaSalle, Washington, and Clark streets. Four granite panels sculpted by John Flanagan flank the main entrance. They show four important functions of city government. The building was extensively remodeled in 1967.

1956   The Village of Schaumburg was incorporated with a population of 130 and an area of two square miles. The area was originally known as Sarah's Grove. But Germans, including many from the Schaumburg-Lippe area, soon owned all the land. O'Hare Airport expansion, new expressways and the Motorola complex touched off a population boom. Today over 75,000 people call Schaumburg home.

1977   In a 4-3 loss to the Vancouver Canucks, Stan Mikita of the Chicago Black Hawks scored the 500th goal of his NHL career. "Stosh" would finish his 22-year career with the Hawks in 1980 with 541 lifetime goals and 1,467 points. At the time, his points total was the second best in hockey history, behind only Gordie Howe.

Chicago 365

1979 "The Snow Queen" upset Mayor Michael Bilandic in the Democratic primary. Bilandic had fired Jane Byrne from her cabinet position, and she was given little chance of winning. But 72 inches of snow buried the city in January and February. The response by the Bilandic administration was inept. It also turned out he had paid his former pal $90,000 to write a snow emergency plan that no one could find.

February 28

1894 Ben Hecht was born in New York. Hecht is best remembered for his play, *The Front Page*. The story was based on his own experiences at the Chicago *Daily News*. Several movies were based on the play, including *His Girl Friday*, with Cary Grant and Rosalind Russell; *The Front Page*, with Walter Matthau and Jack Lemmon, and *Switching Channels*, starring Burt Reynolds and Kathleen Turner.

1903 Vincente Minnelli was born in Chicago. Minnelli directed classics such as *Meet Me in St. Louis, Gigi* and *Designing Women* for MGM. At first Minelli clashed with Judy Garland, his star in *Meet Me in St. Louis*. But they were engaged by the time filming was finished. They were married from 1945 to1951, and named their daughter after the Gershwin song, "Liza."

1963 The mob ended the life of Alderman Benjamin Lewis. Lewis overcame poverty and racism to become the committeeman for the 24th Ward in Douglas Park. As his power grew, he criticized African-American leaders aligned with the Daley machine and appointed dozens of black committeemen. Mobsters manacled Lewis to a chair in his Roosevelt Street office and shot him three times in the head.

1989 Richard M. Daley defeated acting Mayor Eugene Sawyer in the Democratic primary. His father Richard J. Daley served as mayor for 21 years. Richard M. Daley would go on to defeat Timothy Evans and Edward Vrdolyak in the general election. His tenure has been marked by a controversy over closing Meigs Field, but Daley was elected to a fifth term on February 25, 2003.

February 29

1940 Newspaper owner and publisher Robert S. Abbott died. His

Chicago 365

Chicago Defender was the largest selling black newspaper in the nation and spurred migration of blacks to Chicago from the rural areas of the Deep South. During a wave of lynchings, the paper said, "If you must die, take at least one with you." *The Defender* still has a circulation of about 30,000 today.

1960 The first Playboy Club opened in Chicago at 116 East Walton Street. Hugh Hefner went to court to obtain a liquor license after authorities balked at the bunny costumes. Eventually, 40 such clubs described by *Newsweek* as "Disneyland For Adults," would spring up around the world. The Chicago location closed in 1986. The Regal Knickerbocker Hotel occupies the site today.

1968 The "Kerner Commission," named after chairman Governor Otto Kerner of Illlinois, issued its report on the riots that swept major cities across the nation. The commission declared that the United States was "headed towards two societies, one Black and one White – separate and unequal."

March

March 1

1884 A permit was issued for William Le Baron Jenney's Home Insurance Company Building at LaSalle and Adams. A skeleton of steel beams instead of masonry supported the building, paving the way for the first skyscrapers. Architects such as Louis Sullivan and John Wellborn Root were soon designing tall buildings that became known as "The Chicago School" of architecture. The Home Insurance Building was torn down in 1931.

1917 Harry Christopher Carabina was born in St. Louis. Harry Caray played semi-pro baseball briefly before he became a radio announcer at age 19. He called St. Louis Cardinal games from 1945 to 1969, and then worked in Oakland in 1970. In 1971, he came to the Chicago White Sox. Caray moved across town in 1982, and was the beloved voice of the Cubs until his death on February 18, 1998.

1935 Conrad Robert Falk was born in Chicago. The former milkman and singer known as Robert Conrad starred as Tom Lopacka on "Hawaiian Eye." He starred as Jim West on "The Wild, Wild West" from 1965-70. Conrad also played Pappy Boyington in "Baa Baa Black Sheep." The series debuted on NBC in 1976, was cancelled and revived in 1977, and then cancelled again in 1978.

1999 A jury awarded violin prodigy Rachel Barton $29.6 million for the 1995 train accident that cost her a leg. Barton was dragged 366 feet from a Winnetka platform when the strap of her violin case got wedged in the train door. Railroad attorneys said Barton held onto the strap to save her $500,000 violin.

March 2

1891 The Village of Bartlett was incorporated The original forty acre town site was owned by Luther Bartlett, a native of Conway, Massachusetts. He came to the area in 1844. The family used the site as a source of timber for buildings and firewood. Bartlett's population has grown from 360 in 1900, to 3501 in 1970, to 36,706 in 2000.

1908 A Jewish immigrant from Russia, Lazarus Averbuch, stabbed and wounded Police Chief George Shippy. He also wounded Shippy's son and bodyguard before they shot him dead. Convinced the attack was a Jewish plot to avenge the arrest of anarchist Emma Goldman, Shippy ordered hundreds of people rounded up, but he failed to prove a plot. He never returned to the force and died a madman from syphilis in 1911.

1932 Al Capone offered a $10,000 reward for the capture of the Lindbergh baby kidnapers. Capone was in a Chicago jail cell, awaiting appeal of his eleven-year sentence for tax evasion. Scarface denied that he was involved. He said he could help find the real kidnapers if he wasn't in jail.

1992 Ryne Sandberg briefly became the highest paid player in Major League history as he signed a four-year contract worth $28.4 million. In 1994, Sandberg announced his retirement, saying he could not ask Cubs fans to pay his salary when he was not pleased with his performance. It cost him $10 million in salary for the next two seasons. He made a comeback in 1996 and retired for good in 1997.

March 3

1831 George Pullman was born in Albion, New York. He made a fortune after devising a system to raise buildings, lifting Chicago from the mud. He used the money to develop the Pullman Sleeper railroad car. Orders poured in after a sleeper brought Abraham Lincoln's body home. Pullman built a complete town around his factory. But he slashed wages without cutting rents in 1894, and a violent strike erupted. He died a hated man.

1887 Congress officially established a fort on land donated by a group of businessmen who wanted troops to protect property amid the labor unrest. Fort Highwood would be re-named in honor of Army General Philip Sheridan when he died in 1888. Troops arrived in November 1887 and were used during the Pullman Strike of 1894. During World War Two, 500,000 men and women were processed there. Fort Sheridan closed in 1993.

1904 Paul Cornell died. In 1853, the lawyer from New York bought

Chicago 365

300 acres of lakefront land between 51st and 55th Streets. He built a hotel and named the area Hyde Park, after the park in London. Chicago annexed Hyde Park in 1889. The University of Chicago was established there in 1892 and Jackson Park housed the 1893 Columbian Exposition.

1953 Fahey Flynn made his debut on the 10 pm WBBM-TV newscast. For more than 30 years, Flynn would be a comfortable presence in Chicago homes. He was teamed with P.J. Hoff, a very funny man who drew cartoons to illustrate the weather. In 1968, the management of WBBM decided that Flynn's trademark bow tie wasn't hip. So Flynn jumped to rival WLS Channel 7, and led them to the top of the ratings.

March 4

1747 Kasimir Pulaski was born in Poland. He was a heroic Polish freedom fighter who died fighting for our freedom in the Revolutionary War. In 1933, Mayor Edward Kelly changed the name of Crawford Avenue to Pulaski Road, sparking a 20-year legal fight that went all the way to the Illinois Supreme Court. Many people still call it Crawford Avenue to this day.

1837 The Legislature granted a city charter to Chicago. The population stood at about 4,200. William B. Ogden would be elected the first Mayor in May, when 709 citizens went to the polls. A city census showed that there were 398 dwellings, 5 churches, 26 liquor dispensaries, 10 taverns, 19 groceries, 17 law offices and 3 drug stores in the newly chartered city. There was $1,193 in the city treasury.

1888 Knute Rockne was born in Voss, Norway. His family came to Chicago when Knute was five years old and he played football on the sandlots of the Logan Square neighborhood before heading for Notre Dame. He coached the Fighting Irish from 1918 to 1930, racking up five undefeated seasons. Rockne died in a plane crash in Kansas in 1931.

1952 Nancy Davis and Ronald Reagan were married in Los Angeles. She was born Anne Francis Robbins in New York but grew up on Chicago's North Side, after her actress mother married neurosurgeon Dr. Loyal Davis. She graduated from Girl's Latin School and then attended Smith College. As Nancy Davis, she appeared in eleven films between 1949 and 1956, including *Hellcats of the Navy* with Ronald Reagan.

Chicago 365

1978   Chicago's last afternoon newspaper died at the age of 102. The *Daily News* was once home to Carl Sandburg. Columnist Mike Royko became the voice of the working class. Eugene Field, the first daily columnist, wrote for the *Daily News*. His "Wynken, Blynken and Nod" and "Little Boy Blue" first appeared there. Ben Hecht wrote the play *The Front Page* based on his experiences as a *Daily News* reporter during the 1920's.

March 5

1962   Mayor JDaley called it "a great thing for the city" as the first family moved into one of the 28 gleaming towers of the Robert Taylor homes. The 4,400-unit complex along State Street was the largest housing project in the world. Complexes such as Taylor, Cabrini-Green and the Henry Horner Homes were seen as a way to provide decent housing for poor families. But they became a symbol of failed good intentions.

1982   John Belushi died of a cocaine and heroin overdose at the Chateau Marmont Hotel in West Hollywood. His friend Cathy Smith would be charged with involuntary manslaughter for administering the deadly dosage. She was sentenced to three years in prison.   John's "Cheeseburger, Cheeseburger" skit on "Saturday Night Live" was based on the Billy Goat Restaurant in Chicago.

1990   The former dean of the City Council died. Vito Marzullo ran the 25th Ward from 1953 to 1985. He declared, "The mayor don't run the 25th Ward, neither does the news media or the do-gooders. Me, Vito Marzullo, that's who runs the 25th Ward, and on Election Day everybody does what Vito Marzullo tells them." Oakley Boulevard in the Heart of Chicago area carries the honorary name Vito Marzullo Boulevard.

March 6

1831   Philip Sheridan was born in Albany, New York. General Sheridan was a hero of the Civil War who went on to fight Indians on the plains. In 1871, he came to Chicago as General of the Army. Sheridan ordered the destruction of buildings that halted the spread of the Great Fire to the South. Fort Highwood north of Chicago was re-named in his honor when Sheridan died in 1888.

Chicago 365

1928   The Village of Gurnee was incorporated. When the railroad arrived in 1873, the depot was named after Walter Gurnee, a member of the board of directors and a former Mayor of Chicago.   Gurnee may be best known as the home of Six Flags Great America, which opened on May 9, 1976. The Massive Gurnee Mills Shopping Center opened 1991.

1933   Mayor Anton Cermak died. Guiseppe Zangara supposedly was firing at President Franklin Roosevelt when he hit Cermak on February 15th in Miami.   Zangara laughed when he was sentenced to death. Cermak may actually have been Zangara's target.   Some believe that Al Capone ordered Cermak's death in revenge for the shooting of Frank Nitti by Cermak's special police detail.

2000   The Chicago group Earth Wind and Fire were inducted into the Rock and Roll Hall of Fame. Maurice White formed the group in 1969. He studied music composition and percussion at Roosevelt University and recorded at Chess Studios before joining Ramsey Lewis' group in 1967. After leaving Lewis, he formed a group named after the three elements in his astrological chart.

March 7

1958   The Village of Buffalo Grove was incorporated, with a population of 164. Within two years, the population had risen to 670.   The Village became one of the fastest growing areas in the Northwest suburbs. Over 42,000 people live there today. In their book, Lee & Saralee Rosenberg named it one of the *50 Fabulous Places to Raise Your Family*.

1971   Theater owner Barney Balaban died in Byram, Connecticut. Barney and his brother bought the Kedzie Theater at Kedzie and Roosevelt Road in 1908.   The business grew into Chicago's largest theater chain, Balaban and Katz. (Later ABC-Great States Theaters and Plitt Theaters)   Balaban's Theaters were lavish movie palaces. They included the Central Park, Riviera, Granada, the State-Lake and the Chicago.

1979   Hack Wilson was elected to the Hall of Fame. In 1930, the Cubs slugger smacked 56 home runs, a National League record that stood until Mark McGwire and Sammy Sosa came along. Wilson drove in 191 runs in 1930, a record that still stands.   Wilson got his nickname either from wrestler George Hackenschmidt or from Hack Miller, a 5' 9" 195-pound Cubs player of the 1920's.

1998   Eleanor Shuman died in Elgin at age 87. She was one of the last living survivors of the *Titanic* disaster. Shuman was the only survivor to meet *Titanic* director James Cameron. She met him at the Chicago premiere of the movie. Eleanor was just 18 months old when she was placed in the last lifeboat to leave the ship on April 15, 1912. Shuman said she remembered the screams of the dying.

March 8

1857   Margaret McGuiness died from excessive sex and alcohol. She was the most famous prostitute in The Sands, an area dubbed by the *Tribune* as "The vilest and most dangerous place in Chicago." It was said that McGuiness did not have clothes on for three years, and entertained from ten to 40 men per night.

1908   In Chicago, two socialist women, Gertrude Breslau-Hunt and May Wood-Simons, spoke against the exploitation of underpaid women workers. The event is one of those that resulted in March 8th being declared as International Women's Day. In 1968, Chicago women revived the celebration of International Women's Day in the U.S.

2004   A judge approved a new interim agreement between the Chicago Board of Education and the U.S. Justice Department, replacing the original 1980 desegregation decree. The judge said he might end federal oversight by 2006. The Public Schools agreed to issue reports on school-by-school spending and consider new standards for admission to magnet schools.

March 9

1871   Oscar DePriest was born in   Florence, Alabama. In 1915, DePriest became the first African American to serve on the City Council. He would also serve as Cook County Commissioner. On November 6, 1928, DePriest became the first African American to be elected to U.S. House of Representatives in the 20th century. DePriest served in the House until 1934.

1892   Three friends of Ida Wells were lynched in Memphis after opening

Chicago 365

a grocery store across the street from a white-owned store. Wells wrote blistering editorials against lynching in her local black newspaper. She took her crusade to England, and came to Chicago after her life was threatened in Memphis. She married attorney Ferdinand Barrett, and helped form the organization now known as the NAACP.

1915   Henry Legler, head of the Chicago Public Library, declared that he had no intention of banning so-called "sex novels." Legler declared, "There are books that deal with sex relations that have a sureness of touch that make them more moral than many spineless novels."

1943   Bobby Fischer was born in Chicago. Fischer began playing chess at age six and developed an aggressive style. When he defeated Boris Spassky of the Soviet Union to win the world title in 1972, Fischer sparked renewed interest in the game. He lost the title by default in 1975, refusing to play due to a dispute over the rules. Fischer went into seclusion and has not played publicly since.

2002   Winds gusting at nearly 60 miles per hour caused scaffolding to fall 43 stories from the Hancock Building to the street below. Three people in cars on the street were killed as the platforms came down. Eight people were injured. Glass and debris rained down while bystanders tried to help the victims.

March 10

1844   John Quarter was consecrated as the first Catholic Bishop of Chicago. When Quarter arrived, the cathedral was incomplete, there was just one church in Chicago (St. Mary's) and the parish was deep in debt. Quarter opened the first college in Chicago and used much of his own money to complete the Cathedral.

1919   Clyde "Bulldog" Turner was born in Plains, Texas. In 1940, the Detroit Lions were certain that Turner would turn down offers from other teams, so they didn't bother to draft the Hardin-Simmons University prospect. The Bears snapped him up. At center and linebacker, Turner led the Bears to four straight NFL title game appearances and three championships. He was named to the Football Hall of Fame in 1966.

Chicago 365

1933 Six black horses bore the casket of Mayor Anton Cermak from City Hall to Soldier Field. Over 30,000 people marched in the procession, while a crowd of 500,000 lined the streets. A minister, a priest and a rabbi performed the service and at 12:00 noon, the entire city paused in tribute. That afternoon, the man who took a bullet meant for President Roosevelt was laid to rest at Bohemian National Cemetery.

1986 The Wrigley Company raised the price of a seven-stick pack of chewing gum from 25 to 30 cents, the first price increase in six years. When introduced in 1893, a five-stick pack cost five cents. It remained a nickel until 1971 when the firm reluctantly raised the price by putting seven sticks in a ten-cent pack.

March 11

1869 Highland Park was incorporated. Walter S. Gurnee named the railroad depot Highland Park in 1854. Gurnee was an early mayor of Chicago, a railroad board member and the man who gave his name to the Village of Gurnee. The Highland Park residents wanted a city government in order to drive out the saloons. There were eight in the city limits at the time.

1924 Belva Gaertner shot and killed her married lover, Walter Law. The twice divorced caberet singer said, "No woman can love a man enough to kill him. They aren't worth it, because there are always plenty more." She added, "Gin and guns - either one is bad enough, but together they get you in a dickens of a mess" Gaertner was acquitted. The Velma Kelly character in the play and motion picture *Chicago* is based on Gaertner.

1955 Oscar Meyer died. Oscar and his brother Gottfried started out with a leased meat market in Chicago in 1883. The firm sponsored the German exhibit at the Columbian Exposition in 1893 and first applied the brand name in 1904. Oscar Meyer introduced the Weinermobile in 1936 and the Oscar Meyer jingle ("Oh I wish I was an Oscar Meyer Weiner!") made its debut in 1963.

1959 Lorraine Hansbury's play, *A Raisin in the Sun* premiered in New York. Sidney Poitier starred on stage and in the movie version. Hansbury based the story on her childhood experiences as an upper class family in a white Chicago neighborhood. The title comes from a line in a Langston Hughes poem, "What happens to a dream deferred? Does it dry up like a raisin in the sun? Or fester like a sore—and then run?"

March 12

1849   A massive ice jam on the Chicago River broke loose. The ice and resulting flood wiped out the bridges and the docks. It damaged or destroyed four steamships, six steamboats, 24 brigs, 27 canal boats and two sloops. Two children were killed. A falling mast hit one and the other died at the Randolph Street Bridge.

1917   Leonard Chess was born in Poland. Leonard and his brother Phil arrived in Chicago in 1928 and recorded nightclub performers in their garage. Their label was originally known as Aristocrat, but changed to Chess in 1950. The second Chess release was "Rollin' Stone" by Muddy Waters. Chess turned down a young Elvis Presley, but would record performers such as Chuck Berry, Bo Diddley and Howlin' Wolf.

1966   Bobby Hull of the Blackhawks scored his 51st goal of the season against the New York Rangers, becoming the first NHL player to collect more than 50. Hull ended the season with 54. "The Golden Jet" would go on to score 50 goals or more in a season five times in his career.

1989   Some 2,500 veterans and supporters marched at the School of the Art Institute of Chicago to demand removal of an American flag placed on the floor. It was part of a student Scott Tyler's exhibit "What Is The Proper Way To Display A U.S. Flag?" Republican Senator Walter Dudycz led the fight against the exhibit. The school's government funding was slashed following the controversy.

March 13

1848   The Chicago Board of Trade opened above the Gage and Haines flour store with just 82 members. Founded to promote and bring order to commerce in Chicago, the board initially lured members with a free lunch. A grading system for commodities was established in 1856 and the board developed futures contracts in 1865. Today, the BOT is the world's largest futures and options exchange.

1960 Cardinals owner Violet Bidwell Wolfner announced that the team was moving to St. Louis. Just 160,438 fans had paid to see the team play in Chicago during a 2-10 season in 1959. Two home games were played in Minneapolis. Bears owner George Halas had blocked the Cardinals from moving to Dyche Stadium, and was reportedly so eager enough to see the Big Red leave that he helped pay their moving expenses.

1975 A syndicate headed by Chicago White Sox owner Jerry Reinsdorf bought the Bulls. A few days later, Reinsdorf hired Jerry Krause as the new General Manager. Krause drafted Scottie Pippen, Horace Grant, B.J. Armstrong, Will Purdue, and Tony Kukoc. Those players, along with Michael Jordan, would make the Bulls the dominant NBA team of the 1990s.

March 14

1914 A crowd of 5,000 turned out as ground was broken for a new baseball park. Charles Weeghman built Weeghman Park for his Federal League team. When the league folded, Weegham bought the Cubs. The stadium would be renamed after he sold the team to William Wrigley Junior and a group of investors in 1918. Weegham lost his fortune and his restaurant chain backing the Federal League.

1934 Astronaut Eugene Cernan was born in Chicago. The graduate of Proviso Township School in Maywood began astronaut training in 1963. He was a crewmember aboard Gemini Nine and Apollo Ten. In 1972, he commanded Apollo 17. He is the last man to leave his footprints on the surface of the moon. Cernan was the second man to walk in space and is one of only two men to have flown to the moon twice.

1933 Quincy Delight Jones was born in Chicago. Jones first rose to national attention as a trumpet player for Lionel Hampton and became a renowned jazz artist, producer and arranger. In 1962, he wrote "Soul Bossa Nova," better known as the theme from *Austin Powers*. Jones produced Michael Jackson's groundbreaking solo albums, including *Thriller*. He has won over 25 Grammy Awards.

1981 Nineteen people were killed in a fire at the Royal Beach Hotel,

Chicago 365

5523 North Kenmore. The blaze at the four-story apartment hotel for transients also injured 14 people, including two police officers. Firefighters used ladders to rescue 15 tenants and several residents jumped to safety from as high as three stories up.

March 15

1815 Arnold Damen was born in Holland. Damen was a pioneer Catholic educator and the founder of Holy Family Parish. Holy Family Church was dedicated on August 26, 1860. Damen opened a free school for girls and one for boys in 1857. He served as the first president of St. Ignatius Seminary, the forerunner of Loyola University. Robey Street was renamed Damen Avenue in his honor in 1927.

1937 The first blood bank in the United States opened at Cook County Hospital. Doctor Bernard Fantus, Director of Therapeutics, discovered that blood treated with a 2% solution of Sodium Citrate would not clot right away and could be refrigerated. The blood could be stored for only ten days. Fantus coined the term, "blood bank."

1984 Former Deputy Traffic Court Clerk Harold Conn became the first to be convicted as a result of the FBI's "Operation Greylord" investigation. The sting operation uncovered widespread corruption in the Cook County court. Nearly 100 officials would ultimately be convicted, including 15 judges, four court clerks, 13 police officers and 50 attorneys. FBI agents had posed as defendants offering bribes to have cases dismissed.

1999 Eleven people were killed and over 100 injured when the Amtrak City of *New Orleans* collided with an 18-wheeler at a crossing in Bourbonnais, 50 miles south of Chicago. The train was carrying about 215 passengers. Most of the victims were in the sleeper car, which was directly behind the engines and luggage cars.

March 16

1899 Joseph Medill died at the age of 75. One of the founders of the Republican Party, Medill took over the Chicago *Tribune* in 1855 and built it into a powerful paper. He was instrumental in securing the nomination of

Chicago 365

Abraham Lincoln for president. Medill was also a racist who once proposed giving arsenic to the unemployed. After the Great Fire, Medill's optimism got him elected mayor.

1900   Ban Johnson announced that the new American League would field a team in Chicago. Under a deal with NL officials, the team would play its games on the south side and use the nickname, "White Stockings," previously used by the NL team. But the AL team was not allowed to use "Chicago" in the official name.

1993   Fire broke out at the Paxton Hotel, 1432 North LaSalle. Residents were trapped due to bars installed on the first floor windows. Heroic firefighters rescued over 100 people, but 19 residents were killed. The fire spurred formation of the Chicago High Rise Commission, which recommended that sprinkler systems be phased in.

March 17

1850   The early Irish settlers in Chicago were lured by jobs building the Illinois and Michigan Canal. By 1850, 1/5 of the population was Irish. Finley Peter Dunne's "Mr. Dooley" newspaper columns offered a look at their lives in the 1890's and James T. Farrell's Studs Lonigan trilogy told their story during the Great Depression. Irish Mayors of Chicago included John Hopkins, Edward F. Dunne, William E. Dever, Edward J. Kelly, Martin J. Kennelly and Richard J. Daley. Daley's son leads the city today and Michael Flatley of Chicago brings Irish culture to the masses through his roles in "Riverdance" and "Lord of the Dance."

1910   Architect Zachary Taylor Davis kneeled on a piece of genuine auld sod and placed the cornerstone for the "Baseball Palace of the World." The new Comiskey Park opened on July 1, 1910. The spacious park with a double-decked grandstand replaced the South Side Grounds at 39th and Wentworth, a rickety firetrap.

1919   Nathaniel Adams Coles was born in Montgomery, Alabama. His family moved to Chicago when he was four. In high school, Nat and his brother formed the Eddie Coles Solid Swingers and played at the Panama Tavern on 58th Street. He made his first recordings in 1936. Nat "King" Cole went on to record classics such as "The Christmas Song, "Mona Lisa" and "Too Young." He hosted a show on NBC-TV in 1957 and 1958.

Chicago 365

1967 Billy Corgan was born in Chicago. He formed his first band while attending Glenbard North High School in Carol Stream. He went on to form the Smashing Pumpkins, one of the most successful and critically acclaimed bands of the 1990's. The group recorded five albums before breaking up, including *Siamese Dream* in 1993 and the smash *Mellon Collie and the Infinite Sadness* in 1995.

1995 Challenger Hal Baskin hinted that 16th Ward incumbent Alderman Shirley Coleman might be partially to blame for the behavior of her former husband, Hernando Williams. Williams was about to be executed for rape and murder. Baskin said, "She may not have been giving the man what he needed at home." Coleman won re-election.

March 18

1893 The largest piece of hollow forged steel in the world arrived in Chicago. The axle for the Observation Wheel at the Columbian Exposition weighed 89,320 pounds. It was 45 ½ feet long and 33 inches in diameter. Pittsburgh bridge builder George Ferris designed the 264-foot-tall wheel to rival the Eiffel Tower in Paris, built for an exposition in 1889.

1942 Two black players were allowed to work out with the White Sox at spring training in Pasadena. Nate Moreland and a man who excelled at football, track, swimming and baseball at UCLA didn't impress manager Jimmy Dykes. The Major League color barrier was still in full force, and Dykes was none too fond of blacks. That other player's name was Jackie Robinson.

1988 The re-united "Rat Pack," Frank Sinatra, Dean Martin and Sammy Davis Jr., appeared at the Chicago Theatre. In 1962, The Rat Pack played 16 shows in eight days at The Villa Venice in Wheeling. It was an effort to appease owner Sam Giancana. Sinatra had enlisted Giancana's help for the Kennedy campaign, and Giancana became enraged when Attorney General Robert Kennedy came after the mob.

1995 A press release simply announced, "I'm Back." Michael Jordan announced he was coming out of retirement and returning to the Chicago Bulls. Jordan would start and score 19 points the next day as the Bulls lost to Indiana in overtime, 103-96. With Jordan back for the final 17 games of the regular season, the Bulls went 13-4 to finish at 47-35 overall.

March 19

1914 Jay Berwanger was born in Dubuque, Iowa. The quarterback for the University of Chicago won the first Heisman Trophy in 1935. (At the time known as the Manhattan Downtown Athletic Club Trophy) When the NFL began its college draft in 1936, Berwanger was the first player selected. But he walked away when George Halas refused to pay him $25,000 for a two-year deal. Jay never played in the NFL.

1921 Carl Wanderer was executed for killing his pregnant wife and "a ragged stranger" that he claimed had shot her in a staged holdup. Wanderer sang "Dear Old Pal O'Mine" as he went to the gallows. Ben Hecht of the *Daily News* and Charles MacArthur of the *Examiner* had solved the case. MacArthur quipped, "that son-of-a-bitch should have been a song-plugger."

1943 Frank "The Enforcer" Nitti killed himself near his home in Riverside. He had been indicted for shaking down movie industry figures and the claustrophobic mobster couldn't face the thought of more prison time. Nitti had taken over for Al Capone and consolidated the gangs into "The Outfit." He survived a 1932 assassination attempt plotted by Mayor Cermak. Cermak wanted to put his own hoods in power.

1998 The Blackhawks retired Dennis Savard's number 18. Savard was the fifth player in team history to have their number retired. He ranks fourth among Hawks with 377 lifetime goals, second with 719 assists and third with 1,096 points. He scored 473 goals during his career, including his seasons with Montreal and Tampa Bay.

March 20

1933 Giuseppe Zangara went to the electric chair in Florida for attempting to assassinate President Roosevelt and killing Chicago Mayor Anton Cermak instead. He had emerged from a crowd at a Miami park and opened fire on February 15. Zangara was defiant to the end. His last words were, "You give me electric chair. I no afraid of that chair! You one of capitalists. You is crook man too. Put me in electric chair. I no care!"

1944 A near riot broke out in at Goldblatt's Department Store on State

Chicago 365

Street. About 2,500 women trampled guards and floorwalkers to snap up the 1,500 alarm clocks advertised for sale. Alarm clocks had become precious commodities since they were last sold in 1942. Many of the customers were war workers who complained they had no clock to wake them up and relied on someone to nudge them.

1969   A federal grand jury indicted eight police officers and eight demonstrators on criminal charges stemming from the disturbances at the Democratic National Convention the previous summer. The eight demonstrators were Abbie Hoffman, Jerry Rubin, David Dellinger, Tom Hayden, Rennie Davis, John Froines, Lee Weiner, and Bobby Seale.

March 21

1869   Florenz Ziegfeld, Junior was born in Chicago. In 1896, Ziegfield met French actress Anna Held, who suggested a show similar to the Folies-Bergere The first show opened in New York in July 1907. The shows featuring scantily clad chorus girls soon became known as "Ziegfeld Follies." Zeigfeld developed stars such as Will Rogers, Fanny Brice and Eddie Cantor.

1925   Two convicted prohibition agents faced up to four years in prison and $20,000 in fines in connection with a $5 million sacramental wine scandal.   The agents worked with rabbis to form phony Jewish congregations to obtain "sacramental" wine. The Director and ex-director of the Illinois Prohibition department would be indicted.

1928   Capone men killed bootlegger and 19th Ward GOP Committeeman "Diamond Joe" Esposito.   Esposito was an associate of U.S. Senator Charles Deneen, who was running against a slate backed by Capone and Mayor "Big Bill" Thompson. The election was known as "The Pineapple Primary" due to the dozens of bombings aimed at Deneen supporters.

1997   Three white teenagers attacked Lenard Clark, a 13-year-old black boy in Bridgeport. The attack left Clark brain damaged. Frank Caruso, Victor Jasas and Michael Kwidinski were charged in the case. Caruso would be sentenced to eight years in prison for aggravated battery and a hate crime. But Jasas and Kwidinski pleaded guilty to aggravated battery and got off with probation and 300 hours of community service.

March 22

1861 Chicago had no police protection. Mayor John Wentworth had slashed the number of officers to save money. When citizens complained, he imposed a citywide curfew. The legislature formed an independent police board, which insulted "Long John." At 2:00 a.m., he sacked the entire force. It took 12 hours for the Board to find new officers and convince many of the fired cops to return. Only two robberies were committed.

1899 Dancer and choreographer Ruth Page was born in Indianapolis. Page was a major influence on the Chicago dance scene for over 70 years. At a time when foreign countries dominated dance, Ruth broke tradition and created ballet that was unabashedly American. She is also credited with originating the style of combining opera and ballet.

1913 Mladen George Sekulovich was born in Gary. As Karl Malden, he won an Academy Award for his role as Mitch in *A Streetcar Named Desire* in 1951 and was nominated for his portrayal of Father Corrigan in *On the Waterfront* in 1954. He may be best known as Mike Stone in the TV series "Streets of San Francisco," which ran from 1972 to 1977. Malden also starred in American Express commercials for 21 years.

1958 Famed producer Michael Todd died in a New Mexico plane crash. The third husband of Elizabeth Taylor was buried in Beth Aaron Cemetery in Forest Park. His remains disappeared in 1977. Hollywood private investigator Anthony Pellicano led a TV crew to them, claiming mobsters dug up the grave to find a ring. But Pellicano probably did it as a publicity stunt. Todd was reburied under his real name, Avrom Goldbogen.

March 23

1901 The First Chicago Auto Show opened in the Coliseum at 15th and Wabash. More than 65 firms showcased the latest designs as cars sped around a track inside the building. There were several near misses as patrons tried to cross the track instead of using two narrow footbridges. One spectator commented, "If I owned the whole bunch of them I would turn them out in a pasture and let them stay there for all time to come."

Chicago 365

1953 Yvette Marie Stevens was born at the Great Lakes Naval Training Station. An African Shaman gave her the name "Chaka" or "fire" while she was working for the Black Panther school lunch program at age 13. She was soon performing in area clubs under the name Chaka Khan and joined the group Rufus five years later. She left Rufus for a successful solo career in 1978.

1963 President John F. Kennedy made his final visit to Chicago. Kennedy spoke at the dedication of O'Hare International Airport. After laying a wreath at the Lieutenant Edward "Butch" O'Hare monument, the president said, "This is an extraordinary airport, an extraordinary country and it could be classified as one of the modern wonders of the world."

1995 Steinmetz High School was stripped of its state title in the Illinois Academic Decathlon. The working class students at Steinmetz had upset Whitney Young Magnet School in the March 11 competition. But it turned out that coach Gerald Plecki and his students used a stolen copy of the decathlon test to cheat. The incident became the basis for the HBO movie *Cheaters.*

March 24

1913 The first major exhibition of avante garde art caused a sensation at the Art Institute of Chicago. It was known as The Armory Show, because the Metropolitan Museum in New York turned down the show and it was exiled to an armory. The *Tribune* would print a picture of the controversial Marcel Duchamp's *Nude Descending a Staircase*. The thoughtful editor outlined the nude figure in white so readers could find it.

1914 Elmwood Park was incorporated. Inspired by a development in California, John Mills bought 245 acres there in 1926. His Westwood development would include over 1,600 homes and 145 business lots, laid out like spokes on a wheel around the village circle. At the time, it was the largest single-family development ever built by a single firm.

1924 Pope Pius XI elevated George William Mundelein to the rank of Cardinal. Mundelein had served as Archbishop of Chicago since 1915. He bought land in the Village of Area that became St. Mary's of the Lake

Seminary. In 1924, the village changed its name to Mundelein. The Archbishop irritated the German government by publicly criticizing Adolph Hitler before the war. He died in 1939.

March 25

1867   Ground was broken on Chicago Avenue for one of the city's most beloved landmarks. W.W. Boyington designed the new water tower and pumping station, designed to bring water from "the most limpid portions" of Lake Michigan. The *Tribune* was elated that the new system would eliminate "the little fishes, the silvery scales and the fear of pestilence."

1911   Jacob Rubenstein was born in Chicago. He ran errands for Al Capone and was probably involved in the syndicate. Jacob and his brothers later started a novelty company in Chicago and changed their names to Ruby. He moved to Dallas to run strip clubs in 1947. Jack Ruby was well known among Dallas police officers, so he was able to enter the basement of the Dallas City Jail on November 24, 1963.

1925   "Bloody Angelo" Genna met his end at the hands of Hymie Weiss, "Bugs" Moran, and Vincent "The Schemer" Drucci. They opened fire on Genna's car at Ogden Avenue and Hudson. The leader of the powerful Unione Siciliana had $11,000 in his pocket, which he planned to use for a payment on a home for his new bride. The killing was in retaliation for the murder of rival bootlegger Dean O'Bannion.

1950   The Chicago Stags played their last game, losing to the Minneapolis Lakers before 10,182 fans at Chicago Stadium. Pro basketball would not return to Chicago for another 11 years. The Stags were charter members of the Basketball Association of America, a rival to the National Basketball League, founded in 1947. The two leagues merged in 1949 to form the National Basketball Association.

March 26

1968   The Yippies applied for permits to hold a "Festival of Life" during the Democratic National Convention. Founders Abbie Hoffman and Jerry Rubin proposed all sorts of wild events, including plans to run a pig for president. On August 5, city officials denied the permits to sleep in the park and the stage was set for confrontation.

1969 ABC aired a made for T.V. movie entitled "Marcus Welby M.D. On September 23, the medical drama starring Chicago actor Robert Young made its series debut. Young played a patriarchal Santa Monica doctor who mentored Dr. Steven Kiley, played by James Brolin. Young suffered from depression and alcoholism in real life, which reportedly helped him play such an empathetic figure.

1970 The area was digging out from 14.3 inches of snow. That was followed by more than ten inches just six days later. Those storms hold the record for the closest back-to-back snowstorms of ten inches or more. The March 25-26 storm still ranks in the top ten of all time.

1998 The federal government handed down the first indictments in a point-shaving scandal involving the Northwestern University football and basketball teams. Two former basketball players would be convicted of rigging games and four former football players would admit lying to a grand jury investigating sports gambling at the school.

March 27

1886 Ludwig Mies van der Rohe was born in Aachen, Germany. His designs for glass skyscrapers with little ornamentation changed the face of every major city in North America and Europe. Fleeing the Nazis, van der Rohe came to Chicago in 1938. His famous Chicago designs include the twin apartment buildings at 860-880 Lake Shore Drive, some of the first glass skyscrapers in the world.

1898 Residents of Lake Shore Drive were upset to learn of plans for an eleven-story apartment building. At the time, Lake Shore was lined with mansions. John V. Clarke, president of Hibernian Banking, was planning the building on Lake Shore at Geothe. Residents were looking to Palmer Potter to lead the opposition, because his property would be the most affected.

1899 Gloria Swanson was born in Chicago as Gloria May Josephine Svensson. She started out as a teenager with the Essanay Studios and moved to Hollywood after marrying Walter Beery in 1915. After a stint making comedies, Swanson signed with D.W. Griffith. Griffith made her a superstar. Swanson made a comeback in 1950 with her role in *Sunset Boulevard,* a part originally offered to Mae West.

1902　A columnist in the *Chicago Daily News* became the first to refer to the Chicago NL team as the Cubs. At the time, the team was known as the Colts. Sports editor Fred Rayner started using Cubs exclusively. But the *Tribune* held out, even referring to the team as "The Spuds" when Charles Murphy bought the club. The *Tribune* came around in 1907, and Cubs were placed on the team uniforms in 1908.

1939　The very first NCAA Championship basketball game was played at Patten Gym on the Northwestern University campus. At the time, the NIT was the big show, and the NCAA tournament barely rated a mention. The University of Oregon beat Ohio State 46-33.

March 28

1909　Nelson Algren was born in Detroit. He spent his boyhood in Chicago and rode the rails during the Depression. Algren's works often told of the seamier side of Chicago. His most famous book is *The Man With the Golden Arm.* Algren said, "Never play cards with a man called Doc. Never eat at a place called Mom's. Never sleep with a woman whose troubles are worse than your own."

1920　At least four tornados tore a 53 mile path through the Chicago area. A twister hit Elgin hard, and another smashed into Channahon and the Lockport Area. Another tornado touched down near Midway Airport. The twisters killed 28 people. Over 400 people were hurt and damage totaled over $10 million. It ranks as the 3rd worst tornado disaster in Chicago's history.

1925　The *Tribune* moved into new headquarters. Raymond Hood and John Howell's gothic design was picked in a competition for "the most beautiful and eye-catching building in the world." Entries from Eliel Saarinen and Walter Gropius weren't picked, but they went on to greatly influence urban design. The tower contains fragments from many famous structures, including the Great Wall of China and the Coliseum.

1929　Chicago Stadium opened. A boxing match between Tommy

Chicago 365

Loughran of Philadelphia and Mickey Walker of New Jersey was the first event. The Black Hawks played their first game there on December 16, 1929. The arena featured the world's largest pipe organ. It had six keyboards and over 40,000 pipes.

1980   The closure of the Wisconsin Steel Works put 3,000 people out of work. Envirodyne Incorporated gave no notice, simply locking the gates when the last shift ended. Workers were enraged when they learned they had lost most of their pension benefits as well. The Southeast Side faced another blow when U.S. Steel also closed and Republic Steel slashed jobs.

March 29

1859   Oscar Mayer was born in Bavaria. He came to America after the family grocery business failed and worked at the Armour Meat Packing Company and the Kolhammer Meat Market. Oscar and his brothers began making sausages at a rented butcher shop on Sedgwick Street in 1883. In 1936, nephew Carl Mayer came up with the Weinermobile" to promote the company's "German Style Wieners" on the streets of Chicago.

1924   The Chicago *Tribune* took over radio station WJAZ, and began using the call letters WGN.   The inaugural WGN broadcast featured Mayor William Dever, opera singer Edith Mason and "zippy jazz tunes" by Ted Fio Rito and the Oriole Orchestra. WGN as we know it took to the air on June 1, 1924, after the *Tribune* took over the programming and studios of WDAP.

1932   Jack Benny appeared on a radio show hosted by New York *Daily News* columnist Ed Sullivan. He said, "This is Jack Benny talking.   There will now be a slight pause while everyone says, who cares?" An ad executive for Canada Dry liked the performance by the former Benjamin Kubelsky of Waukegan and signed him to host the "Canada Dry Program" on CBS. Benny was soon the most popular comic on the air.

1954   Owner Phil Wrigley asked manager Phil Cavaretta for an honest assessment of the Cubbie's chances.   Cavaretta's answer got him fired for what Wrigley called "a defeatist attitude."   Stan Hack took over as manager, and proved Cavaretta was right as the Cubs finished 7th.

Chicago 365

March 30

1913   Frankie Laine was born in Chicago. Frankie started out as a marathon dancer. He toiled as a singing waiter, a car salesman and a machinist before his big break, replacing Perry Como in Freddy Carlone's band. Hoagie Carmichael discovered him and arranged for his first recording contract. That led to classics such as "Mule Train," "That Lucky Old Sun" and "Cry of the Wild Goose."

1939   This could be considered the birthday of Chicago television. The Zenith Radio Corporation began regularly scheduled programming on experimental W9XZV, Channel One. The first broadcast was a TV version of WLS Radio's "Hoosier Sod Busters" with emcee Don Kelley. Back in 1929, Milton Berle had taken part in a closed circuit broadcast for the American Television Corporation. Berle said about four people saw it.

1992   The Cubs made a great trade with the White Sox. George Bell was shipped to the South Side in exchange for pitcher Ken Patterson, and an outfielder by the name of Sammy Sosa.

2003   Under the cover of night, heavy equipment began carving four X's into the runway at Meigs Field. Not even the FAA knew it was going to happen and the move left 16 planes stranded. The Mayor's office said the airport was closed because of the threat of terrorism. But Daley had proposed closing Meigs Field and turning the area into a park back in 1995.

March 31

1878   The first black heavyweight champion was born. Jack Johnson won the title in 1908. He infuriated racists by romancing white women such as Mae West. Johnson ran the Café de Champion in Chicago. In 1913, he was convicted of taking his white fiancée across state lines for "immoral purposes" and was a fugitive for seven years. He lost the title to Jess Willard in 1915. Johnson is buried in Graceland Cemetery.

1893   Chicago inventor Whitcomb Judson filed a patent for his "slide fastener," a device he designed as a replacement for bootlaces. He marketed it at the Columbian Exposition, but no one was interested.

Chicago 365

Judson sold just 20. On August 29, 1893, he was granted patent No. 504,038 for the invention we now know as the zipper.

1931 Transcontinental-Western Flight 599 crashed near Bazaar, Kansas, taking the life of Notre Dame football legend Knute Rockne. Rockne was on his way to Los Angeles, to assist with the production of a football movie. Rockne was born in Norway but grew up in Chicago, attending North West Division High School. He coached the "Fighting Irish" from 1918 until his death, compiling an amazing winning percentage of .881.

1980 The last Chicago, Rock Island and Pacific train made its final run. The Rock Island dated back to 1852. The railroad went into bankruptcy for a third time in 1975 and was hard hit by a clerk strike in 1979. In 1980, the bankruptcy court ordered that the railroad's assets should be liquidated, the largest railroad liquidation in U.S. history.

APRIL

April 1

1891   After arriving in Chicago with $32 in his pocket, William Wrigley Jr. founded a firm to make soap. He offered free baking powder to merchants who would carry his soap, and was surprised when the baking soda turned out to be more popular. So he switched to baking powder and offered free chewing gum as an incentive. The gum turned out to be much, much more popular.

1924   On primary day, Al Capone's brother died in gunfight with police outside the Western Electric Hawthorne Works. Chicago Police were sent into Cicero because Al Capone was backing a slate of candidates with violence. Plainclothes officers in a caravan of 50 cars spotted Salvatore Capone and took cover, thinking they were in danger. Capone in turn thought rival gangsters were invading and he opened fire.

1930   Prior to an exhibition game in Los Angeles, catcher Leo "Gabby" Hartnett of the Cubs caught two baseballs tossed from a blimp hovering 800 feet in the air. It is estimated that the ball was traveling about 90 miles per hour, but the hard part was locating the ball and following it as it plunged to earth.

1975   Richard J. Daley was elected to an unprecedented sixth term as Mayor of Chicago. He defeated Republican challenger John J. Hoellen by 75%, Daley's largest margin of victory ever. He had already served six years longer than any other mayor in Chicago history. Mayor Daley died of a heart attack on December 20, 1976 at age 74.

April 2

1928   Joseph Louis Bernardin was born in Columbia, South Carolina. After the death of John Cardinal Cody, Pope John Paul II appointed the former Cincinnati and Atlanta Archbishop as new head of the Chicago Diocese on August 25, 1982. Bernardin spoke out against racism, poverty, capital punishment and abortion. He became a Cardinal in February 1983 and died of cancer on November 14, 1996.

1900   The American League White Stockings played for the first time as a Chicago team, defeating the University of Illinois 10-9 in Champaign. The team originally played in Sioux City, IA then St. Paul, MN in the Western League. Charlie Comiskey moved the club to Chicago when the American League was formed.

1956 The latest creation by Chicago TV writer Irna Phillips premiered on CBS. "As the World Turns" was the first half-hour soap opera and at one time was watched by 50% of the viewers in its time slot. Phillips created the very first soap opera for WGN radio in 1930. Her other creations include, "Another World," "Days of Our Lives," and "The Guiding Light."

April 3

1924 Beulah Annan was charged in the murder of Harry Kalstedt. At first she claimed he tried to rape her. Annan later admitted to having an affair with Kalstedt and said she shot him when he tried to break it off. She claimed to be pregnant and an all male jury acquitted her. The Roxie Heart character in the play and the motion picture *Chicago* is based on Annan. She died in 1928 in a mental hospital.

1924 Marlon Brando was born in Omaha, Nebraska. His family moved to Evanston and then Libertyville, where Brando became known as "Bud." In high school he was known for his rebelliousness, pouring hydrosulfate into the ventilating system to create a rotten egg smell. His father sent Marlon to a military school in Minnesota. He was expelled, but not before a drama coach saw that the young man had promise.

1979 Jane M. Byrne was elected as the 1st woman mayor of Chicago. Byrne alienated blacks, fired hundreds of city employees, and axed members of her own administration. She raised taxes and faced strikes by firefighters, the CTA and schoolteachers. Byrne moved into the Cabrini-Green Housing Project for a month in an effort to end violence there. She would lose the next election to Harold Washington.

1998 An emotional sellout crowd of 39,102 cheered and chanted "Harry, Harry, Harry" as Harry Caray's widow Dutchie took his traditional spot in the press box to sing "Take Me Out To The Ballgame" during the 7th inning stretch at Wrigley Field. Harry Caray died in February. Perhaps inspired by Dutchie and a bagpipe version of "Amazing Grace," the Cubs went out and beat Montreal 6-2.

April 4

1915   McKinley Morganfield was born in Rolling Fork, Mississippi. His grandmother gave the child the name "Muddy Waters" when he played in puddles. The singer and guitarist moved to Chicago in 1943. In 1948, he released his first single "I Can't Be Satisfied," and "I Feel Like Going Home." Waters became one of the most influential blues musicians ever. The Rolling Stones took their name from one of his early songs.

1931   The first movie version of *The Front Page* was released. Ben Hecht and Charles McArthur based the play on their experiences in the Chicago newspaper business during the 1920's. The first film starred Pat O'Brien as reporter Hildy Johnson and Adolph Monjou as conniving editor Walter Burns. The story is a vicious satire of utterly corrupt Mayor of Chicago "Big Bill" Thompson and Cook County Sheriff Peter Hoffman.

1987   The Fox Network premiered a new sitcom about the dysfunctional family of a former football hero turned Chicago shoe salesman. "Married With Children" starred Ed O'Neill as the hapless Al Bundy. O'Neill would later appear as the manager of Stan Mikita's Donut Shop in the *Wayne's World* films. The show opened with a shot of the Buckingham Fountain as Frank Sinatra's "Love and Marriage" played.

1989   Democrat Richard M. Daley was elected mayor, defeating Republican Edward R. Vrdolyak and independent Timothy C. Evans. Daley had lost his first bid to follow in his father's footsteps in 1983. Facing a massive budget crisis, Daley privatized 40 city services and got the legislature to grant him unprecedented control over the schools. He was elected to a 5th term on February 25, 2003.

2003   Sammy Sosa hit the 500th home run of his career. The solo blast off Scott Sullivan came during a 10-9 Cubs loss in Cincinnati. Sosa became the 18th player in Major League history to reach 500 career homers.

Chicago 365

April 5

1948 WGN-TV presented its first official broadcast. Lee Bennett hosted the "WGN-TV Salute to Chicago," featuring Joey Bishop, Jack Brickhouse, Bob Trendler and the WGN Orchestra. Regular programming began the following day with a newsreel, the first filmed newscast in Chicago.

1955 One of the most beloved and controversial figures in Chicago history was sworn in as mayor. O'Hare Airport, the Sears Tower, McCormick Place, the expressway system and massive housing projects were constructed during the Richard J. Daley era. But he was criticized for the harsh response to the 1960's riots. He served six terms before dying in office in 1976.

1968 Violence erupted in the wake of the assassination of Martin Luther King Junior. Mobs roamed the West and South Sides. National Guard troops secured the overpasses on the Eisenhower Expressway. Mayor Daley issued a controversial order for police to shoot to kill arsonists and wound looters. By the time the weekend was over, nine people were dead, 162 buildings were destroyed and 1,000 people were homeless.

April 6

1917 The U.S. declared war on Germany. Mayor William Hale Thompson said that with an immigrant population of 225,000, Chicago was the sixth largest German city. His lack of support for the war earned him the nickname "Kaiser Bill." He blasted efforts to help Great Britain, even burning textbooks that he believed glorified King George. But many Chicagoans enlisted and over 5,000 troops from Illinois would die in the war.

1931 James Dewar, manager of the Continental Bakery Chicago plant, came up with a treat that would allow the company to use small baking pans that normally remained idle except during strawberry shortcake season. He was at a loss for a name until he took a business trip to St. Louis and noticed a billboard for Twinkle Toe Shoes. He called his creation "Twinkies."

Chicago 365

1931 Little Orphan Annie debuted on Blue Network over WGN. "Adventure Time with Little Orphan Annie" was the first radio serial to offer premiums successfully. The Ovaltine Company sponsored the show and would issue dozens of items, including coveted Radio Orphan Annie Secret Society paraphernalia. Shirley Bell of Chicago landed the role of Annie at age ten.

1952 Mary Lucy Pilowski, better known as Marilu Henner, was born in Chicago. She attended the University of Chicago before becoming a full-time actress. In 1978, she landed the role of Elaine Nardo on the TV show "Taxi." She returned to TV in 1990's "Evening Shade" with Burt Reynolds. She played herself in the film *Man on the Moon*, the story of "Taxi" cast member and comedian Andy Kaufman.

April 7

1910 Chief of Police Steward issued new rules for public bathers (swimmers). Women would be required to wear bloomers under their bathing suits and to keep their ams covered at least to the elbow. Men were ordered to wear two-piece suits.

1931 Anton Cermack was elected mayor of Chicago, defeating incumbent Bill Thompson by the largest margin ever. Cermack tried to help his favored gangsters take over organized crime. Cermack even ordered a failed assassination on attempt on Frank "The Enforcer" Nitti. In 1933, Cremack was killed by a bullet supposedly intended for President Franklin D. Roosevelt. Some believe the mob ordered the hit on Cermack.

1933 The celebration was orderly as the city welcomed the return of legal 3.2% beer. Trucks lined up for a mile at the Schoenhofen Brewery and 16 carloads of brew arrived from Anheuser-Busch in St. Louis. It was reported that there were few arrests and the crowds at the Morrison, LaSalle, Congress and Stevens Hotels didn't exceed those of a typical Saturday night.

2004 The trial of white supremacist Mathew Hale began in Chicago. Hale would be convicted of soliciting the murder of a federal judge. The leader of the World Church of the Creator had issued a call for "racial holy war. " One of his followers, Benjamin Smith, went on a shooting spree in 1999. Smith wounded nine and killed two, including former Northwestern University basketball coach Ricky Byrdsong.

April 8

1918 A future first lady was born in Chicago. Elizabeth Ann Bloomer's family moved to Grand Rapids when she was two. The dancer who once studied under Martha Graham married Gerald Ford in 1948. As First Lady, Betty fought a very public battle with breast cancer. She later admitted a problem with tranquilizers and alcohol and co-founded the Betty Ford Center in 1982 to help others fight dependency.

1997 Pope John Paul II named Archbishop Francis George, who had led the Portland, Oregon, archdiocese for just 10 months, as the new Archbishop of Chicago. George replaced the late Joseph Cardinal Bernardin. The 60-year-old became the first Chicago native to lead the Archdiocese. He had attended St. Pascal Grade School and studied at St. Henry Preparatory Seminary in Belleville.

2002 Arthur Andersen terminated over 500 employees at the Chicago headquarters and let go another 500 from the training facility in St. Charles, Illinois. As 2002 opened, Andersen was the fifth largest accounting firm in the nation. But the firm's reputation was ruined when it was revealed that employees had destroyed documents relating to audits of the Enron Corporation.

April 9

1924 Sears Roebuck and Company's radio station began tests with the call sign WES, or "World's Economy Store." The first test included singer Grace Wilson and the comedy of Big Ford and Little Glenn. The station officially signed on three days later with the new call letters WLS, for "World's Largest Store." Ethel Barrymore froze at the mike at the start of the broadcast and said loudly on the air, "Turn that damned thing off!"

1926 Hugh Hefner was born in Chicago, a direct descendent of puritan patriarchs William Bradford and John Winthrop. At Steinmetz High School, he penned an essay about our reluctance to discuss sex. "Hef" worked as a promotion copywriter for *Esquire* before deciding to start his own magazine. At age 27 in 1953, he laid out the first *Playboy* in his Hyde Park apartment.

1959   Frank Lloyd Wright died in Phoenix at the age of 92. Wright established his office in Oak Park in 1893 and developed "The Prairie Style." Many believed he was finished when a crazed servant killed his mistress and burned down his retreat in Wisconsin in 1914. But Wright's influence only grew. In his lifetime, the world's most famous architect made 1,141 designs, 532 of which were completed.

1965   "The Girl With the Perfect Face," Linda Darnell, was burned over 80% of her body in a fire at her former secretary's home in suburban Glenview. She died the next day. The night before the fire, she had been watching *Star Dust* on television. It was the movie that made her a star. Darnell had spoken publicly about her fear of dying in a fire when she played a character burned at the stake in *Anna and the King of Siam*.

April 10

1848   The Illinois and Michigan Canal opened, connecting the Great Lakes to the Illinois River. Plans for the canal led to a land speculation boom in the 1830's that spurred the early development of Chicago. But by the time the *A. Rossiter* towed the first boat from the Chicago River to LaSalle, the arrival of the iron horse was rendering the canal obsolete. Today, bicyclists travel along the old towpaths, now a state park.

1879   Sandor Hertz was born in what is now Czechoslovakia. He began his career selling newspapers on the street corners of Chicago and began selling cars in 1904. In 1907, Hertz decided to turn leftover used cars into Taxis and painted them yellow. At that time, taxis were for the rich. Hertz cut prices and improved service. He founded Yellow Cab in 1915. Hertz branched out into the rental car business in 1923.

1914   Tracy C. Drake, president of the Blackstone Hotel Company announced that he and his brother John Drake would build a luxurious new $2 million hotel. The hotel was to be located at Lakeshore Drive and Oak Street. The elegant Drake Hotel opened in 1920, and has housed celebrities and heads of state ever since. The hotel has 537 rooms and 74 luxury suites.

1934 The Blackhawks won their first Stanley Cup, defeating the Red Wings three games to one. Hawks goalie Charles Gardiner was the hero of the series. Gardiner is the only goaltender to have his name engraved on Lord Stanley's Cup as the captain of his team. He died of a tonsil infection just two months after the Hawks victory.

April 11

1872 The first Arbor Day celebration took place. Former Nebraska Governor J. Sterling Morton came up with the idea. His oldest son, Joy inherited the love of nature. In 1886, Joy was living in Chicago and took over the Richmond Salt Company. He changed the name to Morton Salt. In 1922, he dedicated his farm in Lisle as the Morton Arboretum, in honor of his father. Arbor Day is now celebrated on the last Friday in April.

1899 Percy Julian was born in Birmingham, Alabama. Julian won international acclaim for his work in chemistry, creating artificial cortisone and laying the groundwork for the birth control pill and drugs that make organ transplants possible. In 1951, Julian and his family became the first blacks to move into Oak Park. Their home was firebombed twice, but today Oak Park celebrates his birthday as a holiday.

1970 "Vehicle" by the Ides of March entered the *Billboard* Top 40. The band started out wearing wigs on stage to look cool, because Morton West High School in Berwyn didn't allow long hair. The band scored a hit in the Chicago area with "You Wouldn't Listen" before recording the song about "the friendly stranger in the black sedan." Lead singer Jim Peterik went on to great success with the group Survivor.

April 12

1861 Chicago was in an uproar over the news from Fort Sumter. The *Tribune* declared, "Lenity and forbearance have only nursed the viper into life. Let the Cry be, 'THE SWORD OF THE LORD AND OF GIDEON!'" Over 22,000 men from Cook County served. Thousands of Confederates died at Camp Douglas in Chicago. Many of them were originally buried in mass graves in what is now Lincoln Park.

1940 Herbie Hancock was born in Chicago. Hancock began playing the piano when he was seven. At age eleven, he performed Mozart's

Chicago 365

"D Major Piano Concerto" with the Chicago Symphony. He discovered a love for jazz in high school, moved to New York, and later joined with Miles Davis. Hancock began fusing jazz and funk and formed his first group in 1968.

1945 The General Assembly created the Chicago Transit Authority to run the public transportation system. The CTA began operations on October 1, 1947, after taking over the Chicago Surface Lines and the Chicago Rapid Transit Company. In 1952, the CTA bought the Chicago Motor Coach Company, giving it control of all the lines that had once operated as rival companies.

1949 Scott Turow was born in Chicago. From 1978 to 1986, Turow served as Assistant United States Attorney in Chicago, then hit it big his first novel, *Presumed Innocent.* Other best sellers based on his experiences include *Burden of Proof, The Laws of Our Fathers* and *Personal Injuries.* In 1995, Turow won a fight to clear Alejandro Hernandez, who spent eleven years in prison for a crime he didn't commit.

1983 Harold Washington was elected as the city's first African American mayor. Alderman Edward Vrdolyak put together a majority of 29 votes and blocked Washington at every turn during the vicious "Council Wars." But court ordered special elections and redistricting gave Washington a majority in 1986. He was re-elected to a second term but died of a sudden heart attack on November 25, 1987.

April 13

1906 Bud Freeman was born in Chicago. The tenor saxophone player was a member of the Austin High Gang, which included Jimmy McPartland, Joe Sullivan, Eddie Condon and jazz crazy kid named Benny Goodman. Freeman was an important figure in the development of the "Chicago Style" of jazz.

1922 Chicago's second radio station signed on as WGU, operated by the Fair Store and *Daily News.* The station took the WMAQ call letters in October. Charles Correll and Freeman Gosden brought their "Sam and Andy" show from WGN when WMAQ offered syndication on the NBC Network. The show was re-named "Amos and Andy." WMAQ was also the first station to carry Cubs games.

Chicago 365

1992 At 5:30 a.m., a slow leak in an old freight tunnel at the Kinzie Street Bridge blew wide open. Millions of gallons of water poured into the 47-mile tunnel system. City Hall, the Board of Trade and the Mercantile Exchange closed. The disaster cost the city $1.95 billion. In September 1991, a contractor installing pilings had broken through the roof of the tunnel. Cable TV workers discovered the leak in January and had notified the city.

April 14

1912 The *Titanic* struck an iceberg and sank in the North Atlantic. Sixty-seven passengers had some connection to Chicago. Ida Hippach and her daughter Jean survived because John Jacob Astor gave them his seat in a lifeboat. Ida had lost two children in the Iroquois Theater fire. One-year-old Eleanor Shuman and her mother were the last to board a lifeboat. Eleanor met *Titanic* director James Cameron at the Chicago premiere and he said she reminded him of the character Rose.

1925 A regular season Cubs game was broadcast over WGN for the first time. Quin Ryan handled the play-by-play duties from the grandstand roof. Grover Cleveland Alexander got the 8-2 Opening Day win over the Pirates. "Old Pete" helped himself with a single, double and home run.

1973 Murderous mobster "Mad" Sam DeStefano was gunned down in his garage in North Sayre Avenue. DeStefano had murdered his own brother and an ice pick was his weapon of choice in other murders. He once forced a family to urinate on the body of their murdered loved one. But DeStefano had a big mouth and threatened once too often to write an expose about The Outfit.

April 15

1922 Harold Washington was born in Chicago. He served in the Illinois House and Senate, then was elected to the U.S. House of Representatives in 1980. He served time in prison for failing to file his tax returns. But in 1983, he became the first African-American Mayor of Chicago. Mayor Washington increased opportunities for minorities, brought neighborhood groups together and created the Ethics Commission.

1955 Roy A. Kroc opened his first McDonald's on North Lee Street in

Des Plaines. The first day's sales added up to $366.12. Kroc sold mixers used to make malts and noticed that a restaurant in San Bernardino, California owned by Mack and Dick McDonald was using eight at a time. Kroc convinced them to franchise the system of a simple menu prepared quickly. Kroc died in 1984, and the Des Plaines building was torn down. A replica now houses the McDonald's museum.

2004 Donald Trump told Chicago entrepreneur Bill Rancic "You're hired!" The 32-year-old who built an on-line cigar enterprise into a multimillion-dollar business outlasted 15 other competitors on the NBC reality series "The Apprentice." Rancic chose to take over operations at the 90-story Trump International Hotel and Tower, under construction on the site of the *Sun-Times* Building.

April 16

1953 A flash fire killed 34 people at the Haber Corporation factory, 908-14 West North Avenue. Investigators said the sparks from a metal polishing machine may have ignited aluminum and magnesium dust. The four-story building was used to manufacture electrical appliances and parts. Thirty-seven people were injured.

1958 The Calumet Skyway opened. The 7.8-mile expressway includes a bridge soaring 120 feet over the Chicago River. Now known as the Chicago Skyway, it connects the Dan Ryan Expressway (I-90/94) with the Indiana Tollway. It was the first toll road built in Chicago since the plank road to Doty's Tavern in Riverside opened in 1848.

1961 While the city dug out from a major snow storm, sports fans celebrated the first championship by a major Chicago sports team in 23 years. Led by Stan Mikita and the "Golden Jet," Bobby Hull, the Blackhawks defeated Gordie Howe and the Detroit Red Wings to win the Stanley Cup. The Hawks had finished third during the regular season, but stunned the mighty Montreal Canadiens in the semi-finals.

1972 Rookie Cubs pitcher Burt Hooton threw a no hitter in just his fourth Major League start. The 22-year-old hurler and his knucklecurve walked seven and struck out seven as the Cubs won the game 4-0. In his first three starts, "Happy" had held opposing hitters to a .111 average and struck out 15 in one game.

April 17

1852   Adrian Constantine Anson was born in Marshalltown, Iowa. "Cap" Anson dominated 19th century baseball. The first baseman-manager of the White Stockings established records for games, hits, at-bats, doubles, RBI and runs. He hit over .300 in 20 out of his 22 seasons in the NL and was the first player to record 3,000 hits. As manager, Anson led the team to five pennants. He was elected to the Hall of Fame in 1939.

1908   Plans were unveiled for a 20-story hotel at 636 South Michigan. The hotel was named for Timothy B. Blackstone, former head of the Alton Railroad and founding president of the Stock Yards. His home stood on the site. The Blackstone hosted at least a dozen presidents and was home of the "smoke-filled rooms" where Warren G. Harding was chosen as the GOP presidential nominee in 1920.

1915   D.W. Griffith's *Birth of a Nation* prompted a call for censorship from the NAACP. Mayor Carter Harrison II had agreed to allow the film to be shown if two scenes were cut. Officials cited a 1907 law that prohibited the showing of any movie without the approval of the Chief of Police. A 1917 ordinance essentially banned the film. In 1924, the operators of the Auditorium Theater were arrested for showing it.

1951   Just before the Cubs home opener, Sam Snead became the first person to hit the centerfield scoreboard at Wrigley Field with a ball. But it was a golf ball. The Cubs went out and won the game 8-3 over the Reds.

April 18

1857   Clarence Darrow was born in Ohio. He gave up his Chicago law practice to fight for the underdog. In 1924, he saved Nathan Leopold and Richard Loeb from the electric chair. In 1925, John Scopes defied a Tennessee law banning the teaching of evolution. Darrow, an agnostic, defended Scopes against William Jennings Bryan. Scopes was fined $100, but Darrow made Bryan's fundamentalist beliefs look ridiculous.

Chicago 365

1924   A fire at an old dance hall on South Blue Island left eight fire fighters dead. They were buried when the walls of Curran Hall collapsed. One of the dead firefighters had been cleaning a window at the station when the call came in. Frank Leavy left a handprint on the glass that even the strongest cleaner couldn't remove. Twenty years later to the day, a newsboy tossed a paper and broke the glass.

1991   The new Comiskey Park officially opened as the White Sox lost to the Detroit Tigers 16-0 before a sellout crowd of 42,191. Jack McDowell of the White Sox was the first pitcher to take the mound in the new ballpark. Alan Trammel of the Tigers got the first hit and Detroit's Cecil Fielder hit the first home run. The park was renamed U.S. Cellular Field in 2003.

2004   On a windy day at Wrigley Field, Sammy Sosa homered twice to pass Ernie Banks as the all-time Cubs home run leader. A solo shot in the first inning off Paul Wilson of the Cincinnati Reds gave Sosa 513 career home runs. Sosa slugged another in the third. But the Cubs lost the game 11-10 in extra innings when Sammy lost a ball in the sun.

April 19

1903   Eliot Ness was born in Chicago. He came to the Justice Department Prohibition Bureau in 1928 and assembled a crack team of nine agents to shut down Al Capone. In six months, the team shut down 19 distilleries and breweries. Capone offered him a bribe of $2,000 per week. Ness spurned the offer and declared that his men could not be bought. A *Tribune* reporter the next day referred to them as "The Untouchables."

1924   The "National Barn Dance" made its debut on WLS. Sears executives were mortified to hear hillbilly music on their station, but they couldn't deny the popularity of the program. From 1932 to 1957, two sold out shows were presented every Saturday at the Eighth Street Theater. WLS switched to Top 40 in April 1960, and the show moved to WGN, where it ran until 1969.

1961   White Socks owner Bill Veeck made Opening Day memorable. Eddie Gaedel and seven other midgets served as vendors in the box seats, where fans had complained that vendors blocked their view. (Veeck had sent Gaedel up to pinch hit for the St. Louis Browns in 1951) Veeck wanted JFK to throw out the first pitch, so he brought in a man from Oak Lawn with the initials JFK.

1963 The first residents moved into Sandburg Village, a 16-acre complex of high rises aimed at keeping middle class residents in the city. It was a risky move, as the complex was near Cabrini Green and the bars along Wells Street. But 8,000 residents soon lived there. Sandburg Village spurred more redevelopment or "gentrification." Sandburg was converted to apartments in 1979.

April 20

1857 Residents cheered as Mayor Wentworth personally led a column of police on a mission to wipe out the notorious "Sands" red light district along the lake north of the Chicago River. Fifteen saloons and houses of ill repute were torn down or burned. Wentworth arranged a horserace and a cockfight in another neighborhood to make sure the thugs were occupied when he moved in.

1865 The first building in Chicago specifically designed for opera opened. A sellout crowd saw Verdi's *Il Trovatore* at Crosby's Opera House. The construction nearly bankrupted Uranus Crosby. He held a rigged lottery offering the opera and valuable paintings as prizes and caused a controversy by bringing in burlesque. The Great Fire destroyed the building days before it was to reopen after an extensive renovation.

1916 The first National League game was played at Clark and Addison. The Cubs beat Cincinnati Reds 7-6 in 11 innings before over 20,000 fans and one bear cub. Weegham was built for Chicago's Federal League team. It was known briefly as Cubs Field and re-named Wrigley Field in 1926.

1946 A Cubs game was broadcast on television for the first time. WBKB broadcast the home opener, with "Whispering" Joe Wilson handling the play-by-play. The Cubs lost to Harry "The Cat" Breechen and the Cardinals 2-0 before a crowd of 40,887. WGN began its broadcasts two years later.

April 21

1855   Mayor Levi D. Boone, who despised the beer-drinking Germans, had closed the saloons on Sundays and raised license fees by 600%. A mob of angry beer lovers marched on the courthouse where some barkeepers faced trial that day. Shots rang out as police battled the mob at the Clark Street Bridge. Amazingly, there was only one fatality in the Lager Beer Riots, but city was under martial law for three days.

1900   The White Sox played their first game in Chicago. They lost to Milwaukee 5-4 in a ballpark at 29th and Princeton. The addition of the Chicago club assured the stability of the new American League. Under an agreement with the NL, the team was not allowed to use "Chicago" in their name. The AL declared itself a major league in 1901, and the "Chicago" White Stockings made their official major league debut on April 24, 1901.

1967   Tornadoes killed 58 people and injured over 1,000. In Belvidere, 11 children died at the High School as the tornado tossed buses like toys. Another twister ripped through Palos Hills, Oak Lawn, Evergreen Park and the South Side. People died in their cars at the intersection of Southwest Highway and 95th Street. More children died in a skating rink near the highway. It was the worst tornado disaster in area history.

1986   Over 60 million tuned in as Geraldo Rivera unveiled "The Mystery of Al Capone's Vault" at the Lexington Hotel located, at Michigan Avenue and 22nd Street. Capone housed his offices there from 1928 to 1931 and the walls were filled with secret passages. The IRS was there to claim any money that might be found. Crews blasted away the basement wall to find a few empty bottles. The hotel was torn down in November 1995.

April 22

1934   The FBI surrounded the Dillinger Gang at the Little Bohemia Lodge in Wisconsin. Alerted by barking dogs, Lester "Baby Face" Nelson Gillis fled to a nearby home and took hostages. When Special Agents J.C. Newman and W. Carter Baum arrived, Nelson declared, "I'm going down there and get those sons of bitches." He rushed the car and killed the agents. The law caught up with Nelson in November 1934.

Chicago 365

1947 The Chicago Stags lost the first Basketball Association of America Championship to the Philadelphia Warriors four games to one. The league was founded on June 6, 1946. In the fall of 1949, the league would take over several teams from the National Basketball League and change its name to the National Basketball Association. The Stags dropped out of the league in 1950.

1959 CBS began a two-part series dramatizing the life of Eliot Ness and the story of the Untouchables who helped bring down Al Capone. Quinn Martin directed the Desilu Playhouse production. He would go on to produce crime shows such as "The Fugitive," "The Streets of San Francisco," and "Barnaby Jones." The two episodes drew big ratings, and CBS decided to make "The Untouchables" a weekly series.

April 23

1813 Stephen Douglas was born near Brandon, Vermont. The "Little Giant" was elected as the U.S. Senator from Illinois in 1837. In 1858, a young lawyer running for the Senate challenged Douglas to a series of debates. Abraham Lincoln won the popular vote, but the Legislature re-elected Douglas. They met again in the 1860 presidential race.

1860 Carter Harrison Junior was born in Chicago. He was the first mayor of the city to be born here. His father, Carter Henry Harrison II, served five terms as Mayor, from 1897 to 1905 and from 1911 to 1915. He fought a bitter fight with Charles Yerkes, who was trying to obtain a monopoly over the streetcar lines. Towards the end of his term, Harrison shut down the famous Everleigh Club brothel.

1914 The first game took place at Clark and Addison. The Chicago Whales of the Federal League beat Kansas City 9-1. Art Wilson of the Whales hit the first homer. When the Federal League folded after the 1915 season, Charles H. Weeghman bought the Cubs and moved them to his ballpark. Weegham Park became Cubs Park in 1920 after the Wrigley family purchased the team and was named Wrigley Field in 1926.

April 24

1854 Elgin was incorporated as a city. In 1835, James T. and Hezekiah Gifford settled the community on the Fox River, shrewdly locating on a straight line directly between Chicago and the mines at Galena. James Gifford named the settlement after a Scottish city mentioned in a psalm he remembered from boyhood.

1936 Peter Finley Dunne died, nearly forgotten at the age of 68. He was once the most quoted man in Chicago. Dunne's alter ego was Martin Dooley, a philosophizing saloonkeeper who spoke in a thick Irish brogue in the *Evening Post* and the *Journal*. He drew national attention in 1898, when he humorously criticized the Spanish-American War. Dunne compiled Dooley's monologues into several books.

1946 Frank Chance was named to the Baseball Hall of Fame. Legendary Cubs double-play mates Joe Tinker and Johnny Evers were also named to the hall. Tinkers, Evers and Chance actually only combined for 56 double plays. They were immortalized in a poem written by a New York sportswriter in 1910.

2001 The trial of the "The Most Corrupt Cop in Chicago History" ended. Gang specialist Joseph Miedzianowski would be sentenced to life in prison. He ran a Miami to Chicago drug ring, hid a wanted killer, gave weapons to gang members, fixed cases, hindered investigations, and even set up sexual encounters for prisoners. Prosecutors said while behind bars, Miedzianowski plotted to have a U.S. Attorney killed.

April 25

1854 The first streetcar in Chicago began carrying passengers down State Street between 12th and Madison. Chicago's early streetcars were horse drawn. But by the 1880's Chicago, not San Francisco, had the largest cable car system in the world. Electric cars came on line in the 1890's. At their peak, the streetcars carried almost 900 million passengers annually. The last street car disappeared into history on June 21, 1958.

1890 President Benjamin Harrison signed a bill authorizing an exposition to mark the 400th anniversary of the discovery of America by Christopher Columbus. Chicago edged out several cities. During the battle, *New York Sun* editor Charles Dana gave the city its nickname. He wrote, "Don't pay attention to the nonsensical claims of that windy city. Its people could not build a world's fair even if they won it."

Chicago 365

1944   U.S. Army Soldiers carried Sewell Avery, Chairman of Montgomery Ward, out of his office. President Roosevelt ordered the branch seized when Avery defied War Labor Board orders regarding wages and operating a union shop. Avery continued to battle the NWLB. Montgomery Ward stores in several cities were seized in December 1944 and ran by the government until well after the end of the war.

1976   Cubs center fielder Rick Monday rescued an American flag as two radicals tried to set it on fire in the Dodger Stadium outfield. The Cubs lost the game 5-4 in ten innings. The next day, the Illinois Legislature declared May 4th as Rick Monday Day. The Dodgers would get the flag from the LAPD evidence room and present it to Monday.

1982   Cardinal John P. Cody died at the age of 74. Cody had served as head of the diocese since 1965. He was accused of making illegal stock investments and kept dossiers on clergy he considered disloyal. His final year was marked by a federal grand jury investigation. The *Sun-Times* alleged that Cody diverted $1 million in church funds to close friend and step-cousin Helen Dolan Wilson.

April 26

1822   Frederick Law Olmsted was born in Hartford, Connecticut. The landscape architect designed Central Park in New York and park systems in many cities. He laid out the planned community of Riverside along the Des Plaines River, one of the first planned suburbs in the United States. Olmstead also served as the site designer for the 1893 Columbian Exposition and helped found the National Park Service.

1900   Hack Wilson was born in Maryland. He won four batting titles while playing with the Cubs from 1926-1931. In 1930, Wilson hit 56 home runs, which stood as an NL record for 68 years. He also drove in 191 runs, a Major League record that still stands today. Wilson may have earned his nickname because of his resemblance to Russian wrestler George Hackenschmidt.

1941   Wrigley Field became the first in the Major Leagues to have an organ installed. Roy Nelson was behind the keyboard. Nelson's pre-game serenade went well, but the Cubs hit some sour notes. They lost to Max Lanier and the Cardinals 6-2.

1951 A crowd estimated at four million, more than the population of Chicago, lined a parade route to honor General Douglas MacArthur. President Truman had fired the general just 15 days earlier. At a Soldier Field rally, MacArthur accused the Truman administration of operating in a "vacuum." The crowd protested when MacArthur said "my public life is now finished."

1989 Rudy Linares burst into Rush-Presbyterian Hospital. He held police and staff back with a gun and unplugged his son's respirator. Eight months earlier, Sammy Linares had choked on a balloon and suffered irreversible brain damage. Sammy died 30 minutes after his sobbing father pulled the plug. A jury threw out murder charges against Linares, but he was convicted of assault.

April 27

1926 Al Capone opened up on a group of rival mobsters outside the Pony Inn on Roosevelt Road in Cicero. The bullets meant for the O'Donnell Brothers cut down Cook County's "Hanging Prosecutor," State's Attorney William McSwiggin, and two other men. The prosecutor had been drinking with the gangsters. A grand jury would find that McSwiggin was an innocent bystander and Capone was never charged.

1974 "Mighty Mighty" by Earth, Wind and Fire entered the *Billboard* Top 40 chart. It was the first hit for the Chicago group, formed by Maurice White in 1969. The Mario Van Peebles film, *Sweet Sweetback's Baadasssss Song,* featured their music, but the group didn't break through until they added drummer Phillip Bailey in 1972.

1991 The $43 million Oceanarium opened at the Shedd Aquarium. It was the first addition since the aquarium opened in 1930. The Oceanarium includes a Pacific rain forest habitat and is home to whales, dolphins, penguins, seals and birds.

April 28

1796 Augustine Deodat Taylor was born in Connecticut. In 1833, he erected a building in Chicago that spurred a building boom and changed architecture forever. Taylor invented the 2 X 4, nailing them to frames instead of using huge beams held together with complicated joints. His

"Balloon Frame" method was used for the first time during construction of St. Mary's Church at State and Lake.

1908　Fire destroyed the LaPorte, Indiana farmhouse owned by Belle Gunness, formerly of Chicago. Police found the bodies of her three children, and a headless body they presumed to be Belle. Gunness placed newspaper ads to lure potential suitors. She killed at least 14 and maybe as many as 40. Many believe Belle killed her children and a woman she had hired as a housekeeper, set the fire, and made off with the money.

1994　The Black Hawks played the last hockey game at Chicago Stadium. Mike Gartner of the Maple Leafs scored the last goal in the old building in Game Six of the first round playoff series. Jeremy Roenick was the last Hawks player to score there, notching an overtime goal that gave the Hawks a win in Game Four. The Hawks moved across the street to the new United Center in 1995.

April 29

1844　Lake Park was dedicated. Much of the park was built atop landfill from the Great Fire. On October 9, 1901, the park was renamed in honor of Ulysses S. Grant. A. Montgomery Ward fought a court battle for 20 years to prevent development in the park. Today, Grant Park is home to the area's biggest festivals. In 2004, it was extended with the addition of Millenium Park.

1916　Charles H. Weeghman, new owner of the Cubs, announced that fans could keep any ball hit into the stands. The rest of the Major League teams would follow suit.

1934　Luis Aparacio was born in Maracaibo, Venezuela. He played shortstop for the White Sox from 1956-1962 and 1968-1970. The 1956 Rookie of the Year played a total of 2,599 games at shortstop, a record that still stands for the position. Aparacio was elected to the Baseball Hall of Fame in 1984.

1983　Harold Washington was inaugurated as the first black Mayor of the city. In his inaugural address, he declared that the Democratic Machine was dead. That didn't sit too well with Aldermen Edward R. Vrdolyak. He put together a majority of white aldermen dubbed the "Vrdolyak 29" to thwart Washington's every move. For the next three years, the battles earned Chicago another nickname, "Beirut by the Lake."

1997 Mike Royko died at the age of 64. The nationally syndicated columnist stuck up for the common people and blasted politicians. Royko started his column at the Glenview Naval Air Base newspaper. He came to the *Daily News* in the 1950's and then wrote for the *Sun-Times*. He quit in disgust and moved to the *Tribune* when Rupert Murdoch bought the *Sun-Times* in 1984. Royko won a Pulitzer Prize for commentary in 1972.

April 30

1926 After a six-month fight over the number to be assigned to the federal highway from Chicago to Los Angeles, the American Association of Highway Officials proposed 66. The highway was to have been designated as Route 60, but the governor of Kentucky wanted the more important sounding 60 to go through his state. It's a good thing. "Get your kicks on Route 60" doesn't have the same ring to it.

1939 The motion picture *The Story of Vernon and Irene Castle* premiered. Fred Astaire and Ginger Rogers starred in the story of the famous ballroom dancers. The movie was the debut of the song "Chicago, Chicago, That Toddlin' Town." Written in 1922 by Fred Fisher with music by Leonard Bernstein, the song has been recorded by artists such as Frank Sinatra, Count Basie, Tony Bennett and Judy Garland.

1977 An angry crowd gathered on the village green as a small group of neo-Nazi's marched on Skokie. Police met the Nazi's as they exited the Edens Expressway and presented an amended court order blocking the rally in the largely Jewish community. The U.S. Supreme Court would uphold their right to march. But Nazi leader Frank Collin called off the Skokie march after Chicago agreed to allow a rally in Marquette Park.

1995 A horde of media watched as a four-year-old boy cried "I'll be good. Don't make me leave." He was taken from the arms of the woman he knew as mother. The Illinois Supreme Court had awarded custody of "Baby Richard" to his biological father, Otaker Kirchner. Kirchner and the mother were estranged when Kim and Robert Warburton adopted the baby. The Kirchners reconciled, married, and went on to have three children.

Chicago 365
MAY

May 1

1865   Thousands were waiting when the train bearing the body of President Lincoln arrived in Chicago. A memorial arch was erected at 12th Street and Michigan, where the casket was transferred from the train to the hearse for a procession to the Cook County Courthouse.   Over 125,000 paid their respects as Lincoln lay in an open casket at the courthouse. Two days later, Lincoln was laid to rest in Springfield.

1893   A massive crowd, including President Grover Cleveland, poured into the gleaming "White City" as the World's Columbian Exposition opened. Visitors could ride the first Ferris Wheel and see controversial dancer Fahreda Mahzar, known as "Little Egypt. The Post Office issued the first U.S. commemorative stamps for the fair. Among the items introduced or popularized at the fair were Cracker Jacks, Aunt Jemima Syrup, Cream of Wheat, Pabst Beer, Juicy Fruit Gum, diet soda and the hamburger.

1897   The "Sausage King," Adolph Luetgert, killed his wife, boiled her body in acid and disposed of the remnants in a furnace in his factory at Hermitage and Diversey.
Police found Louisa's rings and a small piece of her skull inside a vat. Rumors swept the city that Louisa was ground into sausage, so sales slumped for a while. Luetgert was sent to Joliet for life, where he claimed his wife's spirit haunted him.

1939   The White Sox and Cubs met in a game at Comiskey Park to benefit Monty Stratton. The young White Sox hurler lost his leg in a hunting accident in November 1938. In a show of courage, Stratton took to the mound to pitch on his artificial leg. The game raised nearly $30,000. Stratton went on to pitch successfully in the minors and his life story was told in a movie starring Jimmy Stewart.

May 2

1837   William B. Ogden was elected as the first Mayor of Chicago. Ogden was a land speculator who used some of his own money to pay for early city improvements. He built the first drawbridge in the city, donated the land for Holy Name Cathedral, helped finance Cyrus McCormick's reaper factory and was instrumental in construction of the first railroad in Chicago.

1921 Without ceremony, the Field Museum of Natural History opened. After the Columbian Exposition, railroad tie magnate Edward Ayer asked Marshall Field for money to provide a home for the collection of natural history artifacts from the fair. Field tossed him out of the office, but later gave millions. The collection was initially housed at the exposition's Palace of Fine Arts in Jackson Park, a temporary building.

1927 The Stevens Hotel on South Michigan Avenue opened. The Stevens was the largest hotel in the world with 3,000 rooms, several ballrooms and quarters for pets. Insurance magnate Ernest Stevens owned the hotel. His son John Paul went on to become a U.S. Supreme Court Justice. The Stevens is now the Chicago Hilton and Towers, which contains 1,544 rooms.

1966 The new 31-story Civic Center was dedicated. At the time, the $87 million building was the tallest in Chicago. When the project was proposed in 1960, it was decided that a huge sculpture should be placed in the plaza. The city approached Pablo Picasso, who donated the statue as a gift to the people of Chicago. The building and the plaza were renamed in honor of Mayor Richard J. Daley on December 27, 1976.

1977 Elvis Presley played the second of two shows at Chicago Stadium, his last concert appearance in Chicago. A crowd of 20,000 saw the King in his "White King of Spades" suit. Elvis told the crowd. "In spite of everything that you've heard – rumors, I'm in good health and happy to be here."

May 3

1886 A crowd that had attended a meeting addressed by radical August Spies clashed with strikebreakers at the McCormick Plant. Six strikers were killed. Spies' paper, *Arbeiter-Zeitung* printed handbills calling workers to arms with the bold headline "REVENGE!" The headline was added without his knowledge. The next day, another circular called on workers to "appear in full force" at a rally at the Haymarket.

Chicago 365

1932   Photographers filled the yard of the Cook County jail as Al Capone began his trip to the federal prison in Atlanta. Inmate 40886 lived the good life in the prison, bribing guards and inmates with smuggled money kept inside a hollowed out tennis racket. In August 1933, the government took action. Capone was in the first group of federal prisoners sent to the new prison on Alcatraz Island in San Francisco Bay.

1973   A 2,500 pound girder enscribed with 12,000 signatures was hoisted 1,454 feet over Wacker Drive. The tallest building in the world at the time was topped out as thousands cheered. The Petronas Twin Towers in Kuala Lumpur, Malaysia took the title of world's tallest building in 1996. That is, if you count their 111 foot spires, which are purely decorative. But the Sears Tower is still the tallest in North America.

1997   Developer Lee Miglin died a horrible death at his Gold Coast residence. Andrew Cunanan tortured him with techniques from a "snuff" film, *Target for Torture*. Cunanan stabbed Miglin with pruning shears and slit his throat with a hacksaw. He then drove over the body repeatedly with Miglin's Lexus. Cunanan was wanted for murders in Minnesota and New Jersey. Fashion guru Gianni Versace would be his next victim.

May 4

1886   Anarchist August Spies and others spoke before a worker's rally at the Haymarket, on Randolph between Desplaines and Halstead. The crowd was leaving when Police Inspector John Bonfield sent 178 officers in. No one knows who threw the bomb, but the explosion killed a policeman. Police opened fire, hitting some of their fellow officers. Eight officers and six civilians died. Eight men, including Spies, were convicted in a sham trial of inspiring the violence. Four were hanged and one committed suicide.

1890   A bomber struck the monument honoring the police officers that died at Haymarket Square. The statue was moved to Union Park in 1900, and vandalized on May 4, 1903. A streetcar operator slammed into it on May 4, 1927. It was moved to Randolph Street in 1958. Bombers struck again in 1969 and 1970 and Mayor Daley placed an around-the-clock police guard at the site. The statue moved to Police Headquarters in 1972.

In 1976 it was moved to the Police Academy and can only be seen by making arrangements in advance.

1984   The John Hughes film *16 Candles* was released. Many of the exterior shots in the film starring Mollie Ringwald were filmed at Niles East High School in Skokie. The school was torn down in 1992. Niles North High School provided some of the interior school scenes. The church scene was shot at Glencoe Union Church and other scenes were shot in Evanston, Northbrook and Highland Park.

1991   The DuPage County regional Board of School Trustees voted to close down the last one room schoolhouse in the area. All six students at The McAuley Elementary School in West Chicago had graduated or moved from the district. The little red schoolhouse on Roosevelt Road east of Washington Street opened in 1914.

May 5

1894   The University of Chicago Board of Trustees met to choose a name for the football team. University treasurer Charles Hutchinson originally chose yellow as the team colors. But when a muddy game made the uniforms look terrible, the uniforms were changed to Maroon and the team had a new name.

1905   Robert S. Abbott published the first issue of the *Chicago Defender.* With the motto "American Race Prejudice Must be Stopped, The *Defender* would become the most influential African-American newspaper in the nation. It was widely read in the south, and Abbott encouraged blacks to move to Chicago. Nearly 500,000 blacks would come to north over the next 35 years.

1930   The Merchandise Mart opened. James Simpson, president of Marshall Field's, originally planned The Mart to consolidate the company's 13 wholesale warehouses into one location. Joseph P. Kennedy, father of the 35th president, bought The Mart in 1945. The Kennedy family controlled it until 1998. Today, The Mart is the largest trade center in the world. It hosts major trade shows and over 300 special events each year.

1969   The first Nine Lives Cat Food commercial starring Morris the Cat made its debut in Chicago. Chicago talent scout Bob Martwick rescued the cat from the Hinsdale Humane Society Shelter in 1967. The first commercial was filmed in Chicago in May 1968. But release was delayed while a search continued for an actor to provide a voice for Morris. The identity of that voice is still a closely guarded secret.

May 6

1919 L. Frank Baum died at "Ozcot," his home in Hollywood, California. Baum wrote *The Wizard of Oz* in 1900 while living at 1667 Humboldt Boulevard. In 1967, the Chicago Park district dedicated a park in his honor. Oz Park includes a statue of the Tin Man, made from car bumpers by artist John Kearney. The "Oz Festival" was originally held annually in the 13-acre park, but outgrew the site.

1937 The airship *Hindenburg* burst into flames at Lakehurst, New Jersey. Herb Morrison of WLS was not broadcasting live, but was experimenting with making field recordings using acetate disks. The recording captured Morrison as he cried "Oh the humanity!" SS officers were following Morrison and his engineer, so they went into hiding briefly before leaving for home. WLS aired the recordings the next day

1985 The State of Illinois Center, now the James R. Thompson Center, was dedicated. Architect Helmut Jahn's masterpiece features a multi-colored glass exterior and a 16-story atrium. "Starship Chicago" was controversial, since it cost twice as much as was originally budgeted. The state had to spend more money to fix the air conditioning system, because the sun shining through the glass baked the interior.

May 7

1896 Herman Webster Mudgett, a.k.a. Doctor Henry Holmes, went to the gallows. Holmes may have murdered as many as 200 people in his 100-room "castle" disguised as a hotel at 63rd and Wallace, near the Columbian Exposition. The building was filled with hidden passages and windowless rooms equipped with torture devices, a gas chamber and cremating oven. Holmes used an "elasticity determinator" to test his theory that the human body could be stretched to twice its normal length. Mudgett's story was the subject of the book *The Devil In The White City*.

1928 Al Capone had learned that three of his men plotted to kill him.

Chicago 365

He invited them to a banquet at the Plantation Roadhouse in Hawthorne, Indiana. As John Scalise, Albert Anselmi and Joseph Giunta enjoyed the food, Capone or Tony Accardo picked up a baseball bat and beat each of them. Gunfire finished the job. Scalise and Anselmi were known for coating their bullets with garlic, believing it would cause gangrene.

1989   Groundbreaking ceremonies took place for the new Comiskey Park, now known as U.S. Cellular Field. Jerry Reinsdorf, chairman of the White Sox, had threatened to move the team to Florida unless a new stadium was built. The $167 million ballpark was the first new American League stadium built just for baseball since 1973. Fans showed their approval by turning out in record numbers during the new stadium's first season.

1989   Michael Jordan made "The Shot." It happened in the decisive Game 5 in the first round of the NBA Eastern Conference playoffs in Cleveland. With the series tied at two games each, the Bulls trailed the Cavs by one point with just seconds remaining. Jordan dribbled across the circle and made a fantastic hanging jump shot at the buzzer to win the game.

May 8

1885   The Dearborn Street Station opened. The station with its 12-story Romanesque clock tower was the home of the Santa Fe Railroad, and its memorable long distance trains such as the *Super Chief* and the *El Capitan*. It also served several other lines. In 1971, all of the passenger train traffic there was moved to Union Station. The building was converted to shops and offices in the 1980's.

1924   The name Alphonse Capone appeared in bold headlines for the first time. Capone shot and killed "Ragtime" Joe Howard inside Jacob's Saloon, a speakeasy near the Four Deuces, a nightclub owned by Johnny Torrio. Howard made the mistake of smacking around Capone's friend Jack "Greasy Thumb" Guzik. When confronted by Capone, Howard called him a "dago pimp." That did it.

1926   A plane named *Miss Chicago* inaugurated service at the new Municipal Airport. At the time, airmail service was being flown from Maywood Airfield at First Avenue between Roosevelt and Cermak Roads,

Chicago 365

so it was quiet at first. But by 1932, the airport had earned the title "world's busiest." The city renamed it in honor of the Battle of Midway in 1949. It remained the world's busiest until O'Hare took over in 1962.

May 9

1873 Anton Joseph Cermak was born in Kladno, Bohemia. He rose from the mines to become the force behind the Chicago Democratic machine. He served four terms in the legislature and was an alderman before being elected mayor in 1931. On February 15, 1933 in Miami, he took a bullet meant for President Roosevelt. Cermak died on March 6. Cermak's son-in-law Otto Kerner served as Governor of Illinois from 1961-68.

1948 The first continuously published TV listing magazine was issued in Chicago. Les Viahon and three other men started *Television Forecast* with $750 dollars and published from a basement classroom at Northwestern University. They borrowed staples from the professors to bind the first issue of 16,000 booklets. *Television Forecast* was one of the publications that developed into today's *TV Guide*.

1960 The U.S. Food and drug administration approved the world's first commercially produced birth control pill. G.D. Searle and Company of Chicago manufactured "The Pill," Enovid 10. At the time, the FDA only required that a drug be proven safe, not necessarily effective. But Dr. John Rock insisted on proving the pill was effective. Within four years, four million women were taking it.

1961 In a speech before the Convention of National Association of Broadcasters, Federal Communications Commission Chairman Newton Minnow of Chicago declared that television was a "vast wasteland." *The Tribune* slammed Minnow as a "cultural Kruschev." The producers of the show "Gilligan's Island" would name the castaway's ship the S.S. *Minnow* as a jab at the FCC chair.

1984 The White Sox won the longest game in AL history. The game against Milwaukee at Comiskey Park had been suspended the day before after 17 innings. The next day, the teams had to complete the game before their regularly scheduled contest. The Sox won 7-6 when Harold Baines hit a home run in the 25th. The game took eight hours and six minutes.

Chicago 365

May 10

1869   The completion of the Union Pacific Railroad gave Chicago its first direct link to San Francisco. Over 50,000 people lined Michigan to watch a seven-mile long parade that lasted over four hours. The completion of the Transcontinental Railroad ushered in a period of tremendous growth for the city. By the 1880's, Chicago was the eastern terminus of all the great transcontinental lines.

1959   The Comiskey family sold the White Sox to a syndicate headed by Bill Veeck The Sox would win their first pennant in 40 years and set an attendance record of 1.4 million. The next year, Veeck installed the exploding scoreboard in Comiskey Park. He sold the team in 1961 but returned as owner from 1975-1981. It was his idea to have Harry Caray sing "Take Me Out to the Ballgame" during the 7th inning stretch.

1995   A swarm of media and a raucous crowd of about 2,000 gathered outside the Stateville Correctional Center as midnight approached. Some were dressed as clowns. They laughed and sang while vendors hawked t-shirts. The crowd cheered when the news came that John Wayne Gacy had been executed by lethal injection. "The Killer Clown" had confessed to 33 murders between 1972 and 1979.

2001   Boeing CEO Phil Condit announced that the world's largest aerospace company would move its headquarters to Chicago. Boeing would take up the top 12 floors of 100 North Riverside Plaza. The Chicago, Dallas-Fort Worth and Denver metropolitan areas were considered as the potential locations for the new world headquarters.

May 11

1894   Workers at the Pullman plant walked out. George Pullman had laid out a model community where workers were required to live. But he slashed wages and refused to reduce rents. Workers nationwide refused to handle Pullman cars and federal troops were called in. Violence swept the city. The leaders were arrested and the strike collapsed. Railroad union president Eugene Debs went on to found the American Socialist Party.

Chicago 365

1899 President Donnersberger of the South Park Board led ceremonies opening the golf course at Jackson Park. It was the first public course in the city. Today, the 18-hole course at 63rd Street and Lake Shore Drive remains the pride of the Chicago Parks District courses, described as the best golfing value in Chicago.

1920 Jim Colosimo, one of the most powerful crime bosses in the city, was shot and killed as he entered his nightclub at 2126 South Wabash. Colosimo had fallen in love with a beautiful singer named Dale Winter. His partner Johnny Torrio felt that Colosimo was not paying enough attention to the booze business. Torrio's Lieutenant, Al Capone, brought in Frankie Yale to kill "Big Jim." No one was ever charged.

1978 Carol Schmal and Lawrence Lionberg were murdered in Chicago. Kenny Adams, Willie Rainge, Verneal Jimerson and Dennis Williams spent 18 years behind bars for the murders. Jimerson and Williams were sentenced to death. They were released in 1999 after Northwestern University journalism students under Professor David Protess dug into the case and DNA tests proved their innocence.

May 12

1930 The Adler Planetarium opened, the first planetarium in the United States. Max Adler, a senior officer for Sears, Roebuck and Company, donated the funds to build it. Adler first saw the device that created the image of the night sky while on a trip to Germany in 1928. The Adler added state of the art exhibits and the new 60,000-square-foot Star Pavilion in an extensive 1999 renovation.

1951 Oscar De Priest died in Chicago, a few months after he was hit by a bus. In 1915 De Priest became the first black alderman in Chicago history. His reputation took a beating when he was accused of bribing police and taking payoffs from gamblers. But DePriest went on to become the first black Cook County Commissioner and the first African-American to be elected to Congress since the Reconstruction Era.

1955 "Sad" Sam Jones threw the first no-hitter at Wrigley Field since 1917, defeating Pittsburgh 4-0. It was the first Major League no-hitter for an African American. Jones was known for keeping a toothpick in his mouth. Before the game, Cubs broadcaster Harry Creighton joked he would give Jones a golden toothpick if he threw a no-hitter. Creighton kept his word.

1970   Ernie Banks slugged the 500th home run of his career. It came off Pat Jarvis of Atlanta in the second inning at Wrigley Field. The Cubs won the game 4-3. Frank Secory was the home plate umpire that day. Secory was one of the umpires the day Banks hit his first home run in 1953. Secory played outfield for the Cubs from 1942-46.

May 13

1914   Louis Henry Ford was born in Clarksdale, Mississippi. For over 60 years, Bishop Ford would serve as pastor of St. Paul's Church. He was known for helping the less fortunate. He rose to become the international presiding bishop and chief apostle for the 85 million members of the National Church of God in Christ. On July 27, 1996, the Calumet Expressway was renamed in his honor.

1923   Gangster Samuel "Nails" Morton died when his horse kicked him in the head on the Lincoln Park bridle trail. Dion O'Banion ordered his henchman, Louis "Two Gun" Alterie, to lead the guilty horse to the spot where the accident occurred and put a bullet in the animal's head.

1960   Don Cardwell of the Cubs became the first player to throw a no-hitter in his first start with a new team. Cardwell came over in a trade with the Phillies two days earlier. Right fielder George Altman made a sensational catch in the eighth inning to preserve the no-hitter against the Cardinals. Ernie Banks homered as the Cubs won 4-0.

2004   Floyd Kalber died at the age of 79. For over 30 years, Floyd was a presence in the homes of television viewers. He spent 14 years at WMAQ and came out of retirement in 1984 to take over the 6 p.m. newscast on WLS. He built the newscast into the highest rated in the city and stayed for 14 years. Kalber was a newscaster on NBC's *Today* show for three years.

May 14

1867   William Hale "Big Bill" Thompson was born in Boston. As the utterly corrupt Mayor of Chicago, he allowed the gangsters to rule.

Chicago 365

During World War One, he burned "Pro-British" books seized from the schools and threatened to "Punch King George in the snoot." With help from Al Capone and an anti-prohibition platform, Thompson returned for a third term in 1927.

1881   Tommy Burns of the White Stockings hit a ball that rolled up onto the clubhouse platform in the outfield at Lakefront Park, where owner William Hulbert's dog was sound asleep. Burns rounded the bases as Buttercup Dickerson of the Worcester Ruby Legs had to fight the dog for the ball.

1904   Jack McCarthy of the Cubs stepped on an umpire's broom as he went up to the plate and sprained his ankle. NL President Harry Pulliam would order umpires to carry a small whiskbroom to dust off the plate in the future. The American League made the change in 1905.

1920   Traffic began flowing across the Michigan Avenue Bridge, designed by Edward Bennett. It linked the Loop with the shabby, unpaved Pine Street. Pine was quickly transformed into "The Magnificent Mile" and renamed North Michigan Avenue. The span is the best known example of the trunnion bascule bridge, with two spans that move up or down to allow boats to pass. Chicago has about 50 such bridges today.

May 15

1812   Daniel Brainard was born in Whitesborough, New York. In 1837, he founded Rush Medical College. In 1847, he helped found Cook County Hospital, the first general hospital in Chicago. Brainard was the first surgeon to use ether as an anesthetic. Brainard Avenue is named in his honor.

1856   Lyman Frank Baum was born in Chittennango, New York, He came to Chicago in 1891, working as a reporter for the *Evening Post* and selling china. While living at 1667 Humboldt, he told his children tales from the *Wonderful World of Oz*, a name he came up with after seeing a file cabinet drawer labeled O-Z. In 1900, Baum and illustrator William Wallace Denslow assumed all expenses to publish the book.

1902   Richard Joseph Daley was born. The former member of the state legislature became Cook County Clerk in 1950 and gained massive clout as chairman of the County Democratic Party. He took office as Mayor on April 5, 1955 and was often criticized as racist and corrupt. Some mysterious last minute votes obtained by his machine gave John F. Kennedy the presidency in 1960. He also came under fire for the police tactics during the demonstrations at the 1968 Democratic Convention. Daley died in office in 1976.

1930   Aboard a Boeing Air Transport (BAT) flight from Oakland, California to Chicago, Helen Church became the first airline stewardess. Church was a registered nurse who convinced the predecessor of today's United Airlines that having a nurse on board would ease the public's fear of flying. The first stewardesses were required to be single and were paid $125 per month.

May 16

1832   Philip Danforth Armour was born in New York. Armour's packinghouse helped make Chicago a center of the industry. Henry Ford was inspired after seeing the efficient "disassembly line." Armour also increased revenue by using every part of the animal, producing lard, glue and fertilizer. His reputation took a beating when Upton Sinclair exposed the unsanitary conditions at the plant in *The Jungle*.

1860   The Republican National Convention opened at "The Wigwam," a hastily built hall at Lake and Market Streets. The convention was expected to nominate Senator William Seward of New York. But Seward faced opposition for his outspoken anti slavery stance. When the tally sheets were late in arriving from the printer, the convention adjourned for the night. Those in favor of Abraham Lincoln began maneuvering.

1912   Louis Terkel was born in the Bronx. The family moved to Chicago when he was eleven, and Terkel took the nickname Studs, after James Farrell's novel Studs Lonigan. He is best known for his oral history books, including *Division Street: America*, and the Pulitzer Prize winning *The Good War*. Terkel was blacklisted in the 1950's for refusing to cooperate with the House Un-American Activities Committee.

1985   Michael Jordan was named as the NBA Rookie of the Year. The

Bulls drafted him third in 1984. Sam Bowie and Hakeen Olajuwon were drafted ahead of him. Initially, Bulls GM Rod Thorn actually apologized for drafting Jordan, say,"He is not an overpowering offensive player."

May 17

1673   Father Jacques Marquette and Louis Joliet began their journey down the Mississippi. On the return trip, Indians led them up the Illinois and Des Plaines Rivers to a portage leading to a river feeding into Lake Michigan. In the fall of 1674, an ailing Marquette returned to the site. Marquette and two Frenchmen built a cabin at the present site of Damen Avenue, and became the first white settlement in Chicago.

1890   The community of Berwyn was incorporated. The area includes the former communities of Lavergne, South Oak Park and Upsala, or "Swedetown." Developers Charles Piper and Wilbur Andrews bought 106 acres and asked the CB & Q to build a station. They built their own when the railroad refused. The developers chose the name after seeing Berwyn, Pennsylvania on a railroad timetable.

1925   Chicago's Union Station opened. The $60 million structure was financed by four railroads, the Chicago Burlington and Quincy, the Milwaukee and St. Paul, the Chicago and Alton and the Pennsylvania Railroad. During World War Two, Union Station handled as many as 300 trains and 100,000 passengers daily. Over $35 million was spent to renovate the landmark in 1992.

1969   The debut album by the group Chicago Transit Authority entered the Billboard LP chart. The album peaked at number 17. The jazz-rock group was forced to shorten their name when Mayor Daley threatened legal action. Chicago went on to place 12 singles in the top ten between 1970 and 1977. The group returned to the top of the charts with a revamped lineup in the 1980's.

May 18

1860   The Republican Party nominated Abraham Lincoln for president. New York Senator William H. Seward was thought to have the nomination locked up. But the Illinois chairmen moved Seward's delegates to the side, away from swing state delegations. Hundreds of bogus tickets were handed to Lincoln supporters, who were told to arrive early to displace Seward backers. "Honest" Abe won on the third ballot.

1901   Mr. and Mrs. Robert Shaw arrived home, completing the first automobile trip from New York to Chicago. Their total actual driving time was 98 hours, an average of 11.3 miles per hour.

1934   The most devastating blaze since the Great Fire swept across three square miles of the Union Stockyards. No one knows how it started in the Swift and Company pens at 45th and Morgan. But by the time it was over two days later, over 1,100 people had been hurt, thousands of cattle were dead and several historic buildings were in ashes. Over 1,500 firefighters battled the flames, the wind and a lack of water pressure.

2001   A woman bit off the testicles of a man after he tried to force her to give him oral sex. The woman walked a block to Chicago police headquarters and turned in the evidence. A short time later, a man missing his testicles arrived at the Michael Reese Medical Center. Police said they "put two and two together" and arrested Eric Williams. Doctors were unable to reattach Williams' equipment, and he was left sterile.

May 19

1898   The post office authorized the use of postcards. The Curt Teich Company of Chicago was the world's largest manufacturer. From 1933 to 1958, Teich produced cards spelling out the name of a place in huge block letters, with landmarks inside. Those designs included the words "Greetings From." Such designs were featured on Bruce Springsteen's *Greetings From Asbury Park* album and recently on U.S. stamps.

1924   Chicago Police raided Sieben's Brewery at 1464 North Larabee. Johnny Torrio and 30 other bootleggers were arrested and 128,500 gallons of beer were seized. Northside Boss Dion O'Banion knew his brewery was about to be raided. So he quickly sold it for $500,000 to his rival Torrio. On November 10, 1924, O'Banion was gunned down at his flower shop on North State Street.

Chicago 365

1930   Lorraine Hansberry was born in Chicago. Her play, *A Raisin in the Sun*, was based on her childhood experiences. Seeking to move into Washington Park, the Hansberry family fought racially restrictive housing ordinances all the way to the U.S. Supreme Court. The play opened at the Ethel Barrymore Theatre on March 11, 1959. Sidney Poitier starred in the 1961 film version. Hansberry died of cancer when she was just 34.

1938   Anthony Spilotro was born in Chicago. The mobster was known for gruesome murders, including placing a victim's head in a vise until his eye popped out. He was the basis for Nicky Santoro, played by Joe Pesci in the movie *Casino*. But Spilotro met a horrific end when he disobeyed The Outfit's orders. In June 1986, Anthony and his brother Michael were beaten with baseball bats and buried alive in an Indiana cornfield.

May 20

1826   Potter Palmer was born in New York. He opened a dry goods store on Lake Street in 1852 and was the first to offer special sales and money-back guarantees. Palmer turned the store over to his assistant Marshall Field and Levi Leiter in 1867. He then built the Palmer House Hotel, and a new Field and Lieter store on State Street. Palmer was the first of the elite to move to Lakeshore Drive, which was mostly marshland.

1940   Stan Mikita was born in Sokolce, Slovakia. He played 22 seasons with the Blackhawks, scoring 551 goals, 926 assists and 1,467 points. He led the league in scoring four times and won two MVP awards. Mikita holds the Blackhawk record for lifetime assists and points. He ranks second only to Bobby Hull in goals. He was elected to the Hockey Hall of Fame in 1983.

1988   Laurie Dann, a mentally unstable babysitter from Glencoe, walked into a second grade classroom at the Hubbard Woods School on Chatfield Road in Winnetka. She carried three handguns, and opened fire. Dann killed eight-year-old Nicky Corwin and wounded five others. Dann fled from the school, forced her way into a nearby home, and wounded Phil Andrew. She then turned the gun on herself.

May 21

1924   Bobby Franks headed home from the Harvard School in exclusive Kenwood. He never made it. The nude body of the 14-year-old was found the next day. Police traced a pair of glasses found nearby and a typewriter used to write a ransom note to 19-year-old Nathan Leopold. Loepold and his lover, 18-year-old Richard Loeb, said they did it for thrills. The killer's wealthy parents hired Clarence Darrow to save them from hanging.

1927   Charles Lindbergh landed the *Spirit of St. Louis* at Le Bourget in Paris. Less than a year earlier he had been flying the mail between St. Louis and Chicago. Lindbergh scorned the press, in part because of an incident when he was hired to bring back pictures of the 1925 Illinois tornado disaster for the *Tribune*. A rival Hearst photographer tricked Lindy into flying blank photo plates back to Chicago.

1935   Jane Addams died at the age of 74, just three days after an operation revealed that she had cancer. Thousands lined up to pay their respects at Hull House before Addams was taken to her hometown of Cedarville for burial. She had been in poor health since a 1926 heart attack and was too ill to attend the 1931 ceremony where she became the first woman to win the Nobel Prize.

1952   Lawrence Tero was born in Chicago. One of 12 children, he was raised by a single mother on welfare. Lawrence took up bodybuilding to survive life in the projects. Tero was competing for the title of "World's Toughest Bodyguard" on the TV show "Games People Play," when Sylvester Stallone decided he should star in *Rocky III*. The move role led to "Mister T." winning the role of B.A. Baracus on TV's "The A-Team."

1955   At Chess Studios, Chuck Berry recorded his first hit. "Maybelline" was an adaptation of the country song, "Ida Red," with the new name taken from a line of cosmetics. Berry's idol, Muddy Waters, had introduced Berry to Leonard Chess. Chess turned the record over to influential New York disc jockey Alan Freed, who played it for two straight hours. That might explain why Freed has a writing credit on the record.

Chicago 365

May 22

1849   Bertha Honore Palmer was born in Louisville, Kentucky. The wife of merchant and hotel owner Potter Palmer was the queen of Chicago society. Bertha filled the lavish mansion on Lake Shore Drive with impressionist paintings that she would leave to the Art Institute. When Potter Palmer died, he left money in his will in case his wife married again. The new husband, Palmer said, "would need the money."

1868   The Republican National Convention in Chicago ended. The convention nominated Ulysses S. Grant for President. The delegates also approved a platform supporting reconstruction and the protection of loyal Southerners, oppressed people and immigrants. Over 8,000 spectators and delegates crowded into Crosby's Opera House to unanimously endorse the war hero.

1883   Billy Sunday made his major league debut for the White Stockings. He had a bad day, striking out four times. He would eventually strike out 14 consecutive times. But Sunday would go on to attain much greater fame as an evangelist. The White Stockings won the game 4-3 at Lake Park.

1969   Public school teachers walked off the job for the first time in Chicago history. The strike ended after two days with the teachers agreeing to a one-year contract. The deal included system reforms and raised starting pay from $7,350 annually to $8,400.

May 23

1908   Crowds fought to get a glimpse of Miss Bertha Carlisle as she appeared on the street wearing the first "directoire" gown ever seen in Chicago. The skirt was split above the knee. The newspapers reported that the crowd was denied a bigger thrill because Bertha was wearing trouserettes under the skirt.

1922   Chicago-born Walt Disney formed Laugh-O-Gram, his first studio. The company ended up bankrupt when the distributor didn't pay for the cartoons, so Walt lived in the studio while looking for work. A mouse that scampered about the old building in Kansas City would inspire Walt to create a new character he at first called "Mortimer Mouse." When he raised enough money, Disney left Kansas City and headed for Hollywood.

2001   A federal judge decided not to imprison a woman who stole almost $250,000 from her employer, ruling that she was a shopping addict. Elizabeth Roach faced up to 18 months in prison for embezzlement. But U.S. District Judge Mathew Kennelly found that she ran up $500,000 in credit card bills because she needed expensive clothing and jewelry to "self medicate her depression."

May 24

1861   Colonel Elmer Ellsworth of Chicago became one of the first Union officers to die in the Civil War. Ellsworth had rushed into a hotel in Alexandria, Virginia to tear down a Confederate flag when the hotel manager shot him dead. Ellsworth was a former law student and a close friend of Abraham Lincoln. The president ordered that Ellsworth lie in state at the White House.

1865   Chicago entered the steel age. The first steel rail made in the U.S. rolled off the line at Eber Ward's North Chicago Rolling Mill Company. In 1880, the firm would open a massive plant on the Calumet River. The area from the river to the dunes of Indiana would become the headquarters of the steel industry. In 1906, U.S. steel began construction of its plant and a company town named after lawyer Elbert Gary.

1908   Momo Salvatore "Sam" Giancana was born in Chicago. The former Capone wheelman took over the Outfit in 1955. Giancana was a friend of Frank Sinatra, and his lovers included Judith Campbell Exner, who was also involved with John F. Kennedy. Giancana was involved in the CIA plot to kill Fidel Castro. He was about to testify before a Senate committee about the plot when he was murdered on June 17, 1975.

1934   Jayne Byrne was born Jane Burke in Chicago. In 1979, she upset the Democratic machine by defeating Mayor Michael Bilandic in the primary and became the first female mayor of a major U.S. city. She was blasted for her mercurial management style and her term was marked by crisis. She lost the 1983 primary to Harold Washington, who beat her again in 1987. Byrne lost after challenging Richard M. Daley Junior in 1991.

Chicago 365

May 25

1925   Angelo Genna was the first of the "terrible" brothers to die. The Gennas built a bootlegging operation involving hundreds of Italian families paid to cook alky in their homes. They were behind the murder of Dion O'Banion and defied the other gangs. Earl "Hymie" Weiss and two other gangsters caught up with Genna's car on Ogden Avenue near Hudson.

1950   A Green Hornet Streetcar slammed into a gasoline tanker at State Street and 62nd Place. Thirty-four passengers died as the tanker exploded. Seven nearby buildings burned. Streetcar traffic had been diverted due to a flooded underpass, but the motorman sped through the open switch and skidded into the path of the tanker. Many died because the windows of the streetcar were covered with bars.

1979   At 3:02 p.m., American Airlines Flight 191 roared down the O'Hare runway, bound for Los Angeles. As soon as the DC-10 was airborne, the left engine fell off. The crippled airliner slammed into an abandoned hangar at the old Ravenswood Airport on Touhy Avenue. All 271 people on board the plane and two people in a nearby trailer park were killed in the worst aviation disaster in U.S. history. The NTSB blamed a maintenance crew in Tulsa for damaging the pylon that held the engine to the wing.

1981   Decked out in a Spiderman costume and wearing boots equipped with suction cups, Daniel Goodwin climbed the outside of the Sears Tower. It took him 7 1/2 hours to climb the 1,454 feet. Police were waiting at the top. In 1981, Goodwin climbed the Hancock Tower, despite the best efforts of the Chicago Fire Department. Firefighters turned the hoses on him.

May 26

1880   Ground was broken for George M. Pullman's model town, surrounding his railroad car factory west of Lake Calumet. The company controlled everything. Even the church was expected to turn a profit. A bitter strike broke out in 1894 when Pullman cut wages but refused to lower rents. Pullman died a hated man. The homes narrowly escaped demolition in 1960, and Pullman is now a protected landmark district.

1934   The Century of Progress Exposition opened for a second year. President and Mrs. Roosevelt addressed the crowd through "sound pictures," then pressed buttons to bring the fairgrounds to life. The 1934 exposition featured new buildings and a 670-foot-long fountain, the largest in the world. The fair was extended through 1934 in part due to its popularity, and in part to earn enough to pay off its debts.

1934   The *Burlington Zephyr* shattered the record for the run from Denver to Chicago, making the 1,015 mile trip in 13 hours and five minutes. At the World's Fair, thousands viewed the streamliner that made railroad travel fashionable again. In 1934, the *Zephyr* starred in the film *The Silver Streak*. The *Zephyr* was donated to the Museum of Science and Industry in 1960 and was restored in 1997.

1959   White Sox owner Bill Veeck pulled another stunt. Just before a game at Comiskey Park between the White Sox and Indians, a helicopter landed behind second base. Out jumped four midgets dressed in spacesuits. They "captured" 5' 9" Nellie Fox and 5' 10" Luis Aparicio, presenting them with ray guns. Eddie Gaedel was one of the spacemen. Veeck once sent the diminutive Gaedel up to bat for the St. Louis Browns.

May 27

1933   Energy generated by the rays of the star Arcturus lit the 427 acres of the gleaming "city of the future" lining Lake Michigan. It took 40 years for light to reach Earth from Arcturus, which was how much time had elapsed since the Columbian Exposition. The "Century of Progress" celebrated the anniversary of Chicago's incorporation but focused on the future. Originally planned just for 1933, the fair was extended for another season in 1934. The "Enchanted Island" site later became Meigs Field.

1933   The Museum of Science and Industry opened. Sears and Roebuck president Julius Rosenwald led the effort to raise money to rebuild the temporary structure that served as the Palace of Fine Arts during the 1893 Columbian Exposition. Tourists and school children still come to see the coalmine, the giant Focault Pendulum and to squeeze into the U-505. The exhibits are constantly changed with the times and the technology.

1935   Ramsey Emmanuel Lewis Junior was born in Chicago. He started out as an accompanist at the Zion Hill Baptist Church at age nine. He formed the Ramsey Lewis Trio and signed with Chess Records in 1956. 1965's "The In Crowd" is his biggest hit. Lewis went on to host a radio show and serve as the artistic director of the Jazz in June Festival at Ravinia Park.

1968   George Halas stepped down as coach of the Bears. At the time, he was the all-time winningest coach in football history, with 324 wins, 151 losses and 31 ties. Don Shula of the Miami Dolphins broke the wins record in 1994. Halas served as player-coach of the Bears from 1922-29, coached from 1933 to 1942, returned as coach from 1946-1956 and from 1958-1967.

1992   "The Last Godfather," mob boss Tony Accardo, died of old age and cancer at the age of 86. "Joe Batters" was Al Capone's bodyguard. He may have been involved in the St. Valentine's Day Massacre and beat traitors with a baseball bat.   He took the 5th Amendment 152 times before the Kefauver Committee during its investigation into organized crime in 1952. Accardo bragged that he never spent a day in jail.

May 28

1888   James Francis Thorpe was born what is now Oklahoma. The most outstanding athlete of the 20th century finished his football playing days with the Chicago Cardinals in 1928. In 1917, Thorpe drove in the winning run in a game at Wrigley Field where Chicago's "Hippo" Vaughn and Cincinnati pitcher Fred Toney both had thrown nine-inning no-hitters. Thorpe later became supervisor of recreation for the Chicago Parks.

1978   A package found on a parking lot at the University of Illinois was taken to Northwestern University because of its return address.   It exploded when opened, injuring a security guard.   For the next 17 years, authorities searched for a suspect known as "The Unabomber." On April 3, 1996, authorities arrested Theodore Kaczynski of Evergreen Park. He was sentenced to life for 16 bombings that left three dead and 23 injured.

1993   Fort Sheridan officially ended 106 years of operations as a U.S. Army installation. The post had survived several attempts to close it down since the early 1970's. But the base was no longer needed since the end of the Cold War and Operation Desert Storm. In 1998, a group of developers bought part of the historic district to develop luxury housing. Many buildings have been turned into upscale lofts, condominiums and town homes.

May 29

1848 Wisconsin became the 30th state of the Union. Many sources say the name is a Chippewa word meaning "grassy place." Wisconsin is nicknamed "The Badger State," but it's not named directly after the animal. Early immigrants worked to mine the lead and galena, living in burrows to keep warm and to keep working in the winter. The miners were thus nicknamed "Badgers."

1987 The pride of Gary, Indiana's reputation was starting to take a beating. Reports emerged that Michael Jackson had tried to purchase the remains of the deformed John Merrick, also known as "The Elephant Man." Jackson said the story wasn't true, and still managed to score a huge hit album in '87 with *Bad*. But then stories about his eccentric behavior began to overwhelm the music.

1990 Oakland A's outfielder Rickey Henderson stole the 893rd base of his Major League career, breaking the AL record held by Ty Cobb. He retired with a world record 1,406 swipes. Henderson was born in the back seat of an Oldsmobile in Chicago on December 25, 1958. His father left the family when Rickey was two-years-old. The family moved to Oakland when Rickey was seven.

May 30

1885 Arthur Edward Andersen was born in Plano, Illinois. Andersen and Clarence Delany co-founded an accounting firm in 1913. The firm changed its name to Arthur Andersen in 1918. At one time, Andersen was one of the largest accounting firms in the world, with offices in over 50 countries. Then came the day in October 2001, when Andersen employees started shredding Enron documents.

1909 Benny Goodman was born at 1342 West Washburne. Goodman made his professional debut at the Central Park Theater in 1921. The Harrison High School dropout made his first recording in 1926. An appearance at the Palomar Ballroom in Los Angeles on August 21, 1935 earned him the title "The King of Swing." Goodman helped the cause of integration when he hired Teddy Wilson and Lionel Hampton.

1933   Sally Rand caused a stir with her fan dance routine at the Century of Progress Exposition. She apparently wore nothing but some strategically placed feathers. She was arrested four times, but Judge Joseph Davis refused to order her to stop. Davis said "Lots of people in this community would like to put pants on horses." He called her audience "boobs," but added, "we have the boobs and we have the right to cater to them."

1937   Hundreds of striking steel workers gathered at Sam's Place, headquarters of the Steel Workers Organizing Committee. The Big Steel firms had recognized the union. But Republic and "Little Steel" firms refused. Rocks and bricks flew as the crowd marched towards the Republic Plant. Shots rang out and police waded in with clubs flying. Ten strikers were killed, some shot from behind in the "Memorial Day Massacre." The USWA Local 1033 Union Hall stands on the site of Sam's Place today.

1943   Gale Sayers was born in Wichita. He was raised in the town of Speed, Kansas! During his 1965 rookie season, the Bears running back led the league in scoring and scored six touchdowns in one game. Injuries cut his career short after six seasons, but he racked up 9,435 total yards, 4,956 yards rushing and 336 points. In 1977, he became the youngest player ever named to the Football Hall of Fame.

May 31

1850   Methodist brethren met in a law office above a hardware store at 69 West Lake Street to establish a university for Methodist youth in the interests of "sanctified" learning. John Evans, (for whom Evanston is named) Grant Goodrich and Orrington Lunt founded the first college in Chicago, Northwestern University. A 379-acre site along Lake Michigan was acquired for $25,000 and the first students enrolled in 1855.

1924   Nathan Leopold and Richard Loeb confessed to the murder of 14-year-old Bobby Franks. The teenaged lovers said they did it for the thrill of pulling off the "perfect crime" to show their "superior intellect." The boys showed no remorse. Leopold told a reporter, "It was just an experiment. It is as easy for us to justify as an entomologist in impaling a beetle on a pin."

1950   Tom Berenger was born Thomas Michael Moore in Chicago. He graduated from Rich East High School in Park Forest. He wanted to be a sportswriter, but found himself onstage at the University of Missouri. Berenger is known for his unpredictable roles, including his debut in 1977's *Looking for Mister Good Bar*. He was nominated for the 1987 Best Supporting Actor Oscar for playing the psycho Sergeant Barnes in *Platoon*.

1994   U.S. Representative Dan Rostenkowski was indicted on charges that he misused over $600,000 in federal money. Rostenkowski was forced to resign from his position as chairman of the House Ways and Means Committee and voters tossed him out of office in November. He pleaded guilty to mail fraud and was sentenced to 17 months in prison in 1996. President Clinton pardoned Rostenkowski in 2000.

Chicago 365

JUNE

June 1

1915 Deputy Police Chief Funkhouser banned the film *The Island of Regeneration*. The screen version of The Reverend Cyrus Townsend's novel included three scenes showing a young woman bathing in the nude.

1924 With the words "This is WGN, formerly WDAP," engineer Elliott Jenkins officially launched the new radio station operated by the *Tribune*. The call letters stand for "World's Greatest Newspaper." "Little Orphan Annie" and the show that became "Amos and Andy," made their debuts on WGN.

1975 The stage musical *Chicago* opened on Broadway at the 46th St Theater. Directed and choreographed by Bob Fosse, *Chicago* would run for 947 performances. Gwen Verdon and Chita Rivera starred in the musical based on a play about the 1924 murder trials of Buelah Annan (Roxie) and Belva Gaertner. (Velma) Maurine Watkins, a reporter who covered the trials, wrote the original play.

June 2

1863 Angered by the paper's anti-war stance, General Ambrose Burnside ordered federal troops to seize the offices of the *Chicago Times*. Reaction was swift, with one group forming to seize the offices of the *Tribune*. Another group planned to defend the *Tribune* offices. But Abraham Lincoln stepped in and rescinded Burnside's order.

1904 Peter Jonas Weismuller was born in what is now Romania. Weismuller took up swimming after contacting polio at age nine. Weismuller went on to set 67 world swimming records and win five Olympic gold medals. In 1927, he saved eleven lives when the excursion boat *Favorite* sank in Lake Michigan. Johnny ended his amateur career undefeated before heading to Hollywood, where he starred in 12 *Tarzan* films.

1928 Kraft introduced Velveeta, "A delicious Cheese Food consisting of Kraft Process American Cheese with added milk sugar, milk minerals and water. As digestible as milk itself." Velveeta would not curdle when heated and melted "as smooth as velvet." James L. Kraft started out selling cheese in Chicago back in 1903 and the first Kraft cheese factory was built in Stockton, Illinois in 1914.

1999   The pockets of commuters got a little lighter as the CTA did away with tokens. A new automated fare collection system, using magnetic fare cards, made station agents obsolete.

June 3

1861   Stephen Douglas died at the age of 48. President Lincoln ordered 30 days of national mourning. His widow wanted "The Little Giant" to be buried in Washington, but a group of Illinois politicians convinced her to allow him to rest at his Oakenwald estate along Lake Michigan. The present tomb on 35th Street with its monumental statue by Leonard Volk was completed in 1881.

1908   The School Board announced that in the future, no one over the age of 50 would be hired as a teacher. Superintendent Cooley said that 50 "appears to be the point at which the mental and physical vigor of those who come to us has begun to decline."

1942   Curtis Mayfield was born in Chicago. He started singing at seven and joined the group that became the Impressions at 14. His compositions such as "People Get Ready" and "Keep on Pushing" became civil rights anthems. He went solo in 1970 and hit number one in 1972 with "Superfly." Mayfield was paralyzed from the neck down when a lighting scaffold fell on him in 1990. He died in 1999.

2003   Sammy Sosa shattered his bat while grounding out in the first inning of the game against Tampa Bay at Wrigley Field. Umpire Tim McClelland discovered cork inside the bat, and threw him out of the game. Sosa said he unintentionally picked up a bat normally used to impress fans during batting practice. Major League Baseball X-rayed 76 of Sosa's bats, and they were all found to be free of cork. Sammy served a seven-day suspension

June 4

1944   The *U.S.S. Guadalcanal* task group under Captain Daniel Gallery of Chicago attacked the German *U-505*. Sailors from the destroyer *Pillsbury* boarded the *U-505*, making it the first enemy ship seized by the U.S. on the high seas since the War of 1812. The Navy planned to use it for target practice, but Gallery's brother contacted the Museum of Science and Industry. The *U-505* was dedicated on September 25, 1954.

1977   Rioting broke out in Humboldt Park following the annual Puerto Rican Day Parade. Three people were killed and over 100 injured in the two-day battle with police. A federal panel would blame the riot on "frustration and hopelessness, rage and violence" felt by many in the Puerto Rican community.

1996   Princess Diana arrived in Chicago to raise money for cancer research. Michael Wilkie, a recently-divorced, 280-pound, 55-year-old millionaire tool manufacturer, caused a stir when he asked the princess to dance during a gala at the Field Museum of Natural History on June 5. The princess seemed unconcerned and danced with him briefly, but the British tabliods blasted Wilkie as a "porker" and "savage." During her stay in Chicago, Princess Diana also spoke at at Northwestern University and toured the trauma ward at Cook County Hospital.

June 5

1931   A grand jury indicted Al Capone on 22 counts of income tax evasion. On June 16, Capone pleaded guilty and struck a bargain for a light prison sentence. But the judge refused to be bound by the agreement and Capone changed his plea. On November 24, 1931, Capone was sentenced to eleven years in a federal prison. Capone served seven years, six months and 13 days before he was released, ravaged by syphilis.

1946   A cigarette tossed into an elevator shaft started a blaze at the 23-story LaSalle Hotel, the "largest, safest and most modern hotel in America, outside of New York City." Many died from smoke inhalation or jumped when firemen's ladders couldn't reach past the 8th floor. Sixty- one people were killed. The LaSalle re-opened and remained in business until 1976. The Two North LaSalle office building stands on the site today.

Chicago 365

2002   Chicago R and B star Robert Kelly was charged with producing child pornography. Investigators said a videotape showed the 33-year-old singer having sex with a 14-year-old girl. Kelly admitted he had a "problem with women," but said he was not the man on the tape. Seven of the 21 counts in the indictment were dropped in June 2004.

2004   Former President Ronald Reagan died at the age of 93. Reagan was born in Tampico, Illinois on February 6, 1911. His family lived on the South Side of Chicago in 1914-15 before settling in Dixon. Reagan recreated Cubs games from telegraphed reports while an announcer for WHO in Des Moines in the 1930's. He made a screen test for Warner Brothers in 1937, while attending Cubs spring training

June 6

1884   The Republican National Convention meeting in Chicago nominated James G. Blaine for President and John A Logan of Illinois for vice president. Blaine and Logan lost to Democrats Grover Cleveland and Thomas Hendricks by just 30,000 votes in the general election.

1892   The first trains rattled along what Nelson Algren called "The City's Rusty Heart." The "El," began service over three-and-one-half miles of track from Congress to 39th Street above the alley running between State and Wabash. The *Tribune* noted that people living by the tracks seemed to have forgotten that the trains were starting, "and passengers saw bits of domestic life usually hidden." The line grew to circle downtown in 1897, and the area became known as "The Loop."

1995   Chicago horse broker Richard Bailey was convicted of conspiring to kill candy heiress Helen Brach. Bailey seduced older women and swindled them through bad horse investments. Asked how he could sleep with Brach, Bailey said "I close my eyes and think of the money." Assistant U.S. Attorney Steve Miller also brought down 19 other members of "The Horse Mafia" swindlers, solving several murders dating back to 1955.

June 7

1880   It was a wild night as the Republican National Convention met in Chicago. Fist fights broke out among supporters of U.S. Grant, Senator

Chicago 365

James Blaine, and Treasury Secretary John Sherman. Delegates quit for the night after 28 ballots with no winner. It took 36 ballots before James Garfield emerged as the nominee the following day, a GOP record that still stands.

1953 NBC presented the first network TV broadcast in "compatible color," the system we use today. Chicago's own Kukla, Fran and Ollie starred with the Boston Pops Orchestra, under the direction of Arthur Fiedler, in *St George the Dragon*. Kukla, Fran and Ollie made their regular television debuts on WBKB in 1947. In 1949, the show became the first ever broadcast over the NBC network.

1976 "The NBC Nightly News," with John Chancellor and David Brinkley, aired for the first time. Chancellor was born in Chicago in 1927 and started out as a copy boy for the *Sun-Times*. The partnership lasted until Brinkley moved to ABC News. Chancellor then held the solo anchor spot until 1982. He served as a commentator for NBC until 1993 and died of cancer three years later.

1981 Deputy Police Superintendent James Riordan became the highest ranking Chicago police officer to be murdered. He was off duty in the Captain's Table Dining Room at Marina City when a drunken armed man began bothering diners. Leon Washington shot Riordan as they scuffled. Washington pleaded self-defense and got 35 years. His mother sued the restaurant for serving liquor to her son.

June 8

1867 Frank Lloyd Wright was born in Richland Center, Wisconsin. His mother is said to have put pictures of great buildings in the child's crib. In 1887, the young architect came to work for Louis Sullivan and Dankmar Adler in Chicago. Sullivan fired Wright for moonlighting. Wright started his own firm and developed his signature "Prairie Style." His simple designs used low rooflines, banks of windows and natural materials.

1869 Ives W. McGaffey of Chicago patented the first vacuum cleaner. He built the "Whirlwind" in his basement. The "sweeping machine" wasn't motorized, and sold for a steep $25. The user had to turn a crank and push at the same time. McGaffey did try to add an electric motor in

1900, but he still didn't sell very many. Many companies were already working to improve on his design.

1981   The Morton Grove Village Board of Trustees voted to prohibit the sale and possession of handguns. It was the first such ordinance in the nation. The ordinance was quickly challenged in court as a violation of the Second Amendment, but the Seventh Circuit Court of Appeals allowed the measure to stand. The U.S. Supreme Court refused to hear the appeal.

1982   Millionaire Werner Hartmann was shot 15 times as he stepped out of the shower at his Northbrook home. He had married a stripper who admitted she wanted his money. Debra Hartmann was having an affair with tennis pro Scott Korabick. The "Black Widow," Korabik and a convict named Kenneth Kaenel plotted the murder to cash in on insurance. They were convicted of mail fraud, but were not charged with murder.

1984   Huge crowds turned out for the first Chicago Blues Festival. Performers included John Lee Hooker, Bobby "Blue" Bland, and a "Guitar Showdown" featuring Clarence "Gatemouth" Brown, Johnny Copeland, and Albert Collins. A crowd of over 100,000 attended the festival.

June 9

1883   The first commercial electric elevated railroad in the United States began operation. The first "el" ran around the main exhibition building at the Chicago Railway Exposition. The line operated for just two weeks before the exposition closed. The Electric Railway Company, a New York firm set up to develop inventions by Thomas Edison and Stephen Field, operated the line.

1916   Meeting in Chicago, The Progressive or "Bull Moose" party nominated former president Theodore Roosevelt and picked John Hughes for vice president. Roosevelt launched the party when he ran in 1912. But Roosevelt turned down the 1916 nomination and urged the party to endorse Republican Charles Evans Hughes. The Progressives disbanded before the election.

Chicago 365

1930 *Tribune* police reporter Alfred "Jake" Lingle was gunned down in a Michigan Avenue pedestrian tunnel. The public was outraged at the apparent mob hit. But it turned out that the $65 a week reporter had $63,000 in the bank, was a friend of Al Capone, and was a go-between for corrupt politicians and the police commissioner. Leo "Buster" Brothers was convicted of the crime, though Capone may have been behind it.

1991 Captain Bill Pinkney of Chicago sailed into Boston Harbor aboard his 78-foot sailing ketch, the *Commitment*. Pinkney became the first African-American to sail around the world solo and the fourth American to accomplish the feat. He began the 27,000-mile trip on August 5, 1990.

June 10

1847 The first issue of the *Chicago Tribune* rolled off a hand press in an empty loft at Lake and LaSalle Streets. The first issue consisted of four pages, and 400 copies were printed. Leather merchant James Kelly founded the paper with newspapermen John Wheeler and Joseph K.C. Forrest.

1910 Chester Arthur Burnett was born in Mississippi. He picked up the nickname Howlin' Wolf because of his wild singing style and released his first recording on Chicago based Chess Records in 1950. "How Many More Years" and "Moanin' at Midnight" was a hit and Burnett became a pioneer of the Chicago blues style. His other classics include "Back Door Man," "The Red Rooster," and "Goin' Down Slow."

1915 Saul Bellow was born in Lachine, Quebec. His bootlegger father moved the family to Chicago when Saul was nine. He wrote about his Canadian youth and Jewish heritage in his first novel, *Dangling Man,* in 1944. *The Victim, The Adventures of Augie March* and *Herzog* are among his works that earned critical acclaim. 1975's *Humboldt's Gift* won the Pulitzer, and Bellow was awarded the Nobel Prize for literature in 1976.

1916 At the Coliseum, the Republican National Convention nominated Associate U.S. Supreme Court justice Charles Evans Hughes for president. Just before the convention, 1,200 women met at the Blackstone Theater to organize the first woman's party and push for suffrage.

Thousands marched in a heavy rainstorm. It was reported that $13,000 in clothing was ruined.

1922 The *Tribune* announced a $100,000 contest to design "the world's most beautiful office building" for its new headquarters. New York architects Raymond Hood and John Mead Howells won with their design for a 36-story Gothic tower. Pieces of over 120 famous structures, including the Berlin Wall (a more recent addition), and the Great Wall of China are embedded in the base of the tower on North Michigan Avenue.

June 11

1920 Meeting in "smoke filled rooms" 408 and 410 of the Blackstone Hotel, the Republican Senate leaders selected Senator Warren Harding as a compromise candidate for president. He won the nomination on the 10th ballot. Harding pledged to return the nation to "normalcy" and said he was of good character. He didn't mention his four-year affair with Nan Britton. He also had another mistress, Carrie Phillips.

1964 Police broke up a press conference by the Rolling Stones as traffic came to a halt on Michigan Avenue. Mick and the boys were seated outside when the barber from the Sheraton Hotel threatened them with a pair of scissors. The Stones, described by the *Tribune* as "unkempt" slouches, scurried to a limo. They were in town for a recording session at the Chess Records Studios.

1986 The movie *Ferris Bueller's Day Off* was released. Chicago locations include Wrigley Field, the Sears Tower and the Art Institute. The high school interior scenes were filmed at the former Maine North High School (now the Illinois State Police Station in Des Plaines) and at Glenbrook North. The "Save Ferris" water tower stands next to the Northbrook Library. Scenes were also shot in Glencoe, Highland Park and Winnetka.

June 12

1808 The "President of the Underground Railroad" was born in Vermont. Charles Volney Dyer served as the surgeon at Fort Dearborn and went on to become the head of the Chicago, Burlington, and Quincy

Chicago 365

Railroad. He helped thousands escape, and is reported to have arranged for fugitive slaves to ride in his railroad's boxcars. At one time, Halsted Street was named in his honor.

1986 Bennie Goodman died of a heart attack at his New York apartment at the age of 77. Goodman had continued to play right up to the end, and had even scheduled a concert tour for later in the year. The son of poor Jewish immigrants who lived in the Maxwell Street neighborhood, Goodman was known as the "King of Swing."

1991 The Chicago Bulls won their first NBA championship, defeating the Los Angeles Lakers four games to one. Michael Jordan scored 30 points as the Bulls won Game Five 108-101. Jordan was named as the MVP, averaging of 31.2 points, 11.4 assists and 6.6 rebounds during the series. It marked the first of his six finals MVP awards.

June 13

1903 Harold "Red" Grange was born in Forksville, Pennsylvania. "The Galloping Ghost" shattered records at the University of Illinois. In 1925, George Halas signed him to the Chicago Bears of the fledgling NFL for an unheard of $25,000. Grange became pro football's first superstar, and turned the game into big business. He even appeared in several movies. Grange was elected to the Football Hall of Fame in 1963.

1930 The feds seized 200,000 gallons of booze in a raid at the Wabash Automobile Accessory Shop at 2108 South Wabash. The brewery could turn out 100 barrels each day. Following the raid, the press made a hero out of publicity seeking Assistant Chief Special Agent Eliot Ness. But the man who really hurt Capone was Agent A.V. Dalrymple. He seized over 2,500 stills in a year, but is forgotten today.

1986 Eleven years after the war ended, Vietnam vets finally got their welcome home. More than 500,000 people cheered some 200,000 veterans as they marched the three miles from Olive Park to Grant Park, the scene of violent anti-war protests in 1968. The names of 964 Chicagoans who gave their lives in the war are engraved on the wall at the Vietnam Veteran's Memorial in Washington, D.C.

1994   O.J. Simpson was in town to play golf with some Hertz Rent-a-Car clients when the phone rang in his room at the O'Hare Plaza Hotel. Los Angeles Police told him his ex-wife Nicole Brown Simpson and her friend Ronald Goldman were found dead. Simpson didn't ask how they died. He called his attorney and boarded a flight to Los Angeles.

1997   The Bulls won their fifth NBA Championship in seven years, defeating the Utah Jazz four games to two. Michael Jordan scored 39 points in the clincher, and was named MVP of the finals for the fifth time.

June 14

1671   Sieur de St. Lusson claimed "Le Pays de Illinois" for France. The name came from the Illinewek Indians, whom the French called the Illinois. St. Lusson's claim included all of what are now the states of Illinois, Wisconsin, Iowa and part of Missouri. The area was unexplored until the Marquette and Joliet expedition began in May 1673.

1949   A shooting at the elegant Evergreen Hotel inspired the Roy Hobbs character in *The Natural*. Ruthie Steinhagen lured former Cubs first baseman Eddie Waitkus to her room with a note. Waitkus was playing for the Phillies at the time. Steinhagen said that if she couldn't have him no one could, and shot him in the chest. It took five operations, but Waitkus recovered and came back with the pennant winning Phillies in 1950.

1992   The Bulls clinched their second world championship with a 97-93 win over the Portland Trailblazers. The victory celebration got out of hand when fans sat fire to several businesses on West Madison and broke windows all the way to Michigan Avenue.

1998   The Bulls pulled off another "Three-peat," taking the NBA title over Utah four games to two. The 87-76 win gave Chicago its third straight NBA title and sixth in eight years. Michael Jordan was named regular season MVP, NBA Finals MVP and All-Star Game MVP. He scored 45 points during his final game in a Bull's uniform and hit the winning jumper with five seconds to play.

Chicago 365

1805 William Butler Ogden was born in New York. He came to Chicago in 1835 to sell land bought by his brother-in-law, which he believed was worthless. He stayed and became the first Mayor of Chicago in 1837. Ogden was instrumental in construction of the first railroad here and designed the first swing bridge. He lost everything in the Great Fire. His massive lumber yard in Peshtigo, Wisconsin burned the same day.

1852 Waukegan was officially incorporated as a city. The settlement was originally known as "Little Fort," after a fort constructed as a trading post by French explorers during the 17th century. The town grew into an important harbor and was re-named Waukegan, which is the Potawatomie Indian word for Little Fort. Waukegan is the hometown of Jack Benny and science fiction writer Ray Bradbury.

1956 Commissioner Timothy Dalton disbanded the notorious Chicago special investigative unit named after Scotland Yard in London. Inside their Canalport Station, Scotland Yard detectives beat suspects with rolled up telephone books, which leave no scars. But it wasn't brutality that brought the unit down. Mayor Daley was infuriated when the unit bugged Democratic Party headquarters in the Morrison Hotel.

1964 The Cubs made the worst trade in their history. They sent pitchers Jack Spring and Paul Toth to the Cardinals, along with an outfielder named Louis Clark Brock. The Cubs picked up pitchers Ernie Broglio and Bobby Shantz along with outfielder Doug Clemens. Brock would spark the Cards to a World Championship and end up in the Hall of Fame. Broglio won just seven more games. Shantz only played 20 more games.

1999 The "Cows on Parade" made their public debut. The Chicago Department of Cultural Affairs art exhibit featured some 300 colorfully decorated fiberglass cows placed around downtown. Peter Hanig brought the idea to Chicago when he saw a similar exhibit in Zurich, Switzerland. The exhibit was a huge success, drawing an estimated 2 million people to Chicago. It has since been copied by many other cities.

June 16

1893 Some 266 feet above the gleaming "White City" of the Columbian Exposition, Margaret Ferris lifted a glass of champagne and offered a toast "To the health of my husband and the success of the Ferris Wheel." Invited guests took the first public ride. Fair officials laughed when George Ferris of Pittsburgh first proposed a giant wheel, designed to rival the Eiffel Tower. It could carry 2,160 people at a time.

1970 Bears running back Brian Piccolo died after an eight month battle with cancer. He was just 26. Gale Sayers and Piccolo became football's first interracial room mates before the 1967 season. When Sayers suffered a terrible knee injury, Piccolo helped him both mentally and physically. The television movie *Brian's Song* told their story. The Bears established the Piccolo fund in his honor, raising millions for cancer research.

1981 William Wrigley announced that the Cubs would be sold to the Tribune Company for $20.5 million. The sale ended 64 years of ownership by the Wrigley family. The Cubs were terrible during the strike-interrupted split season. Comedian Tom Dressen said, "Will the lady who lost her nine children at the ballpark please pick them up immediately. They are beating the Cubs 10-0 in the 7th."

1996 The Chicago Bulls defeated Seattle 87-75 in Game Six of the NBA Finals, clinching the Bull's fourth championship in six seasons. Michael Jordan's 22 points and seven assists, Dennis Rodman's 19 rebounds and Scottie Pippen's 17 points and four steals led the team to the win. Jordan won his fourth NBA Finals MVP Award.

June 17

1917 Gwendolyn Brooks was born in Topeka, Kansas. She grew up in the Bronzeville neighborhood of Chicago. Her first book of poetry, *A Street in Bronzeville,* was published in 1945. In 1950, she became the first African American to win a Pulitzer Prize for Poetry with her second collection, *Annie Allen.* Brooks was the poet laureate of Illinois from 1968 until her death in 2000.

1942 Herman Otto Neubauer and Herbert Hans Haupt were among a group of Nazis that came ashore at Ponte Vedra Beach, Florida. They brought equipment and thousands in cash to support a two-year campaign of industrial sabotage. Nueubauer and Haupt were to carry out their mission in Chicago. But they were arrested on June 27th before they could do any harm and were executed on August 8, 1942.

1994   Opening ceremonies took place in Chicago for the second round games of the World Cup. Attendance fell short of the projected 400,000 but the games were declared a huge success. Defending World Cup champion Germany beat Belgium on July 2nd to win the second round.

June 18

1855   Joseph Medill, editor of a newspaper in Cleveland, reluctantly bought the struggling *Chicago Tribune*. Medill, one of the organizers of the Republican party, turned the paper around. He made it into a strong force against slavery and helped get Abraham Lincoln nominated for president. Medill served as mayor from 1871 to 1873, helping to rebuild the city. Three of his grandsons went on to run newspapers.

1914   Police Chief Schuettler offered his comment on women's bathing dress. The chief said bloomers are all right on thin women but "immoral obscene, dangerous and ridiculous on fat women."

1942   Roger Ebert was born. The film critic for the Chicago *Sun-Times* partnered with the late Gene Siskel of the *Tribune* to review films on their TV show. The once bitter rivals were first teamed up on WTTS in 1975. After Siskel died in 1999, *Sun-Times* columnist Richard Roeper joined the show. Ebert has written over 40 books on the cinema and also wrote the screenplay for the 1969 cult classic *Beyond the Valley of the Dolls*.

1961   Eddie Gaedel died of a heart attack at the age of 36 after he was mugged in Chicago. St. Louis Browns owner Bill Veeck sent the 3' 7" 65-pound stage performer to the plate with a toy bat in 1951. Gaedel walked on four straight, and the ML quickly banned midgets. He also appeared in other bizarre Veeck stunts, including serving as a vendor after White Sox fans complained that vendors were blocking their view.

Chicago 365

June 19

1908   The Republican National Convention in Chicago nominated Secretary of War William Howard Taft for President. President Roosevelt had made it clear he wanted Taft to be his successor. But Teddy was angered when Taft failed to push for his agenda. He abandoned the GOP when Taft was nominated again at Chicago in 1912, and formed the Progressive or "Bull Moose" Party.

1928   Ulysses S. Sanabria presented Chicago's first television program. He sent television signals out over The Chicago Federation of Labor's Radio Station, WCFL. The broadcast featured a picture of CFL secretary E.N. Nichols and used Sanabria's bulky mechanical transmission system. A viewer needed a two-foot disc to see a picture roughly the size of a couple of postage stamps.

1947   Preston Tucker unveiled his "car of the future." Just 51 were produced before the company failed amid allegations of fraud. The Tucker was far ahead of its time, with a swiveling headlight, rear-mounted air cooled engine, disk brakes, seat belts, and padded dash. The factory was converted into the Ford City Mall in 1965. Tucker's story came to the big screen in 1988 in Francis Ford Coppola's *Tucker: The Man and His Dream*.

1975   Sam Giancana was shot to death in the kitchen of his Oak Park home. Giancana took over the Chicago mob in the 1950's. He is credited with delivering the votes that put John F. Kennedy in the White House and was involved in the CIA plot to kill Castro. Some say he had Marilyn Monroe killed to get even with the Kennedys for coming after the mob and may have been involved in the assassination of the president.

June 20

1899   The Village of Glenview was incorporated. Originally known as South Northfield and North Branch, it was renamed Oak Glen in 1878. But the railroad already had a station by that name. It was proposed to name the village after Fred Hutchings, who donated the land for the depot. But his wife didn't want their name on the dilapidated old rail car that served as a station. So they settled for Glen View, later Glenview.

1915   William Rand died in New Caanan, Connecticutt. The young printer from Boston opened a shop in Chicago in 1856. In 1864, He teamed up with Andrew McNally, an Irish mapmaker, to found Rand McNally and Company. The firm published the first railroad map in 1869 and began publishing road maps in 1904. Today, the company headquartered in Skokie also markets travel related software.

1980 *The Blues Brothers* was released. It was the first big movie filmed in Chicago since the Daley administration, which extorted kickbacks from filmmakers. This time, City Hall allowed director John Landis to trash the Daley Center and film chase scenes on Lower Wacker Drive. Another big chase was filmed at the abandoned Dixie Square Mall in Harvey. The "Hotel for Men Only Transient's Welcome" stood at 22 West Van Buren.

1993 The Bulls won their third straight NBA championship with a thrilling 99-98 win over the Phoenix Suns in Game Six. John Paxson hit the winning three point shot with just seconds left and Horace Grant blocked a shot by Kevin Johnson as time ran out. Michael Jordan became the first player in history to win the finals MVP award three seasons in a row.

June 21

1882 William Mathias Scholl was born. The grandson of a shoemaker, Scholl developed the "Foot Eazer" in 1903. After graduating from Illinois Medical College, (now Loyola) Doctor Scholl started his own foot care business. In 1911, he took over the Western Wheel Works bicycle factory in the 300 block of West Division. The plant moved to Tennessee in 1981 and the factory became the Cobbler Square Apartments.

1920 As war hero Carl Wanderer returned home with his pregnant wife Ruth, a man followed them into the building at 4732 North Campbell. Shots rang out and Ruth fell dead. Carl was praised for his bravery for killing the "ragged stranger." But reporters learned that Wanderer was a homosexual who staged the robbery. On March 19, 1921, Wanderer sang "Dear Old Pal O'Mine" as he went to the gallows.

1958 For the last time, a streetcar clanked down a Chicago Street. Al Carter was the last person to board Car 7213 on the Vincennes Avenue line before it ended the historic run. Carter made it his business to be a footnote to history. He was the last to enter the ticket gates at the

Chicago 365

Century of Progress Exposition. At one time, Chicago had the largest street rail system in the world. Over 900 million passengers boarded in 1929.

1996 Ceremonies marked the dedication of the largest single space in North America dedicated to contemporary art. German architect Josef Paul Kleihues designed the $46 million Museum of Contemporary Art. The building has five times the space of the old structure, opened in 1967 in a converted bakery on East Ontario that also once housed the *Playboy* corporate offices.

June 22

1908 Chicago's present street numbering system was established. The system set up two lines to begin all numbers, State Street north and south and Madison Street, running east and west. With very few exceptions, 100 numbers were assigned to each 1/8th mile or 800 to each mile. Even numbers indicated a building on the north or west side of the street, and odd numbers were on the south or east side of the street.

1918 A speeding empty troop train smashed into the back of a Hagenbeck-Wallace Circus train just outside Hammond, Indiana. The troop train engineer was asleep at the switch. Eighty-six people died, many of them burned to death. Many of the dead are buried in a mass grave guarded by five elephant statues in the "Showman's Rest" section for circus performers at Woodlawn Cemetery in Forest Park.

1926 Joseph "Yellow Kid" Weil was sent to Leavenworth for handling stolen bonds. Weil was the greatest con man ever. He said anyone crooked enough to go into business with him deserved what they got. His amazing cons included a fake bank, (with hookers posing as tellers) and a fake booking parlor. He even posed as a spiritualist, receiving information on his rich marks through headphones concealed under his turban.

2002 Eppie Lederer, known to millions as "Ann Landers," died at the age of 83 at her East Lake Shore Drive Home. Her syndicated column reached 90 million readers in 1,200 newspapers. Eppie took over from the original advice columnist at the *Sun-Times* in 1955 and moved to the *Tribune* in 1987. Her twin sister Pauline penned an advice column under the name "Dear Abby."

Chicago 365

June 23

1892   The Democratic National Convention nominated Grover Cleveland for president and former U.S. Representative from Illinois Adlai Stevenson for vice president. The convention met in a temporary building with a leaky roof.   The "Wigwam" was located on Michigan between Washington and Madison. The largest indoor meeting space in America at the time was built in just 30 days.

1895   A group called the "Sunday Observance League" led by the Reverend W.W. Clark managed to halt the Cubs game at the West Side Grounds in the third inning. The entire Cubs team has hauled off to jail for aiding "the forming of a noisy crowd on Sunday." The team owner posted bond, the game resumed, and the Cubs beat Cleveland 13-4. The Reverend turned down an invitation to stay for the rest of the game.

1904   The Republican National Convention, meeting at the Second Coliseum, nominated incumbent Theodore Roosevelt for president. The convention wasn't very exciting, because everyone expected Roosevelt to be nominated. His main rival, Senator Mark Hanna of Ohio, died four months before the convention.

1927   Bob Fosse was born in Chicago.   He began dancing at the age of nine and left for Hollywood in 1953. *Kiss Me Kate* was the first film to feature Bob Fosse choreography, although he received no credit. Fosse went on to Broadway, choreographing plays such as *Damn Yankees*. In 1972, he won an Oscar for *Cabaret*. His other films included *Lennie, All That Jazz* and the ill-fated *Star 80*.

June 24

1839   Gustavus Swift was born in Massachusetts. In 1878, the Chicago meat packer hired an engineer to develop the first refrigerated railroad cars. The invention allowed cattle to be slaughtered in Chicago and the meat shipped across the nation. Swift allied his firm with the packing houses of J.O. Armour and Edward Morris, forming a monopoly. The U.S. Supreme Court broke up the "Beef Trust" in 1905.

1922 At the suggestion of Chicago Staleys owner George Halas, The American Professional Football Association changed its name to the National Football League. The Staleys, 1921 APFA champions, changed their name to the Chicago Bears. The Bears are one of only two charter members of the NFL still playing today.

1946 A gunman shot James Ragen in the midst of the Bronzeville neighborhood. Ragen had defied the mob, which was seeking to take over his horse racing wire service. At first it appeared that Ragen would survive. That is, until someone managed to get past the police guarding his room at Michael Reese Hospital. They slipped Ragen a dose of deadly mercury. The Outfit controlled the racing wires.

June 25

1837 Charles Tyson Yerkes Junior was born in Philadelphia. Yerkes organized the Chicago mass transit system, controlled the firms that built it, and nearly gained a monopoly through bribery. Yerkes once had an affair with a married woman and her daughter. He tried to improve his image through philanthropy, donating the money for the Yerkes Observatory and went on to help build London's Underground.

1888 Meeting at the Civic Auditorium, the Republican National Convention nominated Benjamin Harrison of Indiana for President and Levi Morton of New York for vice president. There were at least nine candidates for the nomination, and Harrison won on the eighth ballot. In the presidential election, Grover Cleveland would win the popular vote. But Harrison won the Electoral College vote.

1902 Arthur Rubloff was born in Duluth, Minnesota. In 1947, he coined the term "Magnificent Mile" for his plans to redevelop North Michigan Avenue. Rubloff also built Sandburg Village and worked to redevelop the Old Town Neighborhood. Rubloff donated millions to the Art Institute.

1916 The Municipal Pier opened. The pier was originally designed for recreation and for freight. In December 1927, the City Council changed the name to Navy Pier, in honor of those who served in the Navy during World War One. Today, the renovated pier contains exhibition space, the

Children's Museum, the Skyline Stage outdoor theater, Crystal Garden indoor park and an IMAX theater.

June 26

1878   The first telephone exchange in Chicago was founded. The 75 lines of the Chicago Telephonic Exchange originally served businessmen. When the public began asking for phones, the firm merged with competitors to form the Chicago Telephone Company. That firm published the first Chicago phone book in 1886. It included 291 listings. The Chicago Telephone Company grew into Illinois Bell, now Ameritech.

1913   The Governor signed a measure passed by the General Assembly granting women in Illinois the right to vote for presidential electors and some local officials. Illinois became the first state east of the Mississippi to allow women to vote for president. But women still could not vote for state representatives, congressmen or governor. Women also had to use separate ballots and ballot boxes.

1954   Eight people were killed when a freak tidal wave smashed into the shore of Lake Michigan from Jackson Park to Wilmette. About 20 people were swept from a pier at Montrose Harbor. The dead included a mother of eleven who was rescued, but went back into the lake to search for her missing husband. Officials said the eight-foot high wave was caused by a sudden change in air pressure.

June 27

1848   The *Ireland* became the first ocean-going steam ship to dock at Chicago. The opening of the Illinois and Michigan Canal had made it possible for ships to travel from New York to New Orleans and made Chicago the most important inland port in America. Today, the ports of Metropolitan Chicago handle over 80 million tons of cargo annually.

1921   The case of *State of Illinois versus Eddie Cicotte et al* opened in the Chicago courtroom of Judge Hugo Friend. White Sox players Eddie Cicotte, Chick Gandil, Oscar Felsch, Joe Jackson, Fred McMullin, Swede Risberg, Buck Weaver and Claude Williams were charged with conspiring to throw the 1919 World Series. The players were acquitted, but Commissioner Kenesaw Mountain Landis banned them for life.

1985   The American Association of State Highway and Transportation officials decertified Route 66 and the "Main Street of America" ceased to be an official highway. Today, travelers can speed from to Chicago to Los Angeles via the five interstates that replaced the legendary route, but travelers from all over the world still seek out the landmarks and towns along the old highway.

June 28

1944   Meeting at Chicago Stadium, the Republican National Convention nominated Governor Thomas Dewey of Wisconsin for president and John Bricker of Ohio for vice president. Dewey flew in from Albany to become the first Republican nominee to make an acceptance speech at the convention. The Republicans also endorsed a sweeping civil rights platform, including an investigation into discrimination in the military.

1951   "Amos 'n' Andy" premiered on CBS Television. Freeman Gosden and Charles Correll, who originally brought the characters to life as "Sam and Andy" on WGN radio, produced the show. But they were white, so Alvin Childress starred as Amos and Spencer Williams Junior played Andy on television. CBS cancelled the show two years later, amid protests from the black community.

1966   Actor John Cusak was born in Evanston. He starred in films such as *America's Sweetheat, Being John Malkovich, Say Anything, The Cradle Will Rock* and *Pushing Tin*. He also played Rob Gordon, the owner of a suburban Chicago record store and a compulsive list maker, in *High Fidelity*. His sister Joan has also starred in many movies, including appearances with John in *High Fidelity* and *The Cradle Will Rock*.

1999   Hack Wilson of the Cubs became the only dead man to be credited with an RBI. The Office of the Commissioner determined that Charlie Grimm had been credited with an RBI that belonged to Wilson during a doubleheader against the Reds on July 28, 1930. The change gave Wilson 191 RBI's for the season, a record that still stands.

June 29

1858   Julia Lathrop was born in Rock Island. She met Jane Addams while attending Rockford Seminary. In 1890, she joined Addams at the newly established Hull House. Lathrop worked for reform of institutions for the mentally ill, indigents and children. She also helped found the first juvenile court. In 1912, President Taft appointed her to head the federal Children's Bureau, making her the first woman to head a federal agency.

1889 Chicago quadrupled its population in a single day with the annexation of a 140 square mile area, including Ravenswood, Lakeview, Lake Township, Jefferson Township, South Chicago and Hyde Park. The city limits were extended from 39 to 169 square miles and the population topped one million.

1969 Cubs outfielder Billy Williams set an NL record for most consecutive games played. On "Billy Williams Day" at Wrigley Field, Williams smacked five hits and passed Stan Musial on the all time Iron Man list by playing in his 895th and 896 games. Between September 22, 1963 and September 2, 1970, Williams played in 1,117 consecutive games. Steve Garvey broke the record in 1983.

2003 A third floor balcony crowded with young party-goers collapsed, killing 13 and injuring at least 57. The balcony on a building a few blocks from DePaul University crushed the porches below, which were also crowded with people. Following the disaster, the city inspected thousands of porches and approved new regulations regarding construction and repairs.

June 30

1906 President Roosevelt signed the Food and Drug Act and the Meat Inspection Bill, authorizing federal inspection. Roosevelt was angered after reading the descriptions of conditions in the Chicago Stockyards in Upton Sinclair's *The Jungle*. Meat sales fell by 50% after the public read the book. Roosevelt pressured Congress and Senator Albert J. Beveridge of Indiana introduced the meat inspection measure in the Senate.

1934 The Brookfield Zoo opened. Brookfield was the first completely modern zoo in the United States. The "barless" design of the zoo was soon being copied all over the world. Natural barriers such as moats separated the animals from the guests. That caused a problem at first when the leopards began escaping at night.

Chicago 365

1940   The comic strip "Brenda Starr" made its debut. Dahlia Messick changed her name to Dale when she submitted the idea for a strip featuring a glamorous newspaper reporter to Joseph Patterson of the *Tribune*, because there were no female artists drawing comic strips at the time. Messick was the first female to have her work syndicated and females only draw the strip to this day.

1959   Two balls got into play at once in a game between the Cubs and Cards at Wrigley Field. Stan Musial drew a walk. The ball got behind catcher Sammy Taylor and the ump threw another one into play. Taylor threw that ball into center field. Shortstop Al Dark went back and grabbed the first ball, and threw to shortstop Ernie Banks. Banks tagged out a befuddled Musial. Umpire Vic Delmore was fired because of the incident.

1986   The Chicago Playboy Club closed its doors. The first Playboy Club in the world opened at 116 East Walton in 1960. By 1961, it was the busiest nightclub in the world. Hugh Hefner modeled it after the Gaslight Club, where "Gaslight Girls" served powerful men while dressed in sexy 1890's styles. Hefner adapted the idea for his Playboy Bunnies. The Regal Knickerbocker Hotel stands on the site today.

JULY

July 1

1899   The city of Chicago passed its first law licensing automobiles. Drivers had to convince a licensing board that they were mentally balanced, in good physical condition and have "familiarity with the parts of the automobile which might become disarranged." All vehicles were required to have a working 14-inch bell and speeds were limited to eight miles per hour.

1899   Thomas Dorsey was born near Atlanta, Georgia. The "Father of Gospel Music" moved to Chicago as a teenager. He "Wrote Take My Hand Precious Lord" just one month after his wife died during childbirth in August 1932. The child also died. Dorsey combined the blues with religious music to create an entirely new sound. His other songs include "Peace in the Valley" and "Today."

1910   The White Sox played their first game in "The Baseball Palace of the World" at 35th Street and Shields Avenue. They lost to the St. Louis Browns 2-0. Architect Zachary Taylor Davis designed Comiskey Park with help from pitcher Ed Walsh, which explains why it was 363 feet down the lines and 420 feet in straightaway center field. The White Sox played their last game there on September 30, 1990.

1915   Willie Dixon was born in Vicksburg, Mississippi. At age 17, he left for Chicago to become a boxer. Dixon won the Illinois State Golden Gloves Championship, and then hung up his gloves for a musical career. One of the artists who created the Chicago Blues sound, his songs were recorded by Muddy Waters, Elvis Presley, the Rolling Stones, the Grateful Dead, the Doors, Led Zeppelin and Jimi Hendrix.

July 2

1881   Charles Guiteau, a mentally ill Chicago lawyer, shot President James Garfield. Guiteau flunked out of law school, and started a practice with fake endorsements. He wound up at the controversial Oneida Community, joined an obscure cult, and went wild sexually. After the Oneidas kicked him out, Guiteau gave bizarre unsolicited speeches for Garfield. Guiteau believed he alone was responsible for Garfield's victory.

Chicago 365

1904 The "Place to Laugh Your Troubles Away" opened. Riverview Park was originally known as German Sharpshooter Park, a hunting preserve at Western and Belmont Avenues. The owners added a carousel and rides so women and children would have something to do. "The World's Largest Amusement Park," closed in 1967.

1932 Meeting at Chicago Stadium, the Democratic National Convention nominated Franklin D. Roosevelt for president. Roosevelt broke with tradition and flew in from Albany, becoming the first to make an acceptance speech before the convention. Roosevelt would win the election, and returned to Chicago to be nominated again in 1940 and 1944.

1999 Benjamin Smith killed Ricky Byrdsong as the former Northwestern University basketball coach played with his two children in Skokie. Smith went on a two state shooting spree, killing Won Jon Yoon outside a Korean church in Bloomington, and wounding nine others. The member of Mathew Hale's white supremacist "Church of the World Creator" took his own life following a high-speed chase in Salem, Illinois.

2002 On his sixth attempt, Chicago millionaire adventurer Steve Fossett crossed 117 degrees longitude aboard his balloon the *Spirit of Freedom*, and became the first solo balloonist to circumnavigate the globe. Fossett has swam the English Channel, competed in the Iditarod dog sled race, finished the Ironman triathlon, sailed alone across both the Atlantic and Pacific oceans and driven in the 24 Hours of LeMans.

July 3

1895 Catherine "Kate" O'Leary died at the age of 68. Her cottage survived the fire, but the press unfairly called her a hag and welfare cheat. She was forced to move and became a recluse, leaving her home only when necessary or to attend mass. Some historians now believe Daniel "Peg Leg" Sullivan started the fire while gambling in the barn with Kate's son. In 1997, the City Council absolved Kate and her cow of all blame.

1899 The nation's first juvenile court opened on the West Side. Judge Richard S. Tuthill heard the case of Henry Campbell, an 11-year-old accused of larceny by his mother. Reformers such as Jane Addams had pushed the Illinois legislature to recognize that children were developmentally different from adults.

1911 The high temperature hit 102. It had topped 100 on July 2 and would hit 102 again on July 4. It's the only time in Chicago history that the high temperature climbed over 100 three days in a row.

July 4

1836 Construction began on the Illinois and Michigan Canal. Among the speakers that day was Judge Theophilus Smith of the Illinois Supreme Court. Smith predicted that Chicago would have a population of 50,000 in 50 years and 100,000 in 100 years. A group of men threw water in his face. The "boys" declared that if they hadn't stopped him, the Judge would have predicted a population of a million.

1846 The first university in Chicago opened. Chicago's first Bishop, William Quarter, founded the College of St. Mary's by the Lake. The university occupied part of the site where Holy Name Cathedral stands today. In order to teach young ladies, Bishop Quarter brought the Sisters of Mercy to Chicago.

1895 Paul Boyton opened the first modern enclosed amusement park. His Water Chutes park was located at 61st and Drexel. Its success inspired Boyton to establish another park at Coney Island, New York. Boyton was famous for his water suit that filled with air. It allowed him to swim the Rhine, the English Channel and paddle 2,300 miles down the Mississippi. Boyton even swam out with a torpedo to blow up a warship in Peru.

1909 The man who designed the "White City" of the Columbian Exposition, Daniel H. Burnham, unveiled a 164-page plan for the city. It was prepared with the help of Edward H. Bennett. Much of his plan was implemented, including the lakefront parks, commercial boulevards, a "high grade shopping street" along Michigan Avenue, and transportation routes that became today's expressways.

1904 Esther P. Friedman was born in Sioux City Iowa. Her sister Pauline arrived 17 minutes later. Esther Friedman Lederer won a 1955 *Sun-Times* contest to replace Ruth Crowley, author of the "Ask Ann Landers" advice column. Pauline changed her name to Abigail Van Buren and began her "Dear Abby" column in 1956. The sisters began a very public feud and became most widely read columnists of the time.

July 5

1847   Chicago's first big convention opened. More than 3,000 delegates from 18 of the 29 states of the Union attended the Chicago River and Harbor Convention, to discuss the St. Lawrence River. For the first time, many influential businessmen and bankers from the east saw the investment potential in the city. Abraham Lincoln represented Sangamon County at the convention.

1865   The last Confederate prisoners left Camp Douglas. As many as 6,000 died under horrific conditions there in three years, including over 1,000 in the winter of 1864. Originally buried in mass graves in what is now Lincoln Park, the bodies were moved to Oakwoods Cemetery. A monument stands there today.

1894   In the midst of the Pullman strike, an arsonist started a fire that wiped out what was left of the White City. The blaze destroyed the greatest buildings of the Columbian Exposition, the Court of Honor, Machinery Hall, Electricity Building, Administration Building, Mining Building, and the massive Manufactures and Liberal Arts Building. The Palace of Fine Arts was saved.

July 6

1932   Violet Popovich Valli shot Cubs shortstop Bill Jurges in his room at the Carlos Hotel. Valli was unstable and believed that she was Jurges' girlfriend and had been "jilted" by him. Hit in the hand and side, Jurges missed the rest of the season. But he did not prosecute. Violet became a star in local nightclubs. She was billed as "Violet (What I Did For Love) Valli – The Most Talked About Girl in Chicago."

1933   The first Major League All-Star Game took place at Comiskey Park. *Tribune* sports editor Arch Ward came up with the idea of the exhibition game as part of the Century of Progress Exposition. Gabby Hartnett, Lon Warneke and Woody English represented the Cubs. Jimmie Dykes and Al Simmons represented the White Sox. Babe Ruth hit a two run homer as the AL won 4-2.

1959   Queen Elizabeth II and Prince Phillip arrived. The visit was part of the Chicago International Trade Fair, marking the opening of the St. Lawrence Seaway. The Royal Yacht *Britannia* used the $1 billion 185-mile seaway on the way to Chicago. President Eisenhower welcomed the royals, and two million people lined the streets. At the state banquet, some in the crowd carted off souvenirs, including the royal toilet seat.

1983   The All-Star game returned to Comiskey Park. The American League came into the game having lost eleven All-Star Games in a row. But the junior circuit trounced the National League 13-3. Fred Lynn slugged the first grand slam in All-Star history.

July 7

1890   The *Tribune* reported that British writer Rudyard Kipling had written a scathing report on his visit to Chicago. In his *American Notes*, Kipling wrote, "I have struck a city-a real city-and they call it Chicago.... Having seen it, I urgently desire never to see it again. It is inhabited by savages. Its water is the water of the Hooghly, and its air is dirt."

1894   Mobs supporting striking Pullman workers had burned 7,000 rail cars at the 50th Street Panhandle Yards the night before. A crowd attacked Illinois National Guardsmen at 49th and Loomis and the troops opened fire. Several people were killed. Eugene Debs, leader of the Railroad Workers Union, was arrested.   Federal troops restored order, and the strike died out. At least 13 people had died and the workers gained nothing.

1946   Mother Francis Xavier Cabrini was declared a saint. She was the first U.S. citizen to be so honored by the church. Cardinal Mundelein, who presided over her funeral, also presided over her beatification ceremony in Rome. Mother Cabrini arrived in Chicago in 1899 and founded over 70 schools, orphanages, and hospitals around the world. She died in Chicago on December 22, 1917.

Chicago 365

July 8

1896   William Jennings Bryan made a famous speech at the Democratic National Convention in Chicago. At the time, the big issue was whether the government should pay the holder of paper money in gold, or in both gold and silver. Republicans favored gold only. Bryan said, "You shall not press down upon the brow of labor this crown of thorns; you shall not crucify mankind upon a cross of gold!" He won the nomination.

1892   Deanie O'Banion was born in Aurora. The former choirboy at Holy Name Cathedral became a psychopathic thug, ruler of the North Side. O'Banion pushed mob boss Johnny Torrio too far by hijacking his beer trucks and selling him a brewery that was about to be raided. Torrio gunmen killed O'Banion in his flower shop on November 9, 1924 and the Northsiders launched an all-out war on the Italians.

1932   Roy Brown was born. Brown was an artist and puppeteer who drew the artwork on WGN's *Ray Rayner Show* and was the puppeteer for Cuddly Dudley on the show. He also handed the puppets on *Garfield Goose and Friends*. But Brown is probably best remembered as "Cooky the Cook" on *Bozo's Circus*. He played Cooky from 1968 until 1994. Brown died in January 2001.

2003   Cubs manager Dusty Baker was asked to compare day and night games at Wrigley Field. "Personally, I like to play in the heat," Dusty said. "Most Latin people and minority people do. You don't find too many brothers from New Hampshire or Maine, right? We were brought over here because we could work in the heat. Isn't that history?" Baker refused to apologize after the remarks were criticized as racist.

July 9

1893   Doctor Daniel Hale Williams performed the first successful open heart surgery. The pioneer black surgeon operated on a young man who was rushed to Provident Hospital after being stabbed in a barroom brawl. Williams founded Provident in 1891. It was the first interracial hospital in the U.S, and employed doctors of both races. Williams also opened the first nursing school to admit blacks at Provident.

1978 Over 2,500 people jeered as 22 Nazis heard speeches from American Nazi party leaders Frank Collin and Mike Allen at Marquette Park. The rally ended a legal battle that began in 1976, when the city first denied a permit to the Nazis. Chicago agreed to allow the march after federal courts threw out laws passed by the Village of Skokie to prevent a rally in that largely Jewish community.

1987 A man who made it his business to be a historical footnote died. Al Carter was the last person to enter the Century of Progress Exposition and the first to enter Worlds Fairs in Seattle, New York, Montreal and Knoxville. He was first on the Tri-State Tollway, Northwest Tollway, and the Kennedy, Eisenhower, Ryan and Stevens Expressways. Al was there to open the Sears Tower and was the last to ride on a Chicago Street Car.

1998 A war began in the Ravenswood Neighborhood. The Asian longhorned beetle was discovered infesting the beautiful old trees. The state and federal Departments of Agriculture immediately quarantined the area to halt the spread of the bugs, which can't be killed by any known chemicals. They arrived at a neighborhood hardware manufacturing company in crates from China. Over 1,400 trees were cut down.

July 10

1893 Smoke rose from the wooden tower atop the massive Cold Storage Building at the Columbian Exposition, the "greatest refrigerator on Earth." Firefighters climbed 200 feet to the top of the tower, unaware that burning debris had ignited a fire below them and cut off any escape. Twelve firefighters either fell or jumped to their deaths. Three workers also died.

1910 The *New York Evening Mail* published a poem by sportswriter Franklin Pierce Adams entitled "Baseball's Sad Lexicon." It immortalized the Cubs double-play combination. "These are the saddest of possible words: Tinker to Evers to Chance. Trio of bear cubs, and fleeter than birds, Tinker and Evers and Chance. Ruthlessly pricking our gonfalon bubble, making a Giant hit into a double. Words that are heavy with nothing but trouble: Tinker to Evers to Chance."

1966 Dr. Martin Luther King, Jr. addressed a crowd of over 50,000 at Soldier Field as part of his campaign to end discrimination. The crowd called for the ouster of racist school superintendent Benjamin Willis. Following the rally, King led 38,000 people to City Hall, where he posted his demands on Mayor Richard J. Daley's door. It was a symbolic gesture honoring his namesake, Martin Luther.

1982 Pope John Paul II named Archbishop Joseph L. Bernardin of Cincinnati to succeed the late Cardinal John Cody as head of the Archdiocese of Chicago. Bernardin would fight for liberal causes such as arms control and racial equality. He was installed as a Cardinal in February 1983. President Clinton awarded Bernardin the Medal of Freedom in September 1996. Bernardin died of cancer on November 19, 1996.

July 11

1884 The Democratic National Convention, meeting at Exposition Hall, nominated Grover Cleveland for president and Thomas Hicks for vice president. In Chicago, Cleveland is best remembered for sending in federal troops when striking Pullman workers violated an injunction. He said, "If it takes the entire army and navy of the United States to deliver a post card in Chicago, that card will be delivered."

1886 Captain George Wellington Streeter ran his home made steamboat aground off Superior Street. Streeter encouraged contractors to dump fill around the *Reutan*. Soon, there were 186 acres of new land that Streeter declared the independent "District of Lake Michigan." Streeter defended it with a shotgun until his death in 1921. The battle over the land raged until 1940. Today, the Hancock Building, the Chicago Campus of Northwestern University and exclusive homes occupy "Streeterville."

1950 The All-Star game at Comiskey Park ended in dramatic fashion. The National League won it 4-3, when Red Schoendienst of the Cardinals hit a homer in the 14th inning. Ralph Kiner tied the game with a home run in the ninth inning.

1952 The Republican National Convention in Chicago nominated Dwight D. Eisenhower for President and Richard M. Nixon for Vice President. During the convention, Wisconsin Senator Joseph McCarthy blamed the Democrats for losing "nearly 100 million people a year to

Chicago 365

world communism." The 1952 Republican and Democrat conventions in Chicago were the first to be extensively televised.

July 12

1856   More than 150,000 people rely on commuter railroads every day in the Chicago area. It started on this date with a run over the Illinois Central from downtown Chicago to the distant suburb of Hyde Park. The term "commuter" was born shortly thereafter, when railroads began offering discounted, or "commuted" fares to regular riders.

1893   A flotilla of modern vessels met a Viking longship. Officials with the Columbian Exposition wanted to bring Norway's famous Gokstad Viking ship here. But the ship was too fragile to be transported. Magnus Andersen decided to make the journey in a nearly exact replica of the Gokstad ship to prove that the Vikings beat Columbus to the New World by 500 years. He set sail from Bergen, Norway on April 30, 1893.

1951   Thousands rioted after Harvey Clark and his family moved into an apartment building on West 19th Street in Cicero. Police had beat Clark up when the family tried to move in a few months earlier. Governor Stevenson called in the National Guard as police watched crowds burn and loot the 20-flat apartment building. Over 120 people were arrested. A Cicero grand jury blamed the family and an attorney for the NAACP for the riot.

1979   WLUP Radio personality Steve Dahl organized a rally against what he called "Disco Dystrophy." Fans who brought a disco record to the doubleheader between the White Sox and Tigers at Comiskey Park got in for 98 cents and Dahl planned to blow up the records between games. More than 59,000 showed up and 15,000 were turned away. The rockers went crazy when Dahl lit the fuse, tearing up the field. The Sox forfeited the second game and 37 people were arrested.

1995   Navy Pier reopened as a recreation center after a dramatic $150 million reconstruction. A 148-foot high Ferris Wheel, modeled after the wheel at the Columbian Exposition of 1893, was the most dramatic addition. The pier is home to the Childen's Museum, the Crystal Gardens and a computerized fountain with 240 jets. Today, Navy Pier attracts about eight million visitors each year.

July 13

1912 William Lorimer of Chicago became the first U.S. Senator to be thrown out of office for "corrupt methods and practices." In 1910, the *Tribune* exposed the story of a former state legislator who took a bribe in 1908 to vote for Lorimer. At the time, state legislatures elected Senators. The Lorimer case resulted in measures providing for direct elections.

1925 Opening arguments began in the "Monkey Trial" in Dayton Tennessee. WGN spent $1,000 daily for phone lines to present the first broadcast from a trial. Chicago attorney Clarence Darrow defended John Scopes, charged with violating a law forbidding the teaching of evolution. Darrow faced attorney William Jennings Bryan. Scopes was fined $100, but Darrow's cross-examination made Bryan seem narrow minded.

1942 Harrison Ford was born in Chicago. Ford flunked out of college and was working as a carpenter when he auditioned for *American Graffiti* in 1973. It was his first work with director George Lucas. Ford was still pounding nails when Lucas offered him the role of Han Solo in *Star Wars*. In 1981, he starred in the Lucas/Spielberg film, *The Raiders of the Lost Ark* and became one of the most bankable stars in Hollywood.

1995 The high hit 106 at Midway Airport, the highest ever recorded. The heat had held Chicago in its grip for five days. Refrigerated trailers were set up to handle the stream of bodies. Many victims were elderly, afraid to open their windows. More than 600 people would die of heat-related causes, more deaths than in the Great Fire.

July 14

1874 The "Little Big Fire" showed that Chicago was just as vulnerable to the "fire fiend" as it was prior to the Great Fire of 1871. The second Great Chicago Fire swept 18 blocks on the Near South Side. Over 800 structures were destroyed. At least 20 people were killed and 6,000 were left homeless. Insurance companies threatened to boycott Chicago, pressuring city leaders to enact stricter fire codes.

1927 John William Chancellor was born in Chicago. He rose from a copy boy position at the *Sun-Times* to become a reporter for WMAQ and one of the first reporters for NBC-TV. Chancellor hosted the "Today" Show in 1961-62 and then returned to reporting. He is best remembered for "reporting from somewhere in custody" during the 1964 GOP Convention and for anchoring "NBC Nightly News" from 1970-82.

1966   Eight student nurses from South Chicago Community Hospital died horribly in a townhouse at 2319 East 100th Street. Richard Speck took at least ½ hour to torture and kill each one. One nurse hid under a bed and survived to give police a description. A few days later, Speck tried to slit his wrists on Skid Row and was rushed to Cook County Hospital. A doctor had heard the description and called police when he saw Speck's tattoo. It read "Born to Raise Hell."

2001   The last original production of "Bozo the Clown" aired on WGN. Smashing Pumpkin's frontman Billy Corrigan sang "Forever Young" on the prime time special "Bozo: 40 Years of Fun." Bozo first came to WGN in September 1961.   The original cast included Bob Bell as Bozo, Don Sandburg as Sandy, Ray Rayner as Oliver O'Oliver, Bob Trendley as Mr. Bob and Ned Locke as ringmaster Ned.

July 15

1900   John Alexander Dowie opened his City of Zion. The founder of the Christian Catholic Church left Chicago when his faith healing claims resulted in the deaths of some followers and his own daughter. Dowie's word was law in Zion. He banned tobacco, drugs, alcohol and pork. In 1901, Dowie was denounced after claiming he was Elijah the Restorer. He was ousted amid charges of polygamy and financial misconduct in 1906.

1903   Ernest Pfennig, a Chicago dentist, bought the very first car sold by the Ford Corporation. He paid $850 for the car, just one month after Henry Ford had incorporated. Ford boasted that its new machine was "so simple that a boy of 15 can run it." Ford would produce about 1,700 automobiles during its first year of operation.

1927   "Hold 'Em" Joe Powers came down after 16 days and two hours atop the flagpole at the Morrison Hotel. Powers set a new flagpole sitting record, but he lost six teeth during a violent windstorm. Joe got new bridgework, and a kiss from movie starlet Mary Philbin.

Chicago 365

2003 U.S. Cellular Field hosted the 2003 All-Star Game. For the first time in Major League history, the winner of the game would gain home-field advantage in the World Series. Hank Blalock hit a homer off Eric Gagne in the 8th to give the American League a 7-6 victory.

July 16

1862 Ida B. Wells was born a slave in Holly Springs, Mississippi. She began a campaign against lynching while part owner of *The Free Speech and Headlight*, a black newspaper in Memphis. Ida moved to Chicago in 1895 and married Ferdinand Lee Barnett, founder of the *Conservator*, the city's first black-owned newspaper. Wells fought for women's rights and founded the Negro Fellowship League to help homeless black men.

1938 Samuel Insull died of a heart attack in a Paris subway. Legend says the former utilities tycoon died penniless, but the story isn't true. His wallet was stolen as he lay dying on the platform. At one time, "The House of Insull" controlled the elevated railway system, electricity and natural gas in Chicago. Insull helped made electricity more affordable and widely available, but the Stock Market Crash ruined him.

1958 Michael Flatley was born in Chicago. His mother was an Irish dance champion. He started dancing at age four and became a boxer, winning the Chicago Golden Gloves amateur competition. Flatley first rose to fame for his dance performances with the Irish folk group the Chieftans, then with Riverdance and his Lord of the Dance troupe. Flatley says he burns 4,000 calories during every performance.

2004 Millenium Park officially opened, nearly four years behind schedule. The Jay Pritzker Music Pavilion, designed by Frank Gehry, is the centerpiece of the 24.5-acre park. The park also includes beautiful gardens and a reflecting pool and fountain flanked by 50-foot tall glass towers that show video images. The effort to renovate the northwest part of Grant Park began with a much more modest plan in 1976.

July 17

1906 The City of Gary, Indiana was incorporated. Judge Elbert H. Gary, Chairman of U.S. Steel, planned the largest plant in the world on 12,000 acres in the dunes along Lake Michigan. A few months after it opened,

10,000 workers were living in the new city named in his honor. The layoffs in the steel industry in the 1970's and 80's were a huge blow, but the Gary will be forever known as "Steel City."

1955 Braniff Airways Flight 560 from Kansas City, a twin-engined Convair CV-340, hit a gas station sign, smashed through a fence and came to rest upside down at Midway Airport. Twenty-two passengers were killed. Investigators said the pilot was flying 60 to 80 feet lower than the normal approach path due to the foggy conditions.

1957 The Village of Elk Grove was incorporated with a population of 116. A land development firm from Texas studied the entire area and picked the formerly quiet rural site for a planned community, due to its proximity to the new O'Hare Airport. Today, over 33,500 people live in Elk Grove.

1984 Maurice Goldblatt died at the age of 92. With his brother Nathan, Goldblatt opened their first store in a wooden structure at 1617 West Chicago Avenue. By the 1930's, there were seven locations, and Goldblatts was known as "America's Fastest Growing Department Stores." The chain grew to 47 stores but declined in the 1980's. The old flagship store is now part of DePaul University's downtown campus.

July 18

1893 America's first 18-hole golf course was opened at Belmont. Charles Blair McDonald designed the Chicago Golf Club course, modeled after the legendary St. Andrews in Scotland. Back in 1892, McDonald convinced 30 members to chip in $10 each to construct a nine-hole course on the site, the first golf course west of the Alleghenies. The course is now known as Downer's Grove.

1897 Cap Anson became the first player in Major League history to record 3,000 hits. Hit number 3,000 was a single in the 4th inning, as the Chicago Colts beat Baltimore 6-3. The Chicago newspapers did not even mention Anson's accomplishment. The total included 56 walks, which counted as a hit during the 1887 season.

1925 The largely Protestant town of Area changed its name to

Mundelein, in honor of Chicago's Cardinal. Mundelein had founded St. Mary of the Lake Seminary, which brought prosperity to the town. In return for the honor, Mundelein bought the town a fire engine.

1940 The Democratic National Convention nominated President Franklin Roosevelt for an unprecedented third term. The *Tribune* reported that the nomination was a foregone conclusion, comparing the convention to a Joe Louis fight, "over before the crowd got settled." For the first time, the media called the shots. The big events at Chicago Stadium were scheduled to take place during peak radio listening times.

1936 The first Oscar Mayer "Wienermobile" was unveiled at the General Body Company Factory in Chicago. Carl Mayer, nephew of Oscar Mayer, came up with the idea of a 13-foot-long hot dog on wheels as a promotional vehicle. The original cost $5,000. Today's Weinermobiles can hit 90 miles per hour and are equipped with state-of-the-art audiovisual equipment.

July 19

1916 Phil Cavaretta was born in Chicago. In 1945, Caveretta won the National League MVP honors, hitting .355 and helping lead the Cubs to the pennant. He hit .423 in the World Series, but the Detroit Tigers won it in seven games. It was the last time the Cubs made it to the series. The fan favorite served as player manager of the Cubs from 1951-1953, and then finished his career with the White Sox.

1933 Judge Joseph B. Davis dismissed the case against the sensation of the Century of Progress Exposition. Sally Rand appeared to be wearing nothing but a few feathers during her famous fan dance. (She probably wore a body stocking) Davis said "There is no harm and certainly no injury to public morals when the human body is exposed. Some people probably would want to put pants on a horse."

1944 The Democratic National Convention opened at Chicago Stadium. Many delegates favored vice president Henry Wallace for president and advisor James Byrnes for the vice presidential nomination. But the nomination went to a little known Senator from Missouri named

Chicago 365

Harry S Truman. The Mayor of Minneapolis urged the party to move into "the bright sun of civil rights." His name was Hubert Humphrey.

July 20

1823   Doctor Alexander Wolcott married Ellen Marion Kinzie. It was the first wedding in Chicago. Ellen was the daughter of John Kinzie, and was considered to be the first white child born in Chicago.

1948   An exposition honoring a century of railroading opened at the site of 1933 World's Fair. More than 2.5 million people attended the Chicago Railroad Fair during its 76-day run. The fair featured hundreds of pieces of railroad equipment and was complete with its own narrow gauge railroad. Walt Disney attended the fair. On his way home, he wrote down a plan for his own "magical little park."

1969   Chicago came to a halt on a hot Sunday night as Neil Armstrong became the first man to walk on the moon. His words, "One small step for man, one giant leap for mankind," were relayed to earth over a radio transponder built by Chicago-based Motorola.   Later that summer, Chicago would welcome the astronauts with a huge ticket-tape parade.

2003   The replacement for Ann Landers made her debut in the *Tribune*. Over a year after the death of Eppie Lederer, The *Tribune* hired Amy Dickenson, a former *Time* Magazine columnist and a distant relative of poet Emily Dickinson. The paper dropped the column written by Lederer's daughter, Margo Howard.

July 21

1899   Ernest Hemingway was born in what is now Oak Park. He wrote for the high school newspaper, and became a reporter for the Kansas City *Star*. Bad eyesight kept him out of the army, so he volunteered as a Red Cross ambulance driver and was badly wounded in July 1918. His experiences inspired *A Farewell To Arms*. His other works include *The Sun Also Rises*, and *The Old Man and the Sea*.   Suffering from depression, Hemingway shot himself on July 2, 1961.

1919   The Goodyear dirigible *Wingfoot*, caught fire and crashed through a skylight into the Illinois Trust and Savings Building at 231 South LaSalle

Street. Flaming hydrogen, gasoline, glass and steel rained down on employees. Twelve people died but the bank was open for business the next day. The pilot and mechanic survived by parachuting to the rooftops below. Burning engine oil ignited the hydrogen that filled the blimp.

1924 The trial of Nathan Leopold and Richard Loeb began. Defense attorney Clarence Darrow entered a plea of guilty in the "thrill killing" of Bobby Franks. On August 22, Darrow made an eloquent two-hour plea for the judge to spare the boys' lives. The judge sentenced them to life in prison. Another homosexual inmate murdered Loeb in Joliet on January 28, 1936. Loepold was released on March 13, 1960 and died in 1971.

1952 Robin Williams was born in Chicago. The former mime made his debut as the alien Mork on "Happy Days" on February 28, 1978. Mork starred in his own series from 1978 to 1982. Williams made his film debut in the dud *Popeye* in 1980. His films include *The World According to Garp, Dead Poets Society,* and *Mrs. Doubtfire.* Williams fought drug addiction and said, "Cocaine is God's way of saying you're making too much money."

July 22

1911 The home town of the Jake and Elwood Blues was incorporated. You might recall the movie characters were raised at the "St. Helen of the Blessed Shroud Orphanage" in Calumet City. At the time of incorporation, the village was known as West Hammond. The name was changed in 1924. It comes from the Indian name for the Little Calumet River, "Kalamick."

1934 Anna Sage, who ran a brothel where John Dillinger lived with his girlfriend, alerted FBI agent Melvin Purvis that they would see *Manhattan Melodrama* at the Biograph Theater, 2433 Lincoln Avenue. Sage hoped to escape deportation by wearing an orange skirt so the feds could identify Dillinger. The skirt looked red in the lights, so Sage went down in history as "The Lady in Red." Twenty agents moved in when Dillinger emerged at 10:35 p.m. Dillinger was gunned down as he fled towards the alley.

1967 Carl Sandburg died at his home in North Carolina. Sandburg is best remembered for his poems about Chicago. But later in life, he wrote an acclaimed five-volume biography of Abraham Lincoln. It won him the Pulitzer Prize in 1940. He moved to Flat Rock, North Carolina in 1945 and won a second Pulitzer in 1951 for *Complete Poems*. His ashes were placed beneath Remembrance Rock in his hometown of Galesburg.

1986   The Cubs fired ball girl Marla Collins for appearing in *Playboy*. The photos would appear in the October issue, and showed Collins in her Cubs uniform. Another shot featured a grinning Harry Caray pointing out a tattoo on her thigh.

July 23

1925   Union Station at Canal Street and Jackson Boulevard opened. It replaced the Grand Passenger Station, built in 1881. The concourse was demolished in 1969 to make room for an office building, but the Great Hall survives. The station was renovated in 1992, and more than 50,000 commuters pass through every day. Union Station served as a location during filming of the 1987 film *The Untouchables*.

1934   Cook County Coroner Frank J. Walsh put the body of "Public Enemy Number One" on display at the morgue. People lined up on the other side of a glass panel to be photographed next to the body of John Dillinger. Entrepreneurs near the Biograph sold bits of paper dipped in the gangster's blood for 25 cents and a haberdasher sold out of ties identical to the one Dillinger was wearing when he was shot.

1984   A massive explosion rocked the Union Oil Company facility in Romeoville. The blast was felt 30 miles away. Seventeen people were killed, including ten refinery firefighters. The disaster caused more than $100 million in damage. Investigators found that a crack in a tower had allowed flammable vapors to escape.

July 24

1858   In Chicago, Stephen A. Douglas received a note from his rival for a U.S. Senate seat. A tall rail-splitting lawyer from Springfield proposed a series of debates. Douglas agreed to seven debates, and would argue that the states had a right to self-determination on the slavery issue. Douglas would win the Senate seat. But the man who argued that slavery was a moral wrong would return. His name was Abraham Lincoln.

Chicago 365

1877   The Great Railroad Strike spread to Chicago. Union leaders called for the use of non-violent methods to obtain an immediate 20% wage increase. Several hundred people marched to the railroad yards and shut them down. The mayor would issue a call for 5,000 volunteers and call in federal troops to clear the streets.

1915   Excited employees of Western Electric began boarding a steamer moored on the Chicago River near the Clark Street Bridge. Few among the 2,573 passengers on the planned excursion to Michigan City seemed concerned when the ship listed as they were boarding. But at 7:28 a.m., the *Eastland* slowly rolled over in 20 feet of water. A total of 844 people drowned or were trampled to death in the lower decks. The disaster wiped out 22 entire families.

The Second Regiment Armory on Washington Boulevard was turned into a temporary morgue. The building is now part of Oprah Winfrey's Harpo studios. George Halas arrived too late to board the Eastland. He would go on to found the Chicago Bears.

Historian George W. Hilton wrote in a 1995 book that additional lifeboats added in the hysteria over the sinking of the Titanic probably caused the disaster. They made the ship top-heavy. The owners of the ship were held blameless and most of the lawsuits over the disaster were thrown out. The Eastland was converted into the gunboat *Willmette* for the U.S. government. It was sold for scrap in 1946.

1934   The temperature hit 105 degrees at the University of Chicago. That's the highest official reading recorded in Chicago. It was 109 at Midway, which is the highest temperature ever recorded at any Chicago location. But Midway was not the official weather observatory for Chicago at the time.

July 25

1877   Violence swept the McCormick plant, and spread through the city. Thousands of police, militia and volunteers battled mobs at the Randolph Street Bridge, and at a viaduct near Archer and Halstead. Congressman Carter Harrison said "idlers, thieves and ruffians," not the workers, caused the violence. About 35 people died and 300 were arrested before troops restored order the next day.

Chicago 365

1952 At the International Amphitheater, the Democratic National Convention nominated Governor Adlai Stevenson of Illinois for President. Stevenson had asked that his name not be placed in nomination. But Chicago boss Jake Arvey led the movement to draft Stevenson as the nominee. In his acceptance speech, Stevenson said he wished the nomination had gone to "a better, stronger man."

1954 Walter Payton was born in Columbia, Mississippi. "Sweetness" would play for the Bears from 1975 until 1987, setting records for single game rushing and career rushing. He racked up ten seasons with more than 1,000 yards rushing. In February 1999, Payton announced he was suffering from a rare liver condition, primary sclerosing cholangitis. He died while waiting for a transplant on November 1, 1999.

1948 Steve Goodman was born in Chicago. Goodman wrote the "Best Country and Western Song Ever Recorded," David Allan Coe's "You Never Even Call Me By My Name," and the classic "City of New Orleans." Goodman also wrote "A Dying Cub Fans Last Request," "Daley's Gone," and the song that became the anthem of the 1984 Cubs, "Go Cubs Go." Goodman died of leukemia on September 20, 1984.

July 26

1906 William Rainey Harper died in Chicago. Harper was the first president of the University of Chicago. He paid high wages to insure the school had the finest faculty in the world. He was also one of the first to allow men and women in the same classroom and he brought Alonzo Stagg to begin a football program.

1922 Jason Robards Junior was born in Chicago. The son of an actor who appeared in 170 films, Jason Junior made his debut in *The Journey* in 1959. Robards made over 50 movies, and would win back-to-back Oscars for his roles in *All the President's Men* and *Julia*. But he always said the theater was his first love. Robards won a Tony award for his 1959 role in *The Disenchanted*. He died of cancer on December 26, 2000.

1956 Dorothy Hamill was born in Chicago. The family moved to Connecticut, where she began skating at age eight. Hamill was the U.S. figure skating champion from 1974 to 1976, but was not expected to medal in the Olympics at Innsbruck. She won the gold and the hearts of the nation. Her short, bobbed "wedge" haircut was also a hit. Hamill went on to save the Ice Capades when she became the owner.

July 27

1919 John Harris and his friends went swimming near the black beach at 25th Street. They didn't know that blacks had tried to swim at the whites-only beach at 29th Street, and a melee was underway. A rock hit the 14-year-old in the head as his raft drifted into the area. His death sparked the most violent race riot in city history. By the time 6,200 troops restored order five days later, 38 people were dead, over 500 were injured and hundreds were left homeless.

1960 Vice President Nixon was nominated for president at the Republican National Convention at the International Amphitheater. Nixon would narrowly lose the election to John F. Kennedy, in part because of a flurry of questionable last minute votes from Chicago. The GOP was so bitter about the shenanigans of the Democratic machine that the Republican Convention hasn't returned to the city since.

1970 Sly and the Family Stone were three hours late for a free concert in Grant Park and the 50,000 fans went crazy. Police moved in when the crowd pelted the warm up acts with bottles and chased them from the stage. Chanting "off the pig," the crowd burned squad cars and smashed windows in The Loop. During the five-hour melee, 28 policeman and 33 concertgoers were injured and 148 people were arrested.

1970 Sears announced the company would build the world's tallest building on South Wacker between Adams Street and Jackson Boulevard. Plans called for the Sears Tower to stand 110 stories and 1,450 feet tall. Work on the $100 million project was slated to start the following week and set to be completed in 1974.

1989 The movie *Running Scared*, starring Billy Crystal and Gregory Hines was released. The film features one of the more unusual chase scenes in Chicago cinematic history. The detectives played by Hines and Crystal drive their car in pursuit of another vehicle onto the El tracks from O'Hare to the Loop. The big shootout at the end takes place at the James R. Thompson Center.

Chicago 365

July 28

1914   Mayor Carter Harrison Junior declared war on First Ward aldermen "Hinky Dink" Kenna and "Bathhouse John" Coughlin, the "Lords of the Levee." Harrison pledged he would withdraw patronage from the two aldermen and do all in his power to stamp out segregated commercial vice. Harrison was reacting to a deadly riot that followed a raid on a house of ill repute in the notorious Levee District.

1926   Al Capone surrendered and was brought to the Cook County Jail. He was released the next day after a grand jury refused to indict him for the April 27 murder of Assistant State's Attorney Anthony McSwiggin. McSwiggin's father, a 37-year veteran of the Chicago Police Department, angrily said, "They pinned a medal on him and turned him loose." No one was ever convicted of killing McSwiggin.

1927   The excursion boat *Favorite* sank in a gale off the shore of North Avenue. Famous swimmer Johnny Weismuller and his brother Pete, who was captain of the Oak Street Beach lifeguards, dove repeatedly into Lake Michigan and saved at least eleven lives. But eleven adults and 16 children drowned. Weismuller would go on to greater fame in Hollywood, playing Tarzan.

1998   The body of 11-year-old Ryan Harris was found behind a run down building in the 6600 block of Parnell. She had been sexually assaulted and hit in the head with a brick. Police charged two boys, aged seven and eight, and claimed they had confessed. Charges against the boys were dropped on September 4. Floyd Durr was convicted of the murder in 1999.

July 29

1909   The Chicago Board of Education named Ella Flagg Young as the new superintendent. She was the first woman to head a school district in a major city. Young was a leader in the suffragist movement and became the first female president of the National Education Association in 1910. As superintendent, she faced bitter battles with the male members of the board and retired in 1915.

Chicago 365

1919 The race riot spread to The Loop, where white soldiers and sailors murdered blacks and looted businesses. Mobs continued to burn the homes of blacks that lived in white areas. The following day, Mayor Thompson relented and allowed the governor to send in the militia. Twenty-three blacks and 15 whites were dead. At least 342 blacks and 178 whites were injured. Hundreds of homes were in ruins.

1959 FBI agents planted a microphone nicknamed "Little Al" in a mob hangout at a tailor shop on Michigan Avenue. Al and other bugs provided information on Tony Accardo, Sam Giancana, Murray Humpreys, and others. They also uncovered crooked cops, judges and politicians. President Johnson ordered the bugs removed when he found out the feds were listening in on his political pals, the "Texas Mafia."

1989 The White Sox traded Harold Baines, the team's all-time home run leader, to Texas along with Fred Manrique. The Sox picked up Scott Fletcher, Wilson Alvarez and an outfielder by the name of Sammy Sosa. President George Bush, owner of the Rangers at the time, once said the trade was the biggest mistake he ever made as an adult.

July 30

1880 Robert Rutherford McCormick was born in Chicago. His grandfather was the publisher of the *Tribune*, Joseph Medill. McCormick took over the paper in 1911 and engaged in a fierce war with William Randolph Hearst's *Examiner*. It was McCormick's dream to build a convention center on the lakefront.

1925 The robbers told police, "We'd never done such a foolish thing if we had been sober." Five gunmen burst into the lobby of the Drake Hotel and the house detective opened fire. One robber died at the hotel and police shot and killed another. Two more were captured and later hanged. An innocent bystander was also killed. William J. Mullneschuck managed to get away with about $10,000. He was never seen again.

1936 George "Buddy" Guy was born in Lettsworth, Louisiana. He came to Chicago in 1957, and his career took off after Willie Dixon brought him to Chess Records. Guy played guitar on classics by Howlin' Wolf and Muddy Waters, and made many great solo recordings. Guy

Chicago 365

combined the Blues with contemporary soul and won the approval of the rock audiences, even touring with the Rolling Stones in 1970.

1971 At the stroke of midnight, the Union Stockyards closed forever. For decades, a square mile west of Halsted between 39th and 47th street had been filled with bellowing cows, hogs and sheep. The largest stockyards in the world were considered a must-see tourist attraction for over 100 years. The site is an industrial park today, and only the limestone gate at Exchange Avenue and Peoria Street remains

July 31

1912 Irv Kupcinet was born in North Lawndale. Kupcinet was hired as a sports writer in 1935 for the *Times*. "Kup's Column" made its debut in 1943, and he reported on the rich and famous until just days before his death in 2003 at the age of 91. "Mister Chicago" was a pioneering TV talk show host. His "Kup's Show" ran from 1958 until 1986. The city renamed the Wabash Avenue Bridge in his honor in 1986.

1938 Jake Powell of the Yankees was suspended, two days after he made racist remarks in a post-game interview on WGN. When White Sox broadcaster Bob Elson asked about Powell's off-season job as a policeman in Dayton, Ohio, Powell said he enjoyed "beating niggers over the head and throwing them in jail." Powell added that he would like to "hit every colored person in Chicago over the head with a club."

1968 The Chicago city council voted to change the names of South Park Way and Avenue to Martin Luther King Jr. Drive. In 1966, King led a series of demonstrations in Chicago against segregation in housing. The protests led to an agreement to strengthen enforcement of fair housing laws.

Chicago 365

AUGUST

August 1

1843   Robert Todd Lincoln was born. After his father, President Abraham Lincoln, was assassinated, Robert moved to Chicago and became a successful lawyer and served as the Town Board Supervisor of South Chicago. He was named Secretary of War by President Garfield and Minister to Great Britain by President Harrison. Lincoln repeatedly turned down attempts to nominate him for vice-president.

1900   L. Frank Baum of Chicago filed a copyright application for his new children's book, which he originally called *The Emerald City*. Baum, a former China salesman and reporter for the *Evening Post*, wanted to create the first American fairy tale. But the publisher didn't like the title. Baum noticed a file cabinet drawer labeled "O to Z," and he changed the name to *The Wonderful Wizard of OZ*.

1942   American Federal of Musicians president, James C. Petrillo of Chicago, ordered members not to play on phonograph records. The ban lasted two years. In 1948, he ordered another strike before finally settling with the record industry.

1973   Tempest Bledsoe was born in Chicago. She is best known for starring as Vanessa, the middle child on "The Cosby Show." After the show ended, Bledsoe hosted her own short-lived daytime talk show. Most recently, she had a recurring role in "The Practice" as a single mother.

August 2

1833   The earliest recorded contract for a type of construction that made the rapid growth of Chicago possible was signed. G.W. Snow originated the "balloon frame" style of construction. He eliminated mortised beams and fittings, replacing them with a skeleton of 2x4s s set close together, using studs and cross-members. It was all held together with nails, instead of joints. Snow's innovation is still used today.

1858   Chicago's first paid fire department was organized. Volunteers had protected the city since 1833. An 1835 ordinance required each resident to "to have one good painted leather fire-bucket, with the initials of the owner's name painted thereon" for every stove or fireplace in the building. Businessmen and insurance companies formed a fire brigade to protect property following a blaze that killed 23 people in October 1857.

1921 A jury acquitted eight White Sox players accused of throwing the 1919 World Series. But Commissioner Judge Kenesaw Mountain Landis said, "no player that undertakes or promises to throw a ballgame, no player that sits in conference with a bunch of crooked players and gamblers where the ways and means of throwing a game are discussed and does not promptly tell his club about it, will ever play professional baseball." He banned the eight players for life.

1989 The feds indicted 46 traders on the Chicago Mercantile Exchange and the Chicago Board of Trade. During "Operation Hedgeclipper" and "Operation Sour Mash," FBI agents posed as traders. The media had a field day, but the expensive two-year investigation of 6,000 brokers and traders resulted in just 22 guilty pleas and 13 convictions. The Board and the Exchange were cleared of all major charges.

August 3

1795 Twelve Indian tribes signed the Treaty of Greenville, which set up a boundary between the Indian lands and areas available to settlers. Among the land ceded by the tribes was "one piece of land, six miles square, at the mouth of the Chicago River, emptying into the southwest end of Lake Michigan, where the fort formerly stood."

1936 Jesse Owens won the 100 meter race at the Berlin Olympics, the first of his four gold medals. Legend says Adolf Hitler refused to congratulate Owens for humiliating the "Master Race." But Hitler snubbed another black US athlete, Cornelius Johnson, on the first day of the games. He was not in attendance when Owens won his medals. Owens moved to Chicago in 1949. He worked in public relations and became a jazz disc jockey.

1993 A badly decomposed body was discovered near McColl, South Carolina. Ten days later, authorities identified the body as that of Michael Jordan's father, James. He was killed on July 23 during a robbery in his car outside a country store in Robeson County, North Carolina. Two local teenagers, Daniel Green and Larry Demery, were charged with the murder.

1997   Nellie Fox was inducted into the National Baseball Hall of Fame. Fox played second base for the White Sox from 1950 to 1963. He won the AL MVP award in 1959, when the Sox won their first pennant since 1919. The White Sox retired his uniform number two in 1976.

August 4

1830   Civil engineer James Thompson filed a survey for the town of Chicago. The first legal description of Chicago's location was "in Section nine, Township 39, Range 14." A commission planning construction of the Illinois and Michigan Canal hired Thompson to plat the town on the ½ square mile site. Plans called for lots to be sold and the proceeds used to help build the canal.

1901   Louis Daniel Armstrong was born in New Orleans, Louisiana. In 1922, Armstrong brought his trumpet to Chicago to play with his mentor, Joe "King" Oliver, at the Lincoln Gardens at 459 East 31st Street. Armstrong formed his own band, the Hot Five, later the Hot Seven. The recordings they made are some of the best loved in jazz history.

1938   Sherwood "Sherb" Noble ran a promotion at his ice cream store on South West Avenue in Kankakee. The store offered "all you can eat for 10 cents" to test a "soft serve" product developed by J.F. McCullough. Over 1,600 servings were sold that day. In 1940, Sherb opened the first store to exclusively sell McCullough's product on North Chicago Street in Joliet. McCullough suggested the name "Dairy Queen."

August 5

1822   "The Father of Hyde Park" was born in White Creek, New York. Paul Cornell was an attorney who invested in 300 acres of land between 51st and 53rd Streets in 1853. He donated 60 acres to the Illinois Central, on the condition that the trains stop at his station. Cornell was instrumental in the establishment of Jackson Park, Washington Park and the Midway Plaisance. Hyde Park was annexed to the City of Chicago in 1899.

Chicago 365

1823   Archibald Clybourn arrived at Fort Dearborn. He was the first meat packer in Chicago. Clybourn won a government contract to supply beef to supply the garrisons of the Northwest and made a fortune during the Blackhawk War. He built a lavish mansion, right next door to the stockyards. In 1835, he became the first constable in Chicago. Clybourn Avenue is named in his honor.

1966   A rock struck Martin Luther King in the head at a march at Marquette Park. He staggered, but continued the march. Over 40 people were hurt as the crowd hurled rocks, bottles and firecrackers at the 700 protestors. King said he had never seen anything in the south to compare with the hatred he saw that day in Chicago.

1983   "Operation Greylord" exposed a corrupt Cook County judicial system. A young assistant state's attorney named Terrence Hake wore a wire while posing as a crooked prosecutor and attorney handing out bribes to fix cases. The three-year probe sent 15 judges, four clerks, 15 police officers and 50 lawyers to jail.

August 6

1916   "Howwww do you do, ladies and gentlemen." TV news anchor Fahey Flynn was born in Escanaba, Michigan. He came to Chicago to work at WBBM radio in 1941. In March 1953, he made his debut on Channel Two, wearing his trademark bow tie. Flynn left Channel 2 in 1968 when management tried to make him wear a regular tie. He went on to lead WLS Channel 7 to the top of the ratings through the 70's.

1949   Luke Appling of the White Sox took the field for his 2,154th game at shortstop, breaking the Major League record set by Rabbit Maranville. Appling would retire after the 1949 season with 2,218 consecutive games played. In his 20-year career with the White Sox, Appling never saw post season play. He was elected to the Hall of Fame in 1964.

1998   Jack Brickhouse died of a brain tumor at the age of 82. Brickhouse was the voice of the Cubs from 1948 to 1981. He also broadcast games for the White Sox from 1940 to 1967, and was the voice of the Bears for 24 years. He also called Chicago Bulls, Zephyrs and Packers basketball

Chicago 365

games. Brickhouse was named to the broadcaster's wing of the Baseball Hall of Fame in 1983.

1993   The motion picture *The Fugitive* was released. Harrison Ford starred as Doctor Richard Kimble, a Chicago man wrongly convicted of killing his wife.   Tommy Lee Jones starred as the federal Marshall determined to bring him to justice. Some of the prominent locations in the movie include the 203 North LaSalle Building, the Chicago Hilton, City Hall, Cook County Hospital and the County Jail.

August 7

1812   Orders arrived from General William Hull in Detroit instructing Captain Nathaniel Heald to evacuate Fort Dearborn, "if practicable." Heald was ordered to distribute surplus supplies to the Indians to help ensure a safe departure. But the whiskey and ammunition was destroyed, turning the Indians against the garrison. Heald knew the Indians planned to attack, but he decided to obey Hull's order.

1826   The first election took place in Chicago.   There was no town government at the time and most local officials were appointed by Peoria County, so residents voted for governor, lieutenant governor and congressman. A total of 35 voters went to the polls.

1947   The high temperature reached 85 degrees, ending a record breaking heat wave. For three days, the high topped 100. August of 1947 is the warmest August on record in Chicago. During the month, record highs were set on 15 days.

2001   Former Bears player and pro wrestler Steve "Mongo" McMichael took the mike to sing "Take Me Out to the Ballgame" during the 7th inning stretch at Wrigley Field. Upset over a call that went against the Cubs in the 6th, McMichael said he would "have some speaks" with the umpire after the game. Ump Angel Hernandez threw McMichael out of the game. Mongo said he didn't know he had been tossed until he saw it on TV.

August 8

1907   The man who coined the phrase "There's a sucker born every minute" died.   Michael Cassius McDonald was the first crime boss of

164

Chicago 365

Chicago. From his casino at 176 Clark, known as "The Store," McDonald bought off the police and was a close friend with Mayor Carter Harrison I. His health was ruined when his second wife, Dora, had an affair with a teenager and then murdered the boy in February 1907.

1940 Eleanor "The Blond Tigress" Jarman escaped from the women's reformatory in Dwight. Jarman clawed a storeowner during a robbery attempt and her boyfriend shot him dead. The newspapers put her photo on the body of a tiger and called her "The Most Dangerous Woman in America. " She got 199 years in prison and her boyfriend got the chair. Jarman was never recaptured.

1988 "Let there be lights!" With those words, 91-year-old fan Harry Grossman pressed a button, and night baseball came to Wrigley Field. Wrigleyville residents fought a six-year battle against the lights. The rains came in the fourth inning of the game against Philadelphia that night, so the first complete night game at Wrigley took place the next evening against the Mets.

August 9

1910 Alva J. Fisher of Chicago patented the first electric powered washing machine. The Hurley Machine Company produced "The Thor," which used a wooden drum that tumbled the clothes clean in a galvanized tub. The invention took awhile to catch on, because the first machines were very expensive.

1922 An obscure trumpet player arrived in Chicago aboard an Illinois Central train from New Orleans. Louis Armstrong came here to play with King Oliver's Creole Jazz Band. He moved to New York briefly, but returned to Chicago in 1925, playing at South Side Clubs, including the Sunset Cabaret. Armstrong revolutionized jazz and made it America's original art form music, introducing the extended solo and scat singing

1968 Actress Gillian Anderson was born in Chicago. She was raised in London, but returned here and attended DePaul University. She moved to New York, then to Los Angeles where she earned the part of Dana Scully in the television show, "The X Files." Anderson and co-star David Duchovny tried to prove "The truth is out there" until the last episode aired in 2002.

August 10

1833   The town of Chicago elected its first Board of Trustees. The board passed ordinances banning guns and controlling gambling. The trustees also passed the first Sunday closing law and established the first jail, a log cabin at Madison and Michigan Avenues. In 1835, they appointed the first constable.

1907   Essanay Studios was formed, and Chicago became a movie making center long before Hollywood. The studio at 1333 West Argyle boasted the world's top movie star, Charlie Chaplin. Other Essanay stars included Gloria Swanson and the first movie cowboy hero, studio co-founder Gilbert "Bronco Billy" Anderson. Chaplin left after one of the owners tried to blackmail him, and Essanay folded in 1917.

1915   A grand jury indicted six people for manslaughter and criminal negligence in the Eastland disaster. The indictments named William Hull, manager of the Chicago-St. Joseph Steamship Company; Captain Harry Pederson; Engineer J.M. Erickson; federal inspector Robert Reed; Federal inspector J.C. Eckliff and W.K. Greenbaum, manager of   Indiana Transportation. None of the men were ever prosecuted.

2001   Lou Boudreau died at the age of 94. The 1948 American League MVP moved to the Chicago Cubs broadcast booth in 1958. He would remain behind the mike until 1987, with the exception of the 1960 season, when he switched jobs with Cubs manager Charlie Grimm. The native of Harvey, Illinois was known for ringing a cowbell to celebrate Cub home runs or a big play and for calling players "Good Kid."

August 11

1900   A caravan of 15 autos took part in the first "run" held by the Chicago Auto Club. They traveled from the Auditorium Hotel to the Bismark Garden in Lakeview, then to the Edelweiss Garden on 51st Street. All 15 cars made the entire trip.

1961   Police found the body of mobster William "Action" Jackson stuffed in the trunk of a car in The Loop. It was one of the most horrific mob hits ever. Henchmen for Fifi Buccieri, "Lord High Executioner" for The Outfit, brutally tortured Jackson believing he was about to talk to the feds.

They hung him on a meat hook, beat him and used a cattle prod on his genitals for two days. No one ever went to jail for the crime.

1966   John Lennon held a press conference in Chicago to address the controversy over his remarks that the Beatles were more popular than Jesus. Lennon said he was not anti-religion, " I wasn't knocking it or putting it down. I was just saying it as a fact and it's true more for England than here. I'm not saying that we're better or greater, or comparing us with Jesus Christ as a person or God as a thing or whatever it is."

1991   Left-hander Wilson Alvarez tossed a no-hitter in his very first start for the White Sox and second as a Major Leaguer. The Sox beat the Baltimore Orioles, 7-0, at Memorial Stadium. Alvarez became the first rookie to throw a no-hitter since 1983.

August 12

1833   The Town of Chicago was incorporated. The new town had a population of 350, and was bounded by Kinzie, DesPlaines, Madison and State Streets, an area of about three-eighths of a square mile. The name "Chicago" came from the Indian name for the River, "Checagou." The word reportedly meant wild onion or garlic.

1862   Julius Rosenwald was born in Springfield, Illinois.   Rosenwald became president of Sears, Roebuck and Company in 1908 and oversaw the company's phenomenal growth. In 1925, Rosenwald opened the first Sears retail outlet. Rosenwald is best remembered for his philanthropy. He founded the Museum of Science and Industry.

1911   Massive crowds came to Grant Park as the greatest aviation meet ever held in the United States opened. For eight days, huge crowds watched as 34 aviators competed for $80,000 in prizes. During the meet, the flyers took part in a prophetic demonstration. They dropped sacks of flower on the outline of a ship during the "bomb throwing" competition.

1966   The Beatles made their third and final appearance in Chicago, playing two shows at the International Amphitheater. Tickets ranged in price from $3.75 to $5.75. Chicago was the first stop on the Fab Four's final concert tour. The Beatles didn't perform any songs from their latest album, *Revolver*, because the increasingly sophisticated sound was impossible to reproduce on stage.

August 13

1927   After a two hour flight from Grand Rapids, Michigan, Charles A. Lindbergh and the *Spirit of St. Louis* circled the downtown area three times, then touched down at Municipal Field. Lindy rode in a motorcade to Comiskey Park and to a huge reception staged by Colonel McCormick at Soldier Field. He told the crowd that Chicago should construct a lakefront airport to put the city out in front of its rivals.

1935   The first roller derby began at the Coliseum. Promoter Leo Seltzer recruited 25 teams of one male and one female to skate 3,000 miles around the track. In 1937, Sportswriter Damon Runyan came up with the idea of allowing skaters to push and shove while trying to pass players on the other team and the sport exploded.

1969   An estimated two million people cheered as a ticker tape parade welcomed the Apollo 11 astronauts to Chicago. The crowd jammed the seven-mile parade route and about 100,000 crammed the Civic Center area for the official welcome ceremony. Neil Armstrong, Edwin Aldrin and Michael Collins also stopped at the Grant Park band shell and spoke to 15,000 people, including 4,500 area school children.

1987   Nearly 6.5 inches of rain fell at O'Hare Airport, a record for a single day. The airport recorded a total of 9.35 inches in 18 hours. All of the roads leading to the airport were flooded, and thousands left by walking down the Kennedy Expressway. Areas of the northern and western suburbs became shallow lakes, and damage was put at over $220 million. Chicago recorded a record 15.73 inches of rain that August.

August 14

1939   The White Sox played their first game under the lights at Comiskey Field, beating the Browns 5-2. The White Sox were losing money, and management hoped the lights would boost attendance. Two weeks later, the Sox drew over 50,000 for a night game against the Yankees.

Chicago 365

1945 At 6 p.m., the official word of the Japanese surrender arrived. Within minutes, the bars closed and The Loop was jammed with joyous service personnel dancing in the streets. The *Tribune* reported that a line of 30 sailors "grabbed pretty girls as they passed, kissed them and passed them from one to another" at State and Madison. Churches were also filled, to honor the 22,283 from Illinois who made the ultimate sacrifice.

1958 Hanover Park was incorporated. In 1874, Edwin and Luther Bartlett each donated land for railroad depots. There were two Bartlett Depots, each with a post office. One was renamed Ontario to clear things up and the surrounding area became known as Ontarioville. The community of about 400 people incorporated to avoid annexation by other towns, and the name was changed.

August 15

1812 Captain William Wells led the led the evacuation of Fort Dearborn. Hundreds of Indians lay in ambush near present-day 18th Street and Calumet Avenue. Within minutes, 52 people were dead. Two women were killed and a single brave tomahawked 12 children. Wells killed eight Indians. The Indians cut out and ate Wells' heart, hoping to acquire his courage. The Indians burned the fort and left the bodies to rot.

1859 Charlie Comiskey was born in Chicago. The "Old Roman" was the first to play off the bag at first base. But he is best remembered as an owner and executive. He owned the White Sox from their birth until he died in 1931. In 1910, he built Comiskey Park. But his greed led the White Sox players to throw the 1919 World Series. Comiskey was named to the Baseball Hall of Fame in 1939.

1904 Ravinia Park opened. The amusement park was designed to attract riders to the Chicago and Milwaukee Railroad. Classical music became the main attraction in 1906. Ravinia Park became known as the "Summer Opera Capital of the World" before closing during the Depression. It re-opened in 1936, and has been the summer home of the Chicago Symphony Orchestra ever since.

1930 An orphaned baby gorilla named Bushman arrived at the Lincoln Park Zoo. The "Most Valuable Zoo Animal in the World" was known for hurling food and his waste at the crowds. Bushman grew into the largest gorilla in captivity and made the zoo an internationally known center for gorilla breeding. He died on New Years Day 1951. Bushman was stuffed and still intimidates visitors today at the Field Museum.

1967   With the words "what is strange to us today will be familiar tomorrow," Mayor Richard J. Daley unveiled Pablo Picasso's gift to Chicago. The 50-foot tall sculpture in the plaza at the new Civic Center was greeted with scorn. A member of the mayor's staff wanted it torn down. A city councilman recommended that the untitled work be removed for a statue of Ernie Banks. Today, the Picasso is a beloved symbol of the city.

August 16

1862   Amos Alonzo Stagg was born in West Orange New Jersey. During his 41 years as football coach at the University of Chicago, Stagg invented the huddle, the lateral and the tackling dummy. He also invented five-man basketball and played in the first intercollegiate basketball game in 1896. Stagg coached football for 70 years, until age 98. He lived to be 102.

1926   Julius Rosenwald, owner of Sears and Roebuck, donated $3 million to establish an industrial museum in Jackson Park's Fine Arts Building. The museum was to be modeled after the Deutsches Museum in Munich, which included interactive exhibits and a working coal mine. The museum was originally named for Rosenwald, but he objected. The name was changed to the Museum of Science and Industry in 1928.

1974   "The Night Chicago Died" by Paper Lace hit Number One on the *Billboard* chart. Mitch Murray and Peter Callander of the group from Nottingham, England wrote the song about a fictitious battle between Al Capone and the police. They also referred to the nonexistent "East Side of Chicago." When the band's manager wrote Mayor Daley to ask for a civic reception, the mayor replied, "Are you nuts?"

1989   The motion picture *Uncle Buck* was released. John Candy starred as an obnoxious guy who is forced to baby sit hit three nieces and nephews in the Chicago suburbs. McCauley Culkin also starred. The home used in the picture is at 2604 Lincoln in Evanston. New Trier West High School in Northfield and the Windy City Bowling Alley in Cicero also served as locations.

August 17

1803 Captain John Whistler, his family, Lieutenant James Strode Swearingen, and 67 men arrived at the site where the Chicago River empties into Lake Michigan. Hundreds of Indians watched as they unloaded supplies to begin the construction of Fort Dearborn. The fort was finished in late 1804, but was destroyed in an Indian massacre during the War of 1812. Rebuilt in 1816, the fort stood until 1856.

1957 A search was underway for 15-year-old Judith Mae Anderson. She had not returned home after visiting a friend's house the previous night. On August 22 and 24, her body parts were found inside oil drums floating in Montrose Harbor. Police launched the biggest murder investigation in city history. Over 1,000 officers were involved and thousands of people were interviewed, but the case was never solved.

1966 Martin Luther King Junior and leaders of the Chicago Freedom Movement met with Mayor Daley, prominent citizens and members of the clergy at the Palmer House. King and his supporters were marching to demand enforcement of the 1963 Fair Housing Act by the Real Estate Board. The summit led to the formation of the Leadership Council for Metropolitan Open Communities.

2003 Ozzy Osbourne butchered "Take Me Out to the Ballgame" during the 7th inning stretch at Wrigley Field. The *Tribune* published a translation. "Let's go out to the ballgame. Let's go out to the bluhhhhhn. Take me a ee-yan eeya (humming) the field. I don't care if I ahh-uhn ack. Da da da duh da da da eam. Duh ee, da da da da dahhh. For a fee, two, three strikes you're out at the old ballgame."

August 18

1834 Marshall Field was born in Massachusetts. He came to Chicago in 1856 to work as a wholesale clerk and became a partner in the firm. Field and financial wizard Levi Leiter purchased Potter Palmer's dry goods store in 1865. In 1868, they moved to State Street. Field bought out Lieter in 1888. He donated money for the Field Columbian Museum and the Athletic Field at the University of Chicago, originally known as Marshall Field.

1955 The biggest manhunt in Chicago since the Dillinger days came to an end. Richard Carpenter was wanted for 150 robberies over two years. He killed officer William Murphy on August 15th. Carpenter shot and wounded another officer who spotted him in a theater, then invaded a nearby apartment building and terrorized a family for almost 24 hours. Over 250 cops opened fire on the building and Carpenter surrendered.

1994 The United Center opened, replacing historic Chicago Stadium. In addition to the Blackhawks and Bulls games, the United Center has hosted the 1996 Democratic National Convention, The Rolling Stones, Eric Clapton, Bruce Springsteen, Paul McCartney, U2 and many others.

August 19

1868 Frederick Law Olmstead arrived to inspect a 1,600 acre site on the Burlington and Quincy Railroad and along the Des Plaines River. The famous architect who designed New York's Central Park laid out Riverside, one of the first planned communities in the nation. The entire village was designated a National Historic Landmark in 1970.

1889 Influential architect Louis Sullivan loaned $5,000 to his young assistant to help him build a home in Oak Park. Frank Lloyd Wright would eventually be fired for designing homes on the side. But his designs with cantilevered roofs, natural surfaces, abundant natural interior light and horizontal lines became famous. Oak Park today boasts 27 homes designed by Wright.

1904 The Iroquois Theater re-opened as the Colonial Theater vaudeville house, less than eight months after the fire that killed at least 600 people. Members of the Iroquois Memorial Association protested, calling the move an affront to the dead. The Colonial remained in business until 1925. The Oriental Theater stands on the site today.

Chicago 365

1999 McDonald's opened its 25,000th restaurant in the world, located in Chicago's Bronzeville community at 35th Street and Indiana Avenue. The first franchised McDonald's restaurant was opened in 1955 by McDonald's founder Ray Kroc in Des Plaines, Illinois, about 20 miles from the site of the 25,000th restaurant.

August 20

1856 Michael "Hinky Dink" Kenna was born in Chicago. Kenna was a saloon owner who aligned with fellow First Ward Alderman John "Bathhouse John" Coughlin to build an empire of graft in the notorious First Ward Levee District. Coughlin was the more flamboyant of the two, but it was Kenna who controlled the money. Coughlin and Kenna ran the ward and lined their pockets for over 40 years.

1965 The Beatles played two shows at Comiskey Park, one at 3:00 p.m. and another at 8:00 p.m. Brenda Holloway, the King Curtis Band, Cannibal and the Headhunters and Sounds Incorporated were also on the bill. A total of 52,000 people attended the shows. Ticket prices started at $2.50 and the best seats went for $5.50.

1989 Harold Baines of the White Sox became the first Chicago player to have their uniform number retired while they were still playing. The White Sox had traded Baines to Texas in the deal that brought Sammy Sosa to Chicago. Harold wore number three again when he returned in 1996. He was traded again in 1997, but brought the number back as he again returned in 2000 and 2001.

August 21

1797 Andreas von Zirngibl was born in Russia. He fought against Napoleon at Waterloo before settling in Chicago. When he died in 1855, his will ordered that he be buried on his farm and his grave undisturbed, even if the land changed hands. His grave is still there, surrounded by the rusting hulks at the American Fastener Salvage yard, along East 93rd Street and South Ewing Avenue.

1858 The first debate between Abraham Lincoln and Stephen Douglas took place at Ottawa, Illinois. Both men were running for the U.S. Senate and slavery was the key issue. In the seven debates across the state,

Chicago 365

Lincoln argued that slavery was immoral and Douglas countered that the states had a right to decide. Douglas won the Senate seat, but the debates made Lincoln known across the nation.

1929   The Chicago Cardinals became the first professional football team to go out of town for training camp. The team started practice in Coldwater, Michigan. Doctor David Jones had just bought the team for $25,000.

1959   Jim McMahon was born in Jersey City, New Jersey. McMahon first gained national attention as the quarterback for Brigham Young University. The Bears drafted him in the first round in 1982. In 1985, he became a media sensation as the Bears won Superbowl XX. Hampered by injuries, McMahon was traded to the Chargers before the 1989 season.

August 22

1802   Gurdon Hubbard was born in Windsor, Vermont. He came to Chicago in 1818 and traded with the Indians, who called him "Swift Walker." Hubbard built the first stockyard, was behind the Illinois and Michigan Canal, helped found the first bank, built the first brick hotel and founded the Episcopal Church. The city's first insurance underwriter, he paid all claims from the Great Fire.

1848   Melville Elijah Stone was born in Hudson, Illinois. In June 1873, Stone and William E. Dougherty founded the *Chicago Daily News*. Convinced that the McMullens of the *Post* were stealing their material, Stone published a fake dispatch from Yugoslavia that read "Er us siht la Etsll iws nel lum cmeht. Sure enough, the *Post* published the message, which actually read, "The McMullens will steal this for sure" backwards!

1920   Ray Bradbury was born in Waukegan. One of his best-known works combines social commentary with science fiction. *Fahrenheit 451*, released in 1953, tells the story of a totalitarian society where books are outlawed. In 2004, Bradbury complained that filmmaker Michael Moore used the title without permission for his anti-George W. Bush film *Fahrenheit 911*.

1995   A Chicago jury convicted Democratic Representative Mel Reynolds of sexual misconduct involving a 16-year old former campaign worker. Reynolds was also found guilty of obstructing the investigation. He would be sentenced to five years in prison. In 1997, Reynolds received another prison sentence for bank fraud, wire fraud and election fraud. President Clinton pardoned him in 2002.

August 23

1868 Edgar Lee Masters was born in Garnett, Kansas. He moved to Chicago in 1892 to work as a bill collector and then established a law practice. He was Clarence Darrow's partner for eight years. In 1898 he published his first poetry collection, *A Book of Verses*. He is best known for *Spoon River Anthology*, a collection of poems spoken by the dead in an Illinois graveyard.

1870 The first recorded baseball game between two African-American teams took place at Ogden Park on the West Side. The Blue Stockings of Chicago trounced the Pink Stockings from Rockford, Illinois by a score of 48-14. The Chicago team was made up of players employed at hotels in the city.

1919 "Gasoline Alley" began appearing daily in the *Tribune*. Frank King had been drawing a panel for the Sunday paper featuring the characters Walt, Doc, Avery and Bill. *Tribune* editor Joseph Patterson told King to add a baby to make the strip more appealing to women and Skeezix was abandoned on Walt's porch in February 1921. "Gasoline Alley" was the first strip in which the characters aged normally.

1950 The city banned the movie *No Way Out*. City officials said the movie's theme of racial conflict "could cause trouble." Sidney Poitier and Ossie Davis made their debuts in the film about a black doctor who faces racial hatred when a white patient, a criminal, dies in his care.

August 24

1899 The Village of Niles was incorporated. The area was originally known as Dutchman's Point. Niles is said to have come from the *Niles Register*, a very influential newspaper published in Washington D.C. The city is known for its half size replica of the leaning tower of Pisa, constructed in 1932 by Robert Ilg to cover up a swimming pool water tank. In April 1991, Niles and Pisa were officially named as "sister cities."

1955 Emmett Till, a 14-year-old black boy from Chicago, was visiting relatives in Money, Mississippi. He reportedly whistled at a white woman. Three days later, the woman's husband, Ron Bryant, and his brother in law J.W. Milam killed Till and threw him into the Tallahatchie River. Mamie Till insisted on an open casket funeral, so the world could see "what they did to my boy." An all-white jury acquitted the killers.

1971 Ernie Banks hit his final home run. Number 512 came off Jim McGlothlin in the first inning of a 5-4 Cubs win over Cincinnati. When he retired, Banks stood in a tie for 8th place on the all-time career home runs list with Eddie Mathews.

1971 Cook County State's Attorney Edward Hanrahan was among 14 indicted for conspiracy to obstruct justice in connection with the December 4, 1969 raid on the headquarters of the Black Panther party. Two Black Panther leaders died in a seven-minute hail of gunfire. Hanrahan would be cleared, but his political career was over.

August 25

1819 Allan Pinkerton was born in Scotland. The son of a policeman became a barrel maker in Chicago who aided The Underground Railroad. Chicago's first police detective formed his own agency in 1850. His agents uncovered a plot to kill Abraham Lincoln in 1861 and Pinkerton became head of the new Secret Service. Pinkerton men later became notorious for bombing the home of Jesse James' family and for helping break strikes.

1893 It was "Colored Peoples Day" at the Columbian Exposition. The African-American press urged blacks to stay away, because of discrimination at the fair. That day, vendors offered free watermelons. Frederick Douglass was heckled for taking part. But his speech enthralled the crowd. Douglas said, "We Negroes love our country. We fought for it. We ask only that we be treated as well as those who fought against it."

1968 Over 5,000 people turned out to hear a concert by the MC5 and local bands as The Yippie's "The Festival of Life" opened in Lincoln Park. The police were determined to enforce the 11 p.m. curfew in the park. As several thousand people gathered between Stockton Drive and Clark Street, the officers began clubbing people. It was a scene that would be repeated over and over again in the coming days.

Chicago 365

August 26

1860 Holy Family Church on the near West Side was dedicated. On October 8, 1871, founder Reverend Arnold Damen S.J, vowed that if the church survived, seven lights would burn there forever. The wind shifted, and the lights are still burning today. Holy Family is one of five public buildings to survive the fire and the second oldest in Chicago.

1900 President McKinley dedicated the Coliseum at 14th and South Wabash. Built on the site of the old Libby Prison Civil War Museum, The Coliseum hosted every Republican National Convention from 1904 to 1920. It also briefly hosted the Blackhawks and the Bulls, the first roller derby and the infamous First Ward Balls thrown by Aldermen "Bathhouse John" Coughlin and "Hinky Dink" Kenna. It was torn down in 1982.

1927 Buckingham Fountain was dedicated. Philanthropist Kate Buckingham donated the largest ornamental fountain in the world in memory of her brother, Clarence. Edward H. Bennett modeled it after the Latona Fountain at Versailles. Marcel Loyau created the four bronze seahorses, symbolizing the four states that touch Lake Michigan. During displays, the fountain sprays over 14,000 gallons per minute through 133 jets.

1968 Mayor Daley opened the 1968 National Democratic Convention. That morning, over 1,000 protestors marched towards police headquarters, and then turned to Grant Park and swarmed the General Logan statue. As the 11 p.m. curfew arrived, about 1,000 people refused to leave Lincoln Park. Police again waded in with tear gas and clubs. Some residents were clubbed and police attacked reporters and photographers.

August 27

1865 Charles Gates Dawes was born in Marietta, Ohio. He served as vice-president under Calvin Coolidge from 1925 to 1929. While a banker in Chicago in 1912, Dawes wrote a song called "Melody in A Major." In 1951, songwriter Carl Sigman added lyrics to Dawes' music. Tommy Edwards took the new song "It's all in the Game" to number one in 1958. Dawes is the only Vice President to top the charts.

Chicago 365

1871   Theodore Dreiser was born in Indiana. He held menial jobs in Chicago and became a reporter for the *Daily Globe*. Dreiser released his first novel in 1900. *Sister Carrie* was condemned for its frank portrayal of a country girl who moves to Chicago and is seemingly rewarded for an affair with a married man. The novel sold poorly at first. Today Dreiser is seen as one of the most influential authors of the 20th Century.

1872   Aaron Montgomery Ward started his mail order business. He sent out a list of 163 items to members of Grange farmer's organizations across the Midwest. Rural residents loved the variety of goods offered at lower prices than local merchants. By 1874, the business had grown to the point where Ward issued a 32-page catalog. The last Montgomery Ward "Wish Book" was published in 1985.

1959   The III Pan American Games opened at Soldier Field. It marked the first time the games were held in North America. Cleveland was originally slated to host the games, but the city backed down when Congress cut $5 million in funding. Some 2,263 athletes competed in 18 sports. The U.S. won 236 medals with Argentina, the second place country, winning 39.

2003   Salvador Tapia opened fire with a semiautomatic pistol at a car parts warehouse in Chicago, killing six people before police shot him dead. Tapia had been fired from Windy City Core six months earlier for failing to show up for work and arguing with employees. He had been arrested at least 12 times since 1989.

August 28

1818   Jean Baptiste Pont du Sable died in St. Charles, Missouri. He was 73. Du Sable was born in Haiti. About 1772, he established a trading post at a swampy place the Indians called "Eschikagou," meaning "wild onions" In 1800, he sold the property in what is now the heart of Chicago for $1,200. His was nearly penniless when he died. A Black Heritage Series postage stamp issued in 1987 honors du Sable.

1925   Donald O'Connor was born in Chicago. The role of Peter Stirling in the seven *Francis The Talking Mule* pictures made him a star. But his performance as Cosmo Brown and his performance of "Make 'Em Laugh" in *Singing in the Rain* made him a legend. He appeared in several more big-budget musicals and hosted his own television show. Donald O'Connor died on September 27, 2003.

1968 The violence surrounding the Democratic convention reached its peak. As protestors marched down Michigan Avenue, Deputy Police Superintendent James Rochford ordered the street cleared. The crowd chanted, "The whole world is watching," while police beat the demonstrators. At the Amphitheatre, Senator Abraham Ribicoff railed against "Gestapo tactics on the streets of Chicago" as Mayor Daley shouted profanities. Hubert H. Humphrey won the nomination. By the time it was over, 668 people had been arrested and over 1,000 injured, including 192 police officers. It would be 28 years before the Republicans or Democrats would hold another convention in Chicago.

1990 A tornado tore a 16 mile path across Kendall and Will Counties, killing 29 people and injuring 350. Plainfield suffered 21 fatalities and eight died at an apartment complex in Crest Hill. A coach at Plainfield High School moved a football practice inside just before the storm struck, saving several more lives. Three schools, 106 apartments, 470 homes and dozens of businesses were destroyed. Damage was put at $200 million.

1994 Eleven-year-old Black Disciples Gang member Robert "Yummy" Sandifer killed an innocent bystander, 14-year-old Shavon Dean, while firing at a rival gang member. Sandifer had been arrested 27 times in his short life. Three days later, Cragg Hardaway, age 14, and his 16-year-old brother Derrick executed Sandifer to make sure no gang secrets were revealed. Tupac mentioned Sandifer in his song "White Manz World."

August 29

1856 Charles H. Wacker was born in Chicago. Wacker was the chairman of the Chicago Planning Commission, and worked to raise money to implement Daniel Burnham's plan to beautify the city. Wacker was the most outspoken supporter of the part of the plan that called for replacing the South Water Street Market with a double-decked highway to ease traffic congestion. Wacker Drive opened in 1926.

1927 Mayor "Big Bill" Thompson suspended school superintendent William McAndrew for being a "Stool pigeon for King George V." He charged that sedition was being taught in the schools. McAndrew was

Chicago 365

"tried" before the School Board, which voted to remove him, but his term had already expired. Thompson was so outspoken against the British during World War One that he earned the nickname "Kaiser Bill."

1924 Dinah Washington was born Ruth Lee Jones in Tuscaloosa, Alabama. She worked in the washroom while singing at the Garrick Theater, where Lionel Hampton discovered her. She went on to score hits such as "What a Difference a Day Makes," and "Baby You've Got What it Takes," a duet with Brook Benton. She died from an accidental overdose of sleeping pills in December 1963.

1958 Michael Joseph Jackson was born in Gary, the seventh of nine children. Michael's older brothers and cousins originally formed The Jackson Five in 1964. Michael began singing with his brothers at age 4, and the group first performed at Mr. Lucky's in Gary. Soon, they were performing at Chicago clubs. Bobby Taylor discovered them at the Regal Theater, though Motown credits Diana Ross with the discovery.

1996 The Democratic National Convention, meeting at the United Center, nominated Bill Clinton and Al Gore for re-election. Chicago Police underwent special training to avoid any repeat of the "police riot" that gave the city a black eye in 1968. But some were spotted wearing T-shirts that read "We kicked their father's butt in '68 and now it's your turn."

August 30

1847 Cyrus Hall McCormick and his two brothers purchased land on the north bank of Chicago River, near where the east end of the Michigan Avenue Bridge is today. They erected a three-story plant to produce Cyrus' revolutionary invention, the reaper. His firm grew into International Harvester, now known as Navistar. McCormick's reaper plant was the first major industrial factory in Chicago.

1898 Hazen Shirley "Kiki" Cuyler was born in Harrisville, Michigan. The Pirates traded their star outfielder to the Cubs in November 1928, and he would play in Chicago until 1935. While with the Cubs, he would lead the NL in stolen bases three times, batting .360 in 1929 and .355 in 1930. He was named to the Hall of Fame in 1968.

1948 The first residents began moving into the Park Forest planned community, known better as "G.I. Town." Park Forest symbolized post-war suburb development and the "baby boom." Within five years, 90% of the 25,000 residents had children. Developer Philip Klutznick included parks, schools, churches and a shopping center. Similar developments were spreading across the farmland outside the city.

1981 Arlington Park hosted the world's first million dollar horse race for thoroughbreds. A bronze statue at the track today shows the climax of the first "Arlington Million" race, when jockey Bill Shoemaker rode John Henry to a come from behind victory by a neck. John Henry won again in 1984, the only horse to win the race twice. The top grass horses in the world now come to Arlington every August.

August 31

1864 At the Democratic convention in Chicago, General George B. McClellan was nominated for president and George H. Pendleton of Ohio was nominated for vice president. Fifty people were hurt when part of the men's gallery collapsed in the temporary hall on Michigan Avenue. The Democrats adopted a platform blasting President Lincoln for violating civil rights and issuing the Emancipation Proclamation.

1935 Vern Kennedy of the White Sox threw a no-hitter against the St. Louis Browns. Kennedy also starred at the plate in the first no-hitter ever at Comiskey Park. He hit a triple with the bases loaded as the Sox won 5-0. It was the first AL no-hitter in four years.

1955 The first solar powered car was demonstrated at the General Motors Powerama in Chicago. William G. Cobb of General Motors built the 15-inch long "Sunmobile." It was equipped with 12 selenium photoelectric cells. The energy was converted to electricity and sent to a small electric motor.

1997 Princess Diana and her companion Dodi Al Fayed died in a Paris car crash. Thousands of people would wait for hours to sign a condolence book at the Wrigley Building, the site of the British Consolate. A few days later, more than 1,000 people packed a memorial service at St. James Cathedral. In July 2004, the crash that killed Diana was re-enacted on Lower Wacker Drive for a History Channel program.

Chicago 365

SEPTEMBER

September 1

1845 The first school built by the City of Chicago was erected. The school was established mainly through the efforts of millwright Ira Miltimore. The Dearborn School stood on Madison east of Dearborn and cost $7,523. At the time, the building was seen as much too big for the city, and was derided as "Miltimore's Folly." By 1848, it was hopelessly overcrowded.

1875 Edgar Rice Burroughs was born in Chicago. In 1911, he began working on a tale about John Clayton, a baby raised by a family of apes. "Tarzan of the Apes" appeared in the October 1912 issue of *All Story* Magazine and Burroughs was paid $700. Tarzan grew into a series of books, movies and a television show.

1961 Shortly after takeoff from Midway Airport, TWA Flight 529, a Lockheed L-049 Constellation, crashed into a cornfield field near Hinsdale. All 78 people on board were killed. Investigators found that a bolt had fallen from the elevator system, causing the flight controls to malfunction.

1998 Albert Belle of the White Sox broke the team record for single season home runs. He slugged his 42nd of the season at Baltimore, topping the record set by Frank Thomas in 1993. In the same game, Albert recorded his 337th total base of the season, breaking a record set by Joe Jackson back in 1920.

September 2

1850 Al Spalding was born in Byron, Illinois. Spalding racked up 47 wins in 1876 while leading the White Stockings to the first ever National League pennant. He opened his Chicago sporting goods firm in 1876. He went on to great success as an executive. Between 1882 and 1891 his White Sox teams won three pennants.

1850 Eugene Field was born in St. Louis. In 1883, Field became the first daily newspaper columnist in the country. His humorous "Sharps and

Chicago 365

Flats" column ran in the *Daily News* until his death on November 4, 1895. Field is best remembered for his children's verses, such as "Little Boy Blue" and "Wynken, Blynken and Nod."

1919 The American Communist Party was organized in Chicago. But the radicals and socialists were divided over strict adherence to Marxist ideology, so they ended up forming two parties. The two parties merged in 1922. Membership in the American Communist Party peaked during the Great Depression at about 75,000.

September 3

1856 Louis Henri Sullivan was born in Boston. He trained under architect William Le Baron Jenney and then formed his own firm in 1881. Believing "form follows function," Sullivan designed skyscrapers in the "Chicago Style." The buildings utilized steel frame skeletons and designs that made them appear to soar higher. Frank Lloyd Wright worked for Sullivan, who provided Wright with a loan to build his first home.

1926 A huge crowd waited as the *Lake Shore Limited* stopped at the LaSalle Street Station while carrying screen idol Rudolph Valentino to his grave in Los Angeles. A few months earlier, the *Tribune* noted that Valentino had used pink powder puffs at a swanky hotel. The article criticized the effeminization of the American male, and blamed it on Valentino's influence. Valentino challenged the writer to a fistfight.

1955 Thousands of people waited in line at the Roberts Temple Church of God to view the body of Emmett Till, a 14-year-old Chicago boy brutally murdered in Mississippi. His mother demanded that the casket be left open so people could witness the brutality. An all-white jury acquitted the killers on September 23rd. One juror said it wouldn't have taken so long if they hadn't "stopped to drink a pop."

1984 The first trains arrived at the new O'Hare station, designed by Chicago architect Helmut Jahn. The $189.9 million 7.9 mile extension of the North-Northwest rapid transit line running along the Kennedy Expressway took 4 ½ years to complete. The station was constructed beneath the parking garage at the airport.

Chicago 365

September 4

1850   Gas lights appeared in Chicago. The *Journal* reported that the stores along Lake Street "made a brilliant appearance" and the lights added a glow to items made with gold from California. A total of 36 burners made City Hall "the brightest of all, night being transformed into mimic day." The City Council soon decreed that no lights would be lit until nearby residents paid half the cost of $7.50 per lamp.

1918   Paul Harvey was born in Tulsa, Oklahoma. After working at radio stations in Tulsa, Kansas City and St. Louis, he came to work at WENR in June 1944. He quickly became the top newscaster in the city. In 1951, he launched his "News and Comment" show on the ABC Network. On May 10, 1976, he began a new program called "The Rest of the Story." Harvey is now heard on more than 1,200 stations.

1931   Francesea Mitzi von Gerber was born in Chicago. As Mitzi Gaynor, the former ballet dancer made her movie debut in the 1950's *My Blue Heaven*. She may be best known as Nellie Forbush in *South Pacific*. After her movie career faded, Mitzi became a major attraction in Las Vegas and starred annually in TV specials.

1983   Oprah Winfrey arrived to host "A.M. Chicago" on WLS-TV. Within months, Winfrey's personal style took the show from last to first in the ratings, passing Phil Donahue. It was renamed "The Oprah Winfrey Show" in September 1985. Her success led to a role in Steven Spielberg's 1985 film, *The Color Purple,* and a nomination the Best Supporting Actress Oscar. The program was syndicated nationally in 1986.

September 5

1870   Classes began at Saint Ignatius College on West 12th Street and Hoosier (now Blue Island) Avenue in Chicago. Arnold Damen S.J. served as the first president. In 1909, the Jesuit founded school would be re-chartered as Loyola University. The college is named after St. Ignatius of Loyola, founder of the Jesuits.

1898   The first students arrived at the new St. Vincent's College at Webster and Osgood. (now Kenmore Ave.) The college began operating with seven teachers, about 70 students and no president. Tuition for the

Chicago 365

10-month term was $40. On December 24, 1907, St. Vincent's was rechartered as DePaul University.

1929 George Robert Newhart was born in Chicago. Bob was an accountant who wrote and performed comedy for radio. In 1960, *The Button Down Mind of Bob Newhart* became the first comedy album to hit number one. Bob hosted a variety show in 1961 and the "The Bob Newhart Show" from 1972-78. "Newhart" ran from 1982-1990. A fourth series, "Bob," lasted just one year in 1992.

1940 Raquel Tejada was born in Chicago. As Raquel Welch, she worked as a model and a TV weather girl before making her movie debut in Elvis Presley's *Roustabout* in 1964. *One Million Years B.C.* in 1966 made 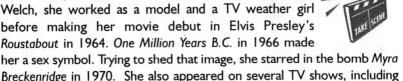 her a sex symbol. Trying to shed that image, she starred in the bomb *Myra Breckenridge* in 1970. She also appeared on several TV shows, including "Seinfeld," and was featured in the 2001 film *Legally Blonde*.

1982 Northwestern ended the worst losing streak in major school college football history to that date. At Dyche Stadium, the Wildcats beat Northern Illinois 31-6 for their first win since September 15, 1979. Running back Ricky Edwards scored four touchdowns in his first start. Eager fans started tearing down the goalposts before time ran out.

September 6

1860 Jane Addams was born in Cedarville, Illinois. She opened Hull House in 1889 to help poor workers through social reform and education. She fought for women's rights and right-wingers called her "the most dangerous woman in the United States." In 1920, she helped form the American Civil Liberties Union. She became the first woman to win the Nobel Prize in 1931. The Hull House Association still helps thousands today.

1901 Anarchist Leon Czolgosz shot President William McKinley in Buffalo. McKinley died eight days later. Czolgosz claimed a speech by Emma Goldman of Chicago inspired him. Police arrested Goldman and nine Chicago anarchists, but they were released. Goldman called McKinley "the most insignificant president the United States ever had," but added, "Still, I do not see what could come out of killing him."

Chicago 365

1955   Chicago's educational television channel signed on the air with a program called "Report to the Teachers." Over 500,000 citizens responded when several educational and cultural organizations sought donations for a non-commercial channel. A year later, WTTW Channel 11 became the first station in the country to offer televised college courses. WTTW is the most watched public television station in the country.

1963   Mike Royko became a writer at the *Daily News*. His first column ran on page 14. But the column soon moved to page three and began running five times each week. When the *Daily News* went bankrupt in 1978, Royko moved to *Chicago Sun-Times*. Disgusted with Rupert Murdoch, he moved to the *Tribune* in 1984. The column continued until Mike was diagnosed with a brain aneurysm in 1997.

September 7

1923   The "Beer Wars" began. Six members of the O'Donnell gang made the rounds of saloons, beating owners who had refused to buy beer from them. Torrio/Capone men confronted the O'Donnells that night, and the brutal Frank McErlane blew the head off Jerry O'Connor at the Klepka Saloon. A rash of killings followed as the other bootlegging gangs worked together to force the O'Donnells to back down.

1928   Tony Lombardo and his bodyguard were killed in front of Raklios Restaurant at the busy corner of Madison and Dearborn. Hundreds ran for cover as the shots rang out. The gunmen escaped. Lombardo was head of the Union Sicilione, an Italian fraternal organization that was a front for the mob. Police said the crime was in revenge for murder of Frankie Uale by Capone's men two months earlier.

1930   Dagwood and Blondie first appeared on the comics page. Chicago native Murat Bernard "Chic" Young created Dagwood, the playboy son of railroad tycoon J. Bolling Bumstead, and Blondie Boopadoop, his flapper girlfriend. Dagwood's family disowned him when they married in 1933 and Dagwood was forced to go to work for Mr. Dithers. After Young died in 1973, his son Dean began writing the strips.

1988   Tony Esposito was inducted into the Hockey Hall of Fame. The Blackhawks picked up the rookie goaltender from Montreal in 1969. In his

Chicago 365

rookie season, Esposito won the Vezina Trophy for best goalie and the Calder Trophy for Rookie of the Year. He set a record with 15 shutouts in 1969-70 and won 30 games or more for seven straight seasons, retiring as the Blackhawk leader with 418 career wins.

September 8

1850 Publisher Victor Lawson was born in Chicago. He founded the *Daily News* in 1876 and turned it into one of the most respected newspapers in the nation. Lawson was the first to send correspondents overseas, and the first to use young boys to hawk papers. The *Daily News* was also home to the first daily newspaper columnist, Eugene Field. Lawson also became president of the Associated Press.

1860 The steamer *Lady Elgin* steamed from Chicago towards Milwaukee on a stormy night. The beautiful side-wheeler carried 400 passengers, mostly Irish members of a Milwaukee paramilitary organization known as the Union Guard on a fund raising excursion. The schooner *Augusta* slammed into the *Lady Elgin* off Winnetka and she went down in 20 minutes. Only 98 people were saved.

1986 The Oprah Winfrey Show, already a hit in Chicago, made its nationally syndicated debut. In less than a year, Oprah had the number one syndicated talk show in the nation. The show won three daytime Emmy Awards in the first year of eligibility. Oprah went on to become the first African-American female billionaire. Today, the show is broadcast in 107 countries and seen by an estimated 23 million viewers weekly in the U.S.

September 9

1968 Mayor Daley slipped up during a press conference in the wake of the violence that marked the Democratic National Convention. Reacting to Senator Abraham Ribicoff's charge that police used "Gestapo tactics," Dailey said, "The policeman isn't there to create disorder, the policeman is there to preserve disorder."

1969 A Mets fan turned a black cat loose on the field at Shea Stadium. Naturally, the cat headed towards the Cub's dugout. He hissed at manager Leo Durocher and ambled past Ron Santo, who was waiting in the on-deck circle. After the cat made his appearance, Tom Seaver got the 7-1 win and the Mets were just ½ game back. Just six days earlier, the Cubs had a five-game lead. They finished second, eight games out.

1971　The Woodfield Mall regional shopping center opened at the Northwest Tollway and Illinois Route 53 in Schaumburg. With 2 million square feet, it is one of the world's largest malls. The name "Woodfield" honored two original tenants, General Robert E. Wood, who was chairman of Sears Roebuck & Company at the time the mall was built, and the Marshall Field and Company

1994　The last basketball game took place at Chicago Stadium. Michael Jordan scored 52 points in a charity game organized by Scottie Pippen. When the game was over, Jordan kneeled down at center court and kissed the floor. Jordan's White Team defeated Pippen and the Red Team 187-150.

September 10

1880　The Archdiocese of Chicago was created and Patrick A. Feehan became the first Archbishop. At the time, the archdiocese covered eighteen counties in the northern part of Illinois, with 194 churches and 204 priests. Today, the archdiocese covers an area of over 10,000 square miles and 375 parishes. The Catholic school system is the 11th largest public or private school system in the world.

1965　The man who boasted that he could "fix anything" died broke at the hands of the mob. Manny Skar built the Las Vegas style Sahara Inn on Mannheim Road. The flamboyant Skar borrowed millions from the mob, and then skimmed the construction money. Skar lost the club and was under indictment for tax evasion when he was gunned down in front of his high-rise apartment building on the Gold Coast.

1986　The restored Chicago Theater re-opened with a performance by Frank Sinatra. The theater at 175 North State Street was built in 1921, but it had fallen into disrepair by 1982 and was about to be demolished. Politicians and civic leaders joined to save the building. The Chicago Theater Preservation Group spent $4.3 million to renovate the 3,800-seat theater.

Chicago 365

September 11

1961 *Bozo's Circus* premiered on WGN. Bozo started out as a character on a 1946 Capitol album and was franchised for television. Bob Bell made Chicago's Bozo the most popular of all. There was a ten-year waiting list for tickets. Bell was the inspiration for the Krusty the Clown character on *The Simpsons.* Joey DeAuria took over in 1984 and the final show aired as a prime-time special on July 14, 2001.

1963 The City Council passed an ordinance forbidding discrimination in the sale or rental of real estate. It passed despite a march on City Hall by 4,000 whites against the measure.

2001 As word of the terrorist attacks reached Chicago, flights were halted at O'Hare and Midway Airports. The Sears Tower and Hancock buildings were evacuated along with the Dirksen Federal Building, Daley Center, Wrigley Building, Merchandise Mart and Aon Tower. Mayor Dayley assured that security was being increased, and banned parking around government buildings. Police ringed the headquarters of United Airlines. Some downtown gas stations raised prices to $6 per gallon and there was some panic buying. Blood donations stretched the system to the limit. Major League baseball cancelled the Cub's home game against Cincinnati and the White Sox game in New York.

2001 A federal judge threw out the conviction of Derrick Hardaway for the 1994 murder of 11-year-old Robert "Yummy" Sandifer. The judge found that the 14-year-old Hardaway should not have been interrogated for 14 straight hours. A court reinstated the conviction in 2002 but said a Chicago youth police officer gave the boy as much help as "a potted plant."

September 12

1859 Florence Kelley was born in Pennsylvania. She stayed at Hull House for seven years in the 1890's, exposing the horrid conditions in the sweatshops. Kelley's work led to an Illinois law that barred children under 14 from working in the factories. After leaving Chicago, Kelley fought to establish a minimum wage and the eight-hour workday. Her socialist beliefs made her a frequent target of FBI investigations.

1913 Jesse Owens was born in Danville, Alabama. Owens won four gold medals at the 1936 Olympics in Berlin, embarrassing Adolf Hitler. But Owens was also snubbed in his own country. President Franklin D. Roosevelt, concerned about upsetting southern voters, 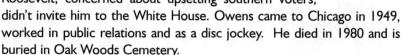 didn't invite him to the White House. Owens came to Chicago in 1949, worked in public relations and as a disc jockey. He died in 1980 and is buried in Oak Woods Cemetery.

1992 Aboard the Space Shuttle *Endeavor,* Mae Carol Jemison became the first black woman in space. During the mission, the 1973 graduate of Morgan Park High School conducted a satellite conference with students at the Museum of Science and Industry. After leaving NASA in 1993, Jamieson went on to found and serve as president of two technology companies.

1995 Cubs broadcaster Harry Caray came under fire for a pre-game interview in which he spoke to Cubs manager Jim Riggleman about Dodger's pitcher Hideo Nomo. Caray said, "Well, my eyes are slanty enough, how about yours?" Caray said he didn't do anything wrong, and "If I did, I'd be the first to apologize."

1998 Sammy Sosa hit his 61st and 62nd home runs of the year, passing Roger Maris for second on the all-time list. The homers also gave him a tie for the National League record for multiple home run games in a single season set by Ralph Kiner in 1947.

September 13

1860 Landscape architect Jens Jensen was born in Denmark. He came to Chicago in 1884 and worked as a gardener in the Chicago West Parks. Jensen was fired as Humboldt Park superintendent for refusing to take part in political graft. He created the "prairie style" of landscape design, planting native wildflowers in parks across the Midwest. He also became a social reformer and helped establish forest preserves around the city.

1925 "The Velvet Fog" was born in Chicago. Melvin Howard Torme was singing in the Blackhawk Restaurant by the age of four. He won first place in a children's singing contest at the Century of Progress Exposition and was hired for a role in a soap opera on NBC radio. At age 15, he scored his first hit with "Lament to Love." His biggest hit was 'The Christmas Song," which Mel wrote with Bob Wells in 1946.

1942   Cubs shortstop Lennie Merullo set a Major League record with four errors in one inning. It happened in the 2nd inning in a doubleheader nitecap against the Boston Braves. Lennie's son was born that day, and the proud parents named him "Boots." The Cubs won the game 12-8, having lost the first game.

1944   Peter Cetera was born in Chicago. Cetera was in a band called The Exceptions when in late 1967 he was recruited to play bass for Chicago Transit Authority. Chicago soon became one of the nation's top bands. Cetera made his first solo album in 1981, but stayed with Chicago until 1985. He hit number one a year later with "The Glory of Love," and scored another hit with "The Next Time I Fall," a duet with Amy Grant.

September 14

1914   Jack Carlton Moore was born in Chicago. As Clayton Moore, he acted in several serials before landing the lead in "The Lone Ranger." With his trusty horse Silver and sidekick Tonto, Moore rode the range until 1952 and again from 1954-57. In 1979, the producers of a new film version got a court order forbidding him from wearing the trademark mask. The movie was a bomb, and Moore got the mask back in 1984.

1927   In Chicago, actress and comedienne Fannie Brice was granted a divorce from Nicky Arnstein. Brice said Nicky lost interest when she had her nose straightened. Arnstein was a con man and thief. But Fannie remained devoted until Arnstein walked away from his wife and two children after his release from Leavenworth. The movie *Funny Girl*, starring Barbara Streisand, was loosely based on Brice's life.

1997   The White Sox retired the uniform number 72 worn by Carlton Fisk. Fisk became the 8th Sox player to have their number retired. The other players are; Nellie Fox (No. 2), Harold Baines (3), Luke Appling (4), Minnie Minoso (9), Luis Aparicio (11), Ted Lyons (16) and Billy Pierce (19).

1978   Na Nu, Na Nu! "Mork and Mindy" premiered on ABC. The show starred Robins Williams as the zany alien from the planet Ork and Pam

Dawber as the down to earth Mindy. A Chicago native, Williams first played the character on a February 1987 episode of "Happy Days." "Mork and Mindy" ran until 1982.

September 15

1926   Unable to find the fogged-in landing field in Chicago, airmail pilot Charles Lindbergh jumped from his plane as it ran out of fuel over Ottawa, Illinois. "Lucky" Lindbergh parachuted to safety, and the three sacks of mail from St. Louis were recovered safely and taken to Chicago by train.

1948   WNBQ Channel Five signed on. Regular commercial programming didn't begin until January 7, 1949. In August 1964, the call letters were changed to WMAQ, to tie in with NBC's radio station. WMAQ was the first television station to offer a 10 p.m. newscast. In 1956, it became the first station to broadcast completely in color.

1979   The sitcom "Working Stiffs" premiered on CBS. The show lasted just three episodes and is notable only because it featured two unknown actors playing Ernie and Mike O'Rourke. The characters were a pair of bumbling janitors working in a Chicago office building. Jim Belushi played Ernie and Michael Keaton played Mike.

1996   Frank Thomas of the White Sox became the all time franchise home run leader. His 215th broke the old mark set by Carlton Fisk. It was just one of three homers he hit in the game that day. On July 14, 2000, Thomas broke the franchise record for RBIs that had stood for 50 years. Luke Appling held the old record of 1,116.

September 16

1909   President William Howard Taft was among the 27,000 on hand at the West Side Grounds. It marked the only time that a President attended a Cubs game while in office. Christy Mathewson got the win as the Giants beat the Cubs, 2-1.

1963   Richard Marx was born in Chicago. His debut album in 1987 was a smash; including the top five singles "Don't Mean Nothing," "Should've Known Better," "Endless Summer Nights," and the Number One hit, "Hold On To The Nights." Critics blasted his big hair and his formulaic music, but the 1989 album *Repeat Offender* gave him two more Number Ones with "Satisfied" and "Right Here Waiting."

1972   "The Bob Newhart Show" premiered on CBS. Visuals showed him driving through Wilmette on his way from his apartment in The Loop to his office at 5500 Lake Shore drive. So much for geography! Newhart played Bob Hartley, a psychologist living in Chicago with his wife Emily, a schoolteacher

1996   Chicago and Paris announced their sister cities partnership. Chicago actually has 22 sister cities, including Athens, Casablanca, Hamburg, Kiev, Mexico City, Milan, Osaka, Shanghai, and Toronto. The first agreement was signed with Warsaw in 1960.

September 17

1879   Andrew "Rube" Foster was born in Calvert, Texas. The young pitcher came to the Chicago Union Giants in 1907, and was soon the manager. He led the team to a record of 123-6 in 1910 and founded the American Giants in 1911. The American Giants often drew more fans than the Cubs or White Sox. Foster founded the Negro National League in 1920. He died on December 9, 1930 in Kankakee.

1920   George Halas of the Decatur Staleys met with representatives of 12 other teams in a Hupmobile showroom in Canton, Ohio to form the American Professional Football Association. Syrup maker A.E. Staley gave Halas the club in 1921, along with $5,000 to keep the Staleys name for one year. In 1922, the Staleys name changed to the Chicago Bears, and the APFA changed its name to the National Football League.

1953   The most popular Cubs player of all time made his Major League debut. Ernie Banks went 0-3 and made an error in his first game. But he replaced Roy Smalley as the Cubs regular shortstop in 1954. In 1955, "Mister Cub" set a record for shortstops with 44 home runs. He won the MVP Awards in 1958 and 1959. He moved to first base in 1962, hit his 500th home run on May 12, 1970 and retired in 1971.

1961   Northwest Orient flight 706 left O'Hare Airport for Miami. About a minute after takeoff, the Lockheed Electra 188C suddenly banked sharply, rolled over, struck some high-tension wires and plunged to earth in Bensenville. All 37 passengers were killed. The accident was blamed on a mechanical failure in the aileron system.

September 18

1881   The *Tribune* reported on a "televide" experiment in Aurora. The paper said a group of electricians saw images sent by wire from Chicago, 42 miles away. The English inventors said that with the "apparatus for conveying the human eyesight" they could expect to see pictures of the church steeples of Chicago from a London observatory in the not too distant future.

1889   Jane Addams and her friend Ellen Gates Starr opened Hull House in an old mansion at Halsted and Polk Streets. The social settlement provided education, day care and the arts to the immigrants of the sweatshops.   Hull House residents led the movement for labor unions, child labor laws, and the first juvenile court. Addams became a peace activist and was the first woman to win the Nobel Peace Prize.

1966   To this day, no one knows why 21-year-old Valerie Percy Percy had to die.   Her father Charles was running for Senate against Paul Douglas when the killer broke into the family mansion in Kenilworth. Valerie was stabbed 14 times. She was the sister-in-law of Senator Jay Rockefeller, but had no known enemies.   One possible suspect killed himself and another died trying to escape from prison.   Charles Percy won the election.

1994   "Chicago Hope" premiered on CBS. At first, the show ran on Thursdays, but was moved after being clobbered by another Chicago based medical drama, "E.R." The show ran for 141 episodes. It featured the first bare breast on network T.V. (In a plastic surgery episode) and the first use of the word "shit" on a regular show. For the record, Mark Harmon uttered the word in context.

September 19

1932   Mike Royko was born in Chicago.   The son of a Chicago cab driver, Royko's columns for the *Daily News*, the *Sun-Times* and then the *Tribune* were among the most widely read in the world. He was known for

Chicago 365

his brash and sometimes sarcastic style, often telling stories of working class Chicago through his alter ego, Slats Grobnik. His commentary won a Pulitzer Prize in 1972. Royko died on April 29, 1997.

1949 Orchard Place Airport was renamed in honor of Lieutenant Edward "Butch" O'Hare. O'Hare won the Medal of Honor for shooting down five Japanese bombers. He was shot down over Tarawa while leading the first night attack from a carrier in 1943. His father was an attorney who turned informant against Al Capone in hopes of getting Butch into the Naval Academy. Capone gunmen killed him on November 8, 1939.

1994 The show "E.R." Premiered on NBC. The long running show is set in the emergency room at Chicago's fictional County General Hospital. The producers originally intended the drama to be set at Cook County Hospital, but changed their minds. The show seldom films in Chicago. Most of the locations, even the snowy city scenes, are filmed in Los Angeles and the Chicago landmarks are added digitally.

2002 A drunken bare-chested man named William Lique Junior and his teenaged son ran onto the field at Comiskey Park and attacked Kansas City Royals first base coach Tom Gamboa. Cook County Judge Leo Holt sentenced Ligue to probation and said baseball was partly to blame. He called Comiskey "The world's largest saloon" and added, "What fan has not seen a pitcher intentionally hurl a baseball at a players head?"

September 20

1890 Ferdinand "Jelly Roll" Morton was born in New Orleans. Morton said he was the inventor of jazz stomp and swing music, and he was probably right. Already a star on the West Coast, the pianist came to Chicago in 1923. The recordings made in Chicago by Morton and his Red Hot Peppers are now considered classics. He was inducted into the Rock and Roll Hall of Fame as an early influence in 1998.

1902 Nixey Callahan fired the first White Sox no-hitter. The win over the Detroit Tigers was the second no-hitter in American League history. The White Sox were victims of the first AL no hitter on May 9, 1901, but they didn't loose the game. Earl Moore of Cleveland threw nine innings of no-hit ball, but the Sox came back to win it won 4-2 in ten innings.

1904 A Cook County Grand Jury returned a true bill against Walter S. Boyle. Boyle had been arrested for violating the state specified speed limit of 15 miles per hour for automobiles. It marked the first time in Illinois that a speeder was prosecuted.

1926 Eleven car loads of hoods led by Hymie Weiss cruised by Al Capone's headquarters at the Hawthorne Hotel in Cicero. The gangsters poured over 1,000 shots into the building. Capone, eating lunch at the restaurant next door, escaped injury. Hymie Weiss would live just 20 more days. On October 11, he was gunned down at his headquarters above Dion O'Bannion's flower shop at 738 North State.

1984 Steve Goodman died of leukemia at the age of 36. Goodman wrote "City of New Orleans" and many songs had Chicago themes, such as "A Dying Cub Fan's Last Request." He was diagnosed with leukemia in 1969, but kept the illness a secret until it prevented him from attending the Harry Chapin Memorial Concert in 1982.

September 21

1903 Preston Tucker was born in Capac, Michigan. Tucker leased an old Dodge aircraft plant at 7401 South Cicero in 1948 and produced "The Car of the Future." The Tucker featured avant-garde styling, disk brakes, seatbelts, and a headlight that moved with the steering wheel. Only 51 were built before the firm collapsed due to dirty tricks by the "Big Three" automakers and the government.

1950 Bill Murray was born in Wilmette. Kicked out of the Boy Scouts and later busted for smuggling pot at O'Hare, he joined his brother in the Second City troupe. Murray came to ABC's "Saturday Night Live With Howard Cosell" in 1975 and moved to NBC's "Saturday Night Live" in 1977. His films include *Caddyshack, Ghostbusters, Rushmore, The Royal Tenenbaums* and *Lost in Translation*.

1997 Ryne Sandberg played his final game at Wrigley Field. He went 2 for 3, before leaving for a pinch runner in the fifth inning. Sandberg returned for a curtain call when Harry Caray sang "Take Me Out to the Ball Game" during the 7th inning stretch. Sandberg retired with the third-highest career fielding percentage for second basemen. (.989)

Chicago 365

September 22

1645 French explorer Louis Joliet was born in Quebec. With Pere Marquette, he would explore the Mississippi basin in 1763. The expedition proved that the Mississippi flowed into the Gulf of Mexico. On the return trip, the Indians led them to a shortcut up the Illinois River to Lake Michigan. They traveled across a swampy stretch of land covered with stinkweed that the Indians called "Checagou."

1920 A Cook County Grand Jury met to investigate charges that eight White Sox players conspired to fix the 1919 World Series. Assistant State Attorney Hartley Replogle subpoenaed several players, including New York Giants pitcher Rube Benton. Benton said he saw a telegram sent to a teammate that said the Sox would lose. Benton said that Chic Gandil, Happy Felsch, Lefty Williams, and Ed Cicotte were in on the fix.

1927 In the seventh round, the "Manassa Mauler" floored the champ before 100,000 at Soldier Field. But referee Dave Barry waited to begin the count over the fallen Gene Tunney. Challenger Jack Dempsey had forgotten the rule that he had to go to a neutral corner. Tunney got back to his feet before the infamous "long count" reached ten. Tunney won the fight and kept the title he had won from Dempsey a year earlier.

1959 When the air raid sirens wailed, some residents of the South Side rushed towards the shelters. But it was a happy day. The "Go-Go" White Sox had beat Cleveland to win the American League pennant. Fire Commissioner Robert J. Quinn fired up the sirens because a city council ordinance called for whistles and sirens to blow if the Sox won. Quinn said the scare actually provided a good test of the city's readiness.

September 23

1908 With the Cubs and Giants tied at 1-1 in the bottom of the 9th, Fred Merkle of the Giants was on 1st and Harry McCormick on 2nd. Al Bridwell singled and McCormick scored. Merkle stopped halfway to second and headed to the clubhouse. Johnny Evers grabbed a ball and tagged 2nd. Umpire Hank O'Day ruled the game ended in a tie. The Cubs won when the game was replayed and "Merkle's Boner" gave them the pennant.

Chicago 365

1912 Harriet Moore published the first issue of *Poetry*. At the time, it was the only magazine in the U.S. devoted exclusively to poetry. The magazine was an important part of the Chicago "Literary Renaissance." Moore introduced many great poets, including Ezra Pound, Robert Frost and T.S. Eliot.

1959 Hoffman Estates was incorporated. The population of Schaumburg Township was just 1,080 in 1950. In 1955, the same year that the Northwest Tollway opened, Sam and Jack Hoffman constructed a subdivision on a 160-acre farm site. About 8,000 people lived in Hoffman Estates when the village was incorporated.

1970 Ziggy the Elephant was freed from solitary confinement at the Brookfield Zoo. The pachyderm was banished to an inside stall when he attacked keeper Slim Lewis in 1941. Lewis led a reluctant Ziggy into the yard. After 40 minutes, he went back inside. School children raised money and billboards urged people to give to the Ziggy Fund to build the private outdoor enclosure. Ziggy died in October 1975.

September 24

1895 Morton Grove was incorporated. When the railroad came through in 1872, the depot was named for a grove of trees surrounding the village and in honor of Levi Parsons Morton, a director of the Milwaukee Railroad who served as Vice President of the United States from 1889-1893. The village may be best known for a 1981 measure making it the first in the nation to restrict private possession of handguns

1943 Just 314 people braved a downpour at Wrigley Field to see the Cubs play the Phillies. The smallest crowd in Wrigley history saw Andy Pafko make his first start for the Cubs. Pafko drove in four runs as the Cubs beat the Phillies 7-4 in a game that was called after five innings.

1969 The "Chicago Eight" trial began. Abbie Hoffman, Jerry Rubin, Bobby Seale, Tom Hayden, Rennie Davis, David Dellinger, John Froines and Lee Weiner were accused of conspiring to incite riots in 1968. The defendants mocked Judge Julius Hoffman, who ordered Seale bound and gagged, and then severed him from the trial. Five were convicted of intent to incite a riot but the convictions were overturned in 1972.

Chicago 365

1984   The Cubs clinched a post-season appearance for the first time since 1945. Rick Sutcliffe tossed a two-hitter for his 14th victory in a row and a 4-1 win in Pittsburgh. Eight days later, Sutcliffe would get the win and hit a home run as the Cubs pounded San Diego 13-0 in the first game of the NLCS.

September 25

1926   The NHL awarded a franchise to Major Frederic McLaughlin, a Chicago coffee tycoon. He bought the Portland Rose Buds of the Western Hockey League and moved the players to Chicago. During World War I, McLaughlin commanded a machine gun battalion of the 85th Army Division. The division was nicknamed the Blackhawks, after a Sauk Indian chief who helped the British during the War of 1812.

1928   Paul Galvin and his brother, Joseph Galvin, incorporated the Galvin Manufacturing Corporation with five employees and $565 in cash. A battery eliminator, which allowed battery-powered radios to run on household current, was the firm's first product. In 1930, they began manufacturing car radios. Paul Galvin came up with a new name for the company. "Motorola" combined "motion" and "sound."

1930   Sheldon Allan Silverstein was born in Chicago. Silverstein's sense of humor made him a beloved author of children's books, including *Where the Sidewalk Ends,* and *The Missing Piece.* He also wrote several hit songs, including "A Boy Named Sue" for Johnny Cash, "On the Cover of the Rolling Stone" by Doctor Hook and "The Unicorn Song," a hit for the Irish Rovers.

1954   The *U-505* was dedicated to serve as a memorial and permanent exhibit at the Museum of Science and Industry. In June, 1944 a task group led by Captain Daniel Gallery of Chicago captured the *U-505* on the high seas. The ship appeared doomed to become a practice target until an effort was organized to bring it to Chicago. The people of Chicago raised $250,000 to tow the boat and install it at the museum.

September 26

1833   The United Tribes of the Chippewa, Ottawa and Potawatomi signed the Treaty of Chicago. For $100,000, the Indians gave up their remaining land in Illinois and agreed to move west of the Mississippi within three years. They were the last tribes to leave the Chicago area.

1870   The original Palmer House Hotel opened at the corner of State and Quincy Streets. Chicago's pioneering architect, John Van Osdel, designed the lavish building. The Great Chicago Fire destroyed the 225-room hotel. But Palmer built an even more lavish hotel at State and Monroe. The Palmer House was billed as the first fireproof hotel and the first to be wired for electricity. The current building replaced it in 1925.

1960   John F. Kennedy and Richard Nixon met at the WBBM-TV studios for the first nationally televised presidential debate. Nixon fidgeted and sweated under the bright lights while Kennedy showed confidence and looked youthful. Before the debate, Nixon was the favorite, but television had changed politics forever. Helped out by some suspicious late votes from Chicago, JFK won the election by just 112,000 votes.

1971   Ernie Banks played his 2,528th and final game. His final hit was a first inning single, giving Banks a career total of 2,583. But the Cubs lost the game to Philadelphia 5-1 at Wrigley Field.

September 27

1885   "The Great Blackstone" was born in Chicago. His real name was Pete Baughton. As Harry Blackstone Senior, he became one of the most famous magicians in the world. His flamboyant signature illusions included "The Vanishing Bird Cage," "The Floating Light Bulb," and "Dancing Handkerchief." Harry Blackstone Sr. passed away on November 16, 1965. His son, Harry Blackstone Junior, also became a great magician.

1910   Walter Brookins, a student of Wilbur Wright, made the first airplane flight over Chicago. Over 20,000 spectators watched as Brookins took off from Grant Park and flew at 2,500 feet for 20 minutes. Two days later, Brookins and his bi-plane raced an Illinois Central train to Springfield. He set a record for distance at 169 miles and for the longest sustained flight at 88 miles. Wilbur Wright was a passenger on the train.

1919   Charles Percy was born in Pensacola, Florida. He held four jobs at once while attending New Trier High School in Winnetka. Percy worked in the Bell and Howell student-training program, and was president of the firm by the time he was 29. In 1966, he won election to the US Senate, defeating Paul H. Douglas. Paul Simon upset Percy to take the seat in 1984.

1930 Hack Wilson of the Cubs hit his 55th and 56th home runs of the season as the Cubs beat the Reds 13-8 at Wrigley Field. Wilson sat a National League home run record that would stand until Mark McGwire and Sammy Sosa came along in 1998.

September 28

1878 Upton Sinclair was born in Baltimore. In 1904, Fred Warren, publisher of the Socialist journal *Appeal to Reason*, commissioned Sinclair to write a novel exposing the Chicago meatpacking industry. Initially rejected by six publishers, *The Jungle* became a sensation and inspired passage of the Pure Food and Drug Act. It also led to the growth of investigative journalism, derided by President Roosevelt as "muckraking."

1901 William Paley was born in Chicago. The young cigar executive became interested in radio after buying time on a Philadelphia station. Paley bought the struggling network that became CBS in 1929. He had the foresight to commit to television early. Paley introduced performers such as Lucille Ball and Ed Sullivan and backed groundbreaking programs like "All in the Family" and "M*A*S*H."

1908 Stories of the lewdness at the First Ward Ball staged by Aldermen "Bathhouse John" Coughlin and "Hinky Dink" Kenna spurred ministers to action. They issued a resolution calling the gathering of politicians, hookers and criminals "an annual insult to the people and a carnival of crime." Hinky Dink declared that the ball would go on. He said it was "as nice a social affair as you will find."

1938 Cubs manager Gabby Hartnett hit the famous "Homer in the Gloaming." As darkness settled over Wrigley Field, the blast off Pittsburgh's Mace Brown in the bottom of the ninth broke a 5-5 tie and put the Cubs in first place ahead of the Pirates by ½ game. The umpires had decided to call the game due to darkness as soon as Hartnett completed the at bat.

Chicago 365

September 29

1901 Enrico Fermi was born in Rome, Italy. Fermi and his team of scientists at the University of Chicago created the first controlled nuclear reaction at a makeshift lab in a squash court beneath the Stagg Field stands on December 2, 1942. In 1945, Fermi was placed in charge of the Manhattan Project, which created the first atomic bomb.

1920 "Shoeless Joe" Jackson walked out of the Cook County Courthouse after admitting that the Sox conspired to throw the 1919 World Series. A boy asked, "It ain't true, is it?" Jackson replied, "Yes, kid, I'm afraid it is." A legend grew that the boy had said, "Say it ain't so Joe." A jury acquitted Jackson and seven other members of the "Black Sox." But Commissioner Kenesaw Mountain Landis banned them for life.

1982 The parents of 12-year-old Mary Kellerman gave her a Tylenol for her cold. She was dead by morning. By October 1, seven people in the area were dead after taking Extra-Strength Tylenol capsules laced with cyanide. Tylenol was pulled from shelves nationwide. So many people played 2880 (the lot number of the deadly pills) that lottery officials halted betting on the number. The case was never solved.

2003 *Sports Illustrated* called it "The Eyesore on Lakeshore." The controversial new Soldier Field, a modern stadium built around the historic colonnades of the old, opened with a game between the Bears and the Green Bay Packers. Taxpayers paid much of the $660 million cost. The project included an additional 17 acres of green space, with a sledding hill and a park for children.

September 30

1850 A group of 300 blacks met at Quinn Chapel on Wells near Washington, the first black church in Chicago. They were protesting the passage of the Fugitive Slave Act. The group resolved to form a black police force to patrol the city and keep an eye out for slave catchers.

1861 William Wrigley Junior was born. He came to Chicago to sell soap his father's soap in 1891 and offered baking soda with each purchase. The

Chicago 365

customers liked the baking soda better than the soap, so he switched to baking soda and gave away chewing gum with each purchase. Again, the premium was more popular, so he started marketing chewing gum in 1892. Juicy Fruit and Wrigley's Spearmint were introduced in 1893.

1990   Harold Reynolds grounded out, clinching a 2-1 White Sox win over Seattle, and 42,849 fans sang "Na-Na Hey-Hey Goodbye" as the curtain came down on the oldest park in the majors. Comiskey was also home for the NFL Chicago Cardinals for 35 years, hosted the first baseball All-Star game in 1933, and the Negro League All-Star games from 1933-50. The Beatles performed two concerts at Comiskey in 1965.

OCTOBER

October 1

1892   Classes opened at the University of Chicago. The American Baptist Education Society turned to John Rockefeller for help founding the school. Rockefeller called it the "best investment I ever made." Marshall Field donated the land. Over 70 Nobel Prize winners either attended the university or were members of the faculty. Alumni include John Ashcroft, Carol Moseley Braun, Carl Sagan and Kurt Vonnegut.

1919   As Game One of the 1919 World Series opened in Cincinnati, the White Sox were heavily favored. Sox pitcher Eddie Cicotte hit the first Reds batter with a pitch. It was a signal to gambler Arnold Rothstein that the fix was in. Weary of skinflint owner Charles Comiskey, eight players agreed to accept money to throw the series. Cicotte gave up six runs and went less than four innings as the Sox lost 4-1.

1927   Tom Bosley was born in Chicago. He made his debut on stage while attending DePaul University. In 1959, Tom won a Tony for his portrayal of New York Mayor LaGuardia in *Fiorello*. He is best known for his role as Howard Cunningham on "Happy Days" from 1974-83. He then appeared on "Murder, She Wrote" and starred as a Chicago priest with a knack for solving crimes on "The Father Dowling Mysteries."

1932   Babe Ruth hit a home run in the first inning off Charlie Root in Game Three of the World Series at Wrigley. The Babe was heckled as he came up in the 5th inning. He took two strikes, appeared to point to the bleachers, and slammed the next one out. Asked if he "called" his shot, Babe said, "Why don't you read the papers? It's all there." A film surfaced in 1994 that appeared to show Babe was just gesturing to his tormentors.

October 2

1938   Charlie Weegman died of a heart attack in his suite at the Drake Hotel. Weegman ran a chain of ten fast food restaurants decades before McDonald's. He sunk his fortune into a Federal League baseball team, the Chicago Whales, and built a new stadium at Addison and Clark. Weegman bought the Cubs after the Federal League folded, but went broke in 1918. William Wrigley bought the team and re-named the stadium.

Chicago 365

1967 The South Side mourned for Major Robert H. Lawrence, killed a day earlier in a plane crash at Edwards Air Force Base. Lawrence became the first black astronaut when he began training in 1966. But because he never actually flew in space, the Astronauts Memorial Foundation refused to etch his name onto the Space Mirror at Kennedy Space Center with other astronauts who died. His name was finally added in December 1997.

1995 Bulls fans were stunned when Will Purdue was traded to Detroit for the hated Dennis Rodman. Rumor had it that Michael Jordan pushed for the acquisition of "The Worm" after playing with him on the set of the movie *Space Jam*. Rodman would lead the NBA in rebounding for three straight seasons as the Bulls won three straight titles. He also changed his hair color repeatedly, dated Madonna and insulted Mormons.

October 3

1897 The Union Loop opened. Transit magnate Charles Tyson Yerkes financed the two miles of elevated tracks. He had had the political pull to build the overhead structures on the streets and pull rival transit companies together. The "Loop" was actually named after a cable car roundabout built in 1882 as part of Marshall Field's system designed to bring customers to his store.

1897 The great Cap Anson played his last game. He hit two home runs as St. Louis beat the Colts 10-9 in the first game of a doubleheader. At 46, he was the oldest player in Major League history to hit two homers. He went 0-3 in game two as the Cubs won 7-1. With Anson gone, the Chicago papers began calling the team "The Orphans." The name stuck until March 27, 1902 when the *Daily News* suggested a new name, the Cubs.

1967 Chicago was stunned to learn that "the place to laugh your troubles away" was closing. Riverview Amusement Park opened in 1904, and occupied a 74-acre site bounded by Western and Belmont Avenues, the Chicago River and Lane Tech High School. "The Bobs" rollercoaster, the "Pair-O-Chutes," and "The Ghost Train" were among the rides. Today, the DeVry Institute of Technology and a shopping center stand on the site.

Chicago 365

October 4

1833 A 142-block area originally set aside for the schools was auctioned off. Lots in the School Section sold for an average price of $60 per acre. That was quite an improvement from three years earlier, when the land was worth about $1.25 per acre. The sale did bring in money for the schools, but that land is now in the heart of The Loop, and the most expensive real estate in the Midwest.

1924 John Charles Carter was born in Evanston. His mother, Lila Charlton, married Chester Heston and the family moved to Winnetka. Charlton Heston started acting at New Trier High School and made his first movie appearance in 1950's *Dark City*. He won the 1959 best actor Oscar for *Ben Hur*. Heston was president of the National Rifle Association from 1998 until 2003 and announced he had Alzheimer's in 2002.

1931 The comic strip "Dick Tracy" made its debut. Chester Gould created the strip, but wanted to call it "Plainclothes Tracy." Captain Joseph Patterson of the *Tribune* syndicate came up with the new name and dubbed Tracy's girlfriend "Tess Trueheart." The square jawed detective became a staple of radio, TV and movies.

1979 Few people had heard of Karol Cardinal Wojtyla the first time he visited Chicago in 1976. But this time, a huge crowd was waiting as his plane arrived at O'Hare Airport. Wojtyla was now Pope John Paul II. He visited Holy Name Cathedral two nights in a row, and heard religious music by Luciano Pavorotti and the Chicago Symphony Orchestra during his visit.

October 5

1902 Ray Kroc was born in Chicago. Ray sold milk shake machines and was intrigued when a restaurant in San Bernardino, California ordered eight mixers. Kroc visited Dick and Mac McDonald's restaurant and tried to talk them into starting a chain so Ray could sell more mixers. The brothers said Kroc could franchise their stores. Kroc opened the first McDonald's franchise at 400 Lee Street in Des Plaines on April 15, 1955.

Chicago 365

1937 President Franklin D. Roosevelt dedicated the outer drive bridge over the Chicago River. He took the opportunity to make a major foreign policy speech comparing the spread of international violence to a virus that needed to be "quarantined" to prevent it from spreading. The bridge connected the main stream of city traffic with the superhighway along Lake Michigan.

1950 Senator Estes Kefauver brought his organized crime hearings to Chicago. Captain Dan "Tubbo" Gilbert, chief investigator for the State's Attorney's office, admitted that he had never raided a bookie joint during his 18 years on the job. "The World's Richest Cop" was actually the political boss of the Police Department and a member of the syndicate. Gilbert said he gained his wealth trading in grain futures and stocks.

1979 Pope John Paul II said an open-air mass at Five Holy Martyrs Church in Brighton Park. He spoke in his native Polish. Before 350 American Bishops at Quigley Preparatory Seminary South, The Pope spoke out against abortion, homosexuality and divorce. Then it was on to Grant Park, where over 200,000 people waited for a three-hour mass, the largest ever in Chicago.

October 6

1945 Tavern owner "Billy Goat" Sianis bought a box seat for his goat for Game Four of the World Series. But ushers refused to admit the goat and owner P.K. Wrigley denied a personal appeal, saying that the goat smelled. Sianis put a "goat curse" on the Cubs. The Tigers tied the series that day and went on to win. Sianis sent a telegram to Wrigley saying, "Who smells now?" The Cubs haven't been back to the fall classic since.

1965 Bolingbrook was incorporated. Between 1961 and 1965, the Dover Construction Company built homes along Illinois 53 north of Old Route 66 in an area originally known as Welco. The subdivision sections were known as Westbury, Colonial Village and King's Park, and the whole development was named the Bolingbrook Subdivision.

1969 The radical "Weather Underground," faction of the Students for a Democratic Society, (SDS) attempted to blow up the statue erected in honor of the policemen who died in the 1886 Haymarket Incident. It was the first in a series of violent protests against the trial of the Chicago Eight that the Weathermen called the "Days of Rage." Two days later, hundreds rioted downtown. Six people were shot and 70 arrested.

1993   Michael Jordan announced his retirement. Jordan said basketball no longer offered any challenge for him. He also cited the recent murder of his father and media scrutiny of his gambling as reasons for hanging it up. In 1994, Jordan signed a minor league deal with the White Sox but was unsuccessful as a baseball player. On March 18, 1995, Jordan announced, "I'm back," and returned to basketball.

October 7

1871   Traveler and lecturer George Francis Train declared that his talk that night in Farwell Hall at Madison and Clark would be the last given there "A terrible calamity is impending over the city of Chicago," he said. The *Times* called him "The Prince of Blatherskites." Within hours, a fire swept a four-block area south of the business district. Several pieces of equipment were lost. The next morning, the *Tribune* reported that due to a lack of rain "a spark might set a fire which would sweep from end to end of the city."

1984   Walter Payton broke Jim Brown's all-time rushing record of 12,312. He broke it on a six-yard run in the 3rd quarter of a 20-7 Bears win over New Orleans at Soldier Field. Payton finished the day with 32 carries for 154 yards. It was the 59th time that Payton had gained over 100 yards in a game, which also broke a record established by Brown. Payton would retire with 16,726 yards.

1991   The $144 million Harold Washington Library Center at State Street and Congress Parkway was dedicated. The city's first library was housed in an old water tank that survived the Great Fire. The library on Michigan Avenue opened in 1897. But by the mid 70's the library had outgrown the building, and it was renovated into the Cultural Center. Mayor Harold Washington authorized construction of the new building in 1987.

1997   The Chicago City Council passed a resolution which absolved Mrs. O'Leary's cow of any blame for the Great Fire. Legend has it that the

Chicago 365

fire started when the cow kicked over a lantern that Mrs. O'Leary had brought out to the barn. A couple of reporters for the *Evening Journal* made up the cow story.

October 8

1871 Just before 9:00 pm, fire broke out in the cow barn behind the home of Patrick and Catherine O'Leary at 137 DeKoven Street. The Courthouse watchman thought the flames were coming from an area burned out in a large fire the night before, and struck the alarm for the wrong location. He soon realized his mistake and called down for the fire alarm operator to strike a different box. Operator William J. Brown refused to strike an alarm for the new location, claiming both boxes were nearby anyway and it would cause confusion. By the time fire crews sorted out the location, a brisk southwest wind was whipping the flames over the shanties in the next block – and towards the heart of the city.

1871 As the Chicago Fire began, another blaze raged 240 miles away. William Ogden, the first mayor of Chicago, had built a sawmill that turned Peshtigo, Wisconsin into a boomtown. For days, fires had been burning in the drought stricken woods around the town of 2,000. Suddenly, the winds turned the blazes into a tremendous firestorm that swept over 2,400 square miles. Over 1,100 people died, including 800 in Peshtigo, but the tragedy received little attention because of the Chicago Fire.

1846 Elbert Gary was born near Wheaton. The suburban Chicago lawyer worked as general counsel for Illinois Steel Company and then opened his own steel firm. In 1901, he helped combine eight companies into U.S. Steel. In 1909, U.S. Steel opened a massive plant along the southern edge of Lake Michigan. The town around the plant was named in Gary's honor.

1941 Jesse Louis Jackson was born in Greenville, South Carolina. In 1959, he came to the University of Illinois on a football scholarship and also attended the Chicago Theological Seminary. In 1965, he joined the Southern Christian Leadership Conference and became a top civil rights leader. He quit the SCLC in 1971 to form Operation PUSH (People United to Save Humanity). Jackson ran for president in 1984 and 1988.

1949 The Edens Expressway was dedicated. The important north-south highway (I-94) is named in honor of William G. Edens, a Chicago banker and early advocate for good roads. Edens sponsored the first state highway bond in 1918. The Edens Parkway, as it was known at the time, was built to connect the Skokie Highway (U.S. 41) with the proposed expressway now known as the Kennedy.

October 9

1871 Whipped by winds of up to 60 M.P.H., the fire jumped across the river and spread to the North Side as thousands fled. By 3 a.m., the waterworks were destroyed and all hope was lost. The wind finally eased and rain began falling about 11 p.m. About 300 people were dead, but only 120 bodies were recovered. A four-mile long, one-mile wide area was in ruins. Over 100,000 people were homeless and 17,500 buildings were destroyed. Damage was put at over $190 million. But a new Chicago would begin rising from the ashes almost immediately.

1873 Charles Rudolph Walgreen was born in Galesburg, Illinois. He lost part of a finger in a shoe factory accident, and his doctor convinced him to become a druggist. Charles bought Isaac Blood's store in Barnett's Hotel at Cottage Grove and Bowen in 1901 and owned seven stores by 1916. Walgreen's introduced the "malted milk" and were the first stores to have lunch counters with soda fountains.

1893 On the anniversary of the Great Fire, 716,881 people came to the Columbian Exposition for "Chicago Day." The figure shattered the record for attendance set at the Paris Exposition in 1889. The festivities included a huge "night pageant" in front of the Manufactures and Liberal Arts Building, the largest structure with a roof ever built. The celebrations included lavish ceremonies, parades, concerts and fireworks.

1924 The Grant Park Municipal Stadium opened. The firm of Holibird and Roche designed the stadium for the South Park Commission. A year later, the Chicago Gold Star Mothers requested that the stadium be named Soldier Field. It was officially dedicated during the Army-Navy game on November 27, 1926. A controversial $600 million reconstruction was completed in 2003.

Chicago 365

October 10

1848   For the first time, a locomotive arrived in Chicago. The *Pioneer* went into operation on the Galena and Chicago Union Railroad, constructed to connect Chicago with the lead mines at Galena. In 1850 the Galena and Chicago Union Railroad was completed as far as Elgin. From those modest beginnings, Chicago would grow into the largest railroad center in the world.

1871   As the city still smoldered, the Chamber of Commerce passed a resolution calling for rebuilding to begin at once. The Western Union office re-opened with boards laid over barrels serving as desks. A few days later, Jonathan Scammon broke ground for a store and office block. Real estate man William Kerfoot hastily built a small shack with a sign that read "All gone but wife, children and energy." That afternoon, the *Tribune* managed to publish an extra edition and a relief train arrived from St. Louis. Governor John Palmer sent three carloads of supplies and called for a special legislative session to approve funds for relief. President Grant contributed $1,000 of his own money.

1897   Elijah Poole was born in Georgia. He took the name Elijah Muhammad, and became an assistant to Wallace Fard, founder of the Nation of Islam. Fard disappeared mysteriously in 1934. Amid rumors of foul play, Muhammad came to Chicago and founded the Black Muslim movement. He declared that Fard was Allah and had chosen him to be God's messenger. Cassius Clay would become his most famous convert.

1944   An ad read, "$5,000 reward for the killers of Officer Lundy on Dec. 9, 1932. Call GRO-1758." Joe Majczek and Ted Marcinkiewicz were convicted of killing Lundy during a deli holdup. But the ad placed by Joe's mother led a pair of *Times* reporters to discover that the state's key witness ran a speakeasy in the deli, and lied on the stand. Joe and Ted were freed. The Jimmy Stewart film *Call Northside 777* was based on the story.

October 11

1883   The General Time Convention met at the Grand Pacific Hotel in Chicago and adopted "Standard Time" for trains beginning on November 18th. Solar time was used prior to 1883. When it was noon in Chicago, it was 11:50 in St. Louis and 12:24 in Cleveland. There was a minute difference between the east and west side of Chicago. The *Tribune* listed 38 local times in Wisconsin, 27 in Illinois, and 23 in Indiana.

1926   Hymie Weiss walked towards his office above Schofield's flower shop, where Dion O'Bannion was killed in 1924. As the man who coined the phrase "Take him for a ride" passed Holy Name Cathedral, machine guns opened up from a rooming house at 740 N. State. The bullets nearly wiped out the inscription on the Cathedral's cornerstone, "At the name of Jesus every knee should bow- those that are in heaven and on earth." Weiss fell dead. The bullet holes on the church are hidden behind a remodeled stairway today.

1975   William Jefferson Clinton, age 29, and 27-year-old Hillary Rodham were married in Fayetteville, Arkansas. Hillary was born in Chicago, the oldest of three children of Hugh and Dorothy Rodham. She grew up in suburban Park Ridge and graduated from Wellesley in 1969. Hillary studied law at Yale, where she met the future president.

1976   Jane Pauley was named to succeed Barbara Walters on NBC's "Today." At age 24 in 1975, Pauley became the first woman to co-anchor a regular weeknight newscast when she was teamed with Floyd Kalber on WMAQ. A *Tribune* reporter visited Pauley at WISH in Indianapolis and blasted her. He wrote, "This future dispenser of news to countless Chicagoans knows virtually nothing about Chicago."

October 12

1868   The new Field, Lieter and Company store on State Street opened. Marshall Field started in the dry goods business in 1856. Field and Levi Leiter bought Potter Palmer's dry goods business on Lake Street in 1865. Lake was the heart of the city. But the new "marble palace" helped turn State Street into "that great street." Field died in 1906, just as work began on a larger store, with a massive clock and Tiffany glass dome.

1907   The Cubs clinched the World Championship with a 2-0 win in Game Five over the Tigers in Detroit. Mordecai "Three Fingers" Brown tossed the shutout. The Cubs were becoming baseball's first "dynasty," appearing in the World Series for the second season in a row.

1918   The flu epidemic held Chicago in its grip. In eight weeks, over 8,500 people died. Theaters, dance halls, pool halls and bowling alleys were closed. Anyone caught spitting in public was arrested. Businesses, churches and schools remained open because of the war effort and to help people stay positive. Public funerals were banned and private funerals were limited to ten people, including the undertaker.

1986   Walter Payton rushed for 76 yards and caught a pass for 30 more in the Bears 20-7 win over the Houston Oilers, to become the first NFL player to rack up over 20,000 total yards from scrimmage. When Payton retired in 1987, he had amassed 21,803 yards, with 16,726 running, 4,538 receiving and 539 on kickoff returns.

October 13

1917   Burr Tillstrom was born in Chicago. He worked for the park district puppet theater and made his own puppets after work. In 1936, Russian ballerina Tamara Toumanova dubbed one "Kukla," Russian for doll. During the 1939 World's Fair, his "Kuklapolitans" demonstrated the new medium of television. Kukla, Fran Allison and Ollie made their debut on WBKB on October 13, 1947 and went national on NBC in 1948.

1983   The cellular revolution began in Chicago as Ameritech started the first commercial cellular service in the U.S. Robert Barnett, an Illinois Bell executive, placed the first call to Alexander Graham Bell's grandnephew. David Meilahn was the first customer. The Motorola phones cost around $3,000 and about $200 per month! In 1997, Meilahn donated his clunky 1983 cell phone to the Museum of Science and Industry.

1992   His mother was holding his hand as seven-year-old Dantrell Davis walked to school from the Cabrini-Green Housing Project. A stray shot from a gang member's assault weapon slammed into the boy's head and Dantrell became one of 61 children killed in Chicago that year. Anthony Garrett, who had been firing from a 10th story window at rival gang members below, was sentenced to 100 years in prison.

1994   Two boys, ages ten and eleven, dropped five-year-old Eric Morse from the 14th floor of a vacant apartment in the Ida B. Wells complex. The boys killed Eric because he had refused to steal candy for them. The incident created outrage across the country, and led to calls for reform of the state's juvenile justice system. Lawmakers lowered the age at which children can be incarcerated for murder from 13 to 10.

October 14

1906   Three Finger Brown got the win as the White Sox took Game Six, and won the all-Chicago World Series. The Sox were helped out in their 8-3 victory when a South Side policeman kicked Wildfire Schulte of the Cubs as he tried to snag a fly ball. The ball fell in for a double.

1908   The Cubs clinched the 1908 World Series, beating the Tigers in Game Five 2-0. Just 6,210 fans attended the final game in Detroit, the smallest crowd in World Series history. The Cubs became the first team to appear in the World Series three times in a row.

1925   Cook County Sheriff Peter M. Hoffman was sentenced to 30 days in jail and fined $2,500 for "outrageous flouting of the processes of this court." Hoffman bribed the warden to arrange for his favorite beer runners to take "vacations" from the Cook County Jail. The utterly corrupt and inept Hoffman was the model for the sheriff character in *The Front Page*.

1945   The Chicago Cardinals beat the cross-town rival Bears, 16-7, to end the longest losing streak in NFL history. The Cards had lost 29 in a row going into the game. Ten of the losses came in 1944, when they played as Card-Pitt in a merger with the Pittsburgh Steelers because of the World War II manpower shortage.

October 15

1928   The first televised wedding took place at a radio station in Des Plaines. The reverend Gustave A. Klenle of St. Luke's Evangelical Church married Cora Dennison and James Fowlkes of Kansas City. In June of the same year, Ulysses S. Sanabria had set up Chcago's first television station. It used WCFL radio to broadcast pictures and WIBO to transmit the sound.

Chicago 365

1966 The Chicago Bulls won their first game, downing the St. Louis Hawks 104-97. There were two pro teams that played in Chicago before the Bulls. The Stags were charter members of the Basketball Association of America, which became the NBA. The team folded in 1950. The Packers played here for two seasons beginning in 1961, but moved to Baltimore and eventually became the Washington Bullets.

1959 "The Untouchables" premiered on ABC. Robert Stack starred as Eliot Ness. The Italian community blasted the show for using stereotypes and the Capone family sued producer Desi Arnaz, who was once a classmate and a friend of Capone's son. The FBI said the show gave Ness too much credit. It did include some of the earliest appearances by actors such as Charles Bronson, Leonard Nimoy and Robert Redford.

October 16

1909 Glenn Curtiss made the first airplane flight in the Chicago area. He soared 60 feet over the Hawthorne Race Track in Cicero. The next day, he made two more flights, reaching an altitude of 100 feet. Curtiss was the first person to receive a U.S. pilot's license. He was the first to manufacture and sell a commercial aircraft and made the first aircraft capable of landing or taking off from a ship at sea.

1943 Mayor Edward Kelly cut the ribbon to open Chicago's first Subway. Construction of the 4.9 mile State Street Subway took nearly five years and cost $34 million. The subway included modern amenities such as fluorescent lights, "moving stairs," (escalators) and soundproof phone booths.

1955 Anton Schuessler, his brother John and their friend Robert Peterson disappeared after the suburban boys visited the city. Their bodies were found in a ditch two days later. Inter agency squabbling left the crime unsolved. Then a federal informant in the 1977 disappearance of Helen Voorhees Brach said Kenneth Hansen bragged about the murders to his male sex partners. Hansen was convicted in 1995 and in a 2002 retrial.

1955 The first "Ann Landers" column by Eppie Lederer appeared in the *Sun-Times*. The housewife won a competition to choose a successor to the paper's original Ann Landers, a nurse whose real name was Ruth Crowley. Lederer moved to the *Tribune* in 1987 and died on June 22, 2002. Her twin sister, Pauline Esther Freidman, wrote a copycat column called "Dear Abby."

October 17

1918   The great influenza epidemic peaked in Chicago on "Black Thursday." About 500 people died and 1,200 more caught the disease in a 24-hour period. Hotels served as hospitals, the city ran out of hearses and trolley cars draped in black were pressed into service to haul bodies. Newspapers reported that the crime rate had dropped by 43%. The disease killed over 8,500 people in just eight weeks.

1931   After deliberating for nine hours, a jury found Al Capone guilty of five counts of failing to file tax returns. A week later, Judge James H. Wilkerson sentenced Capone to eleven years, $50,000 in fines and court costs of another $30,000. Capone was sent to the Cook County Jail to await a trip to a federal penitentiary. Initially, Capone lived like a king at the Atlanta prison. But in August 1934, he was sent to Alcatraz.

1948   George Wendt was born in Chicago. His grandfather was Tom Howard, a photographer for the *Tribune* who took the famous photo of Ruth Snyder in the electric chair at Sing Sing. Wendt played Norm Peterson on "Cheers." The character also appeared on "Wings," "St. Elsewhere," "The Tortellis" and "Frazier." It was estimated that Norm's bar tab at Cheers reached $64,218 after eleven seasons.

2003   Six people died as a fire sent choking smoke into the hallways and stairwells of the 35-story Cook County Administration Building. Some of the victims were not found until after the fire was out. A state commission would blame the fire department for several errors, including mishandling 911 calls and attacking the blaze from the wrong stairwell. The report also cited building management for locking the stairwells.

October 18

1892   The first long-distance telephone line between Chicago and New York opened. Alexander Graham Bell placed a call to the Chicago Mayor

Chicago 365

Carter Harrison Senior. The circuit could only handle one call at a time. Callers were charged $9 for the first five minutes.

1924 Harold "Red" Grange of the University of Illinois put on the greatest performance in football history as the Illini stunned heavily favored Michigan. Grange scored four touchdowns in the first 12 minutes of the game. In the second half, he rushed for a TD and threw a pass for his sixth. Michigan had only allowed four TDs in two seasons. The "Galloping Ghost" single-handedly turned college football into a big time sport.

1938 A man who would change the look of the city arrived in Chicago. Ludwig Mies van der Rohe emigrated from Nazi Germany, where he headed the Bauhaus School of design. Mies believed "less is more." The high-rise apartments at 860 and 880 Lake Shore Drive were his first Chicago designs. They ushered in the modern age of steel and glass towers with little ornamentation.

1939 Mike Ditka was born in Carnegie, Pennsylvania. The All American from the University of Pittsburgh was the top draft pick for the Bears in 1961. He was one of the first tight ends to make frequent pass receptions and was the 1961 Rookie of the Year. He coached the Bears for 11 years, leading them to a Super Bowl in 1985. In 2004, he was mentioned as a possible candidate for Senate, but turned down the offer.

October 19

1857 Twenty-three people died in a fire that broke out in a whorehouse and burned much of business district around Lake and South Water Streets. A mass funeral was held for the victims and the Reverend W.W. King called the fire "a slight breaking out of volcanic fires burning beneath our feet," and condemned "The complicity between authority and vice and crime by which our city is cursed and degraded."

1897 George Pullman died. The man who invented the sleeping car was condemned for exploiting workers living in his company town of Pullman. His greed led to a violent strike in 1894. To keep former employees from desecrating the grave at Graceland Cemetery, he was buried in a lead-lined casket in an eight-feet deep pit lined with concrete. The grave was covered with more concrete, asphalt and steel rails.

Chicago 365

1932   Robert Reed was born John Robert Rietz in Highland Park. Rietz was a serious Shakespearean actor, who despised his role as Mike Brady on "The Brady Bunch." He frequently argued with creator and producer Sherwood Schwartz and was written out of the final episode when he complained about the script where Greg's hair turned orange due to cheap hair tonic. Reed died of cancer and AIDS in 1992.

1946   Michael "Hinky Dink" Kenna died in Chicago. Kenna was an alderman from 1897 until 1923. The corrupt "Hinky Dink" and "Bathhouse John" Coughlin ruled the Levee red light district. They threw annual balls at the Coliseum, bringing together criminals, businessmen and politicians to line their pockets. The depravity and near riots at the First Ward Balls forced Mayor Fred Busse to halt them in 1909.

1980   Stanislav Gvoth Mikita became the first player ever to have his number retired by the Blackhawks. Number 21 played 22 seasons for the Hawks, becoming the first player in hockey history to win the Hart, the Ross, and the Lady Byng Trophy in the same season. Mikita was inducted into the Hockey Hall of Fame in 1983.

October 20

1926   Wacker Drive opened. Mayor William Dever called the $8 million two level roadway "The greatest improvement of its kind in world history." It was named for Charles H. Wacker, chairman of the Chicago Plan Commission, who supported Daniel Burnham's original idea. Wacker runs north, south, east, and west, connecting. seven major north/south streets and nine east/west streets.

1930   WGN premiered a show called "Painted Dreams," the very first soap opera. Irna Phillips created, wrote and acted in the program. It ran until 1932 when Phillips left WGN. At WMAQ, she would create several programs, including "The Guiding Light," which came to television in 1952. Her other TV soap creations include "As the World Turns," "Another World" and "Days of Our Lives."

1932   William Christopher was born in Evanston. The graduate of New Trier High School was originally supposed to make occasional appearances on "M*A*S*H" as Father Mulcahy. But his performance convinced the

Chicago 365

producers to make the character a regular. After the 4077th folded its tents for good, Christopher appeared with Harry Morgan and Jamie Farr in the forgettable "After MASH."

1974 Thieves made off with $4.3 million from the Purolator warehouse at LaSalle and Huron Streets, the largest cash heist in U.S. history. Disgruntled employee Ralph Marrera gave the crooks the combinations. They tried to burn the remaining millions, but the flames died when the vault doors closed. The FBI found $2.2 million buried under a home owned by Marrera's grandmother, but $1.2 million was never recovered.

October 21

1891 Leo Burnett was born in St. Johns, Michigan. Burnett founded an ad agency in Chicago in 1933 and was told he would soon be out on the street selling apples. His agency went on the create characters such as The Jolly Green Giant, Charlie Tuna, the Pillsbury Doughboy, Tony the Tiger, and Morris the Cat. Burnett always kept apples around the office for employees to munch on as a reminder of how he started out.

1892 The Columbian Exposition grounds in Jackson Park were dedicated. Vice President Levi Morton took part in the ceremonies at the Manufacturers and Liberal Arts Building. Officials planned to provide lunch for the 70,000 people expected to attend, but twice that many showed up. The ceremonies included one of the earliest public recitations of the Pledge of Allegiance, written just a few months earlier by Francis J. Bellamy.

1912 Sir Georg Solti was born in Budapest, Hungary. Solti was performing piano concerts by the age of 13 and rose to conductor of the Budapest Opera. After fleeing the Nazis, he worked all over Europe, including at the Royal Opera Covent Garden in London. Solti conducted of the Chicago Symphony from 1969 until 1991. He brought worldwide recognition to the symphony, but never actually lived in Chicago.

1946 The University of Illinois opened its two-year branch campus on the Navy Pier. About 4,000 students were enrolled on the first day. "Harvard on the Rocks" provided educational opportunities for thousands of returning soldiers. In 1965, the University of Illinois moved to the new Circle Campus. At that time, the future looked bleak for Navy Pier.

Chicago 365

October 22

1892   The University of Chicago and Northwestern University squared off in the first intercollegiate football game. The game was played at the 39th Street Grounds, future home of the White Sox, and ended in a 0-0 tie. Alonzo Stagg coached the University of Chicago team and played in the game.

1895   Ignaz Schwinn and his partner Adolph Arnold incorporated Arnold Schwinn and Company. They began building bikes in a rented factory at Lake and Peoria Streets. The first Schwinn was the single speed "Roadster" model, which weighed 191 pounds. The firm went on to build classic models such as the "Stingray" and the "Black Phantom." Schwinn went bankrupt in 1993 and Pacific Cycle bought the brands in 2001.

1963   Over 200,000 black students boycotted classes on "Freedom Day." Thousands marched on City Hall to protest against discrimination symbolized by the "Willis Wagons," portable trailers used as classrooms. Racist school superintendent Benjamin Willis set up the trailers instead of building new schools in black neighborhoods. In 1965, the city would admit running a segregated school system.

2001   The Enron Corporation announced that the Securities and Exchange Commission was investigating the firm's accounting practices. David Duncan, the Arthur Andersen partner in charge of the Enron account, ordered employees in London, Portland and headquarters in Chicago to shred thousands of Enron related documents. After 89 years in the accounting business, Arthur Andersen was ruined.

October 23

1835   Adlai Ewing Stevenson was born. He was a Representative from Illinois and vice-president from 1893 to 1897. He favored "free silver," when the rich wanted U.S. currency based on gold. When Grover Cleveland had surgery it was kept secret, for fear businessmen would panic at the thought of a Stevenson presidency. His grandson was a great statesman and the Democratic presidential nominee in 1952 and 1956.

1930   As Joseph Aiello left his apartment at 205 North Kolmar, a machine gun blasted him from an apartment building across the street. He staggered around the corner into a hail of bullets coming from another building and died with 59 slugs in him. Aiello led an Italian gang that was aligned with Bugs Moran against Al Capone. He once offered a chef $10,000 to put acid in Capone's soup.

1942 Michael Crichton was born in Chicago. He attended medical school at Harvard, but quit to become a writer. Many of his novels have been based on the world of medicine. Chrichton created the critically acclaimed TV show "E.R.," set at the fictitious County General Hospital in Chicago. His best-selling novels include *The Andromeda Strain*, *Rising Sun*, *Disclosure*, *Airframe*, and *Timeline*.

1975 David Mamet's classic *American Buffalo* premiered at the Goodman Theater. Mamet promised theater management that the play would win the Pulitzer Prize for Drama. J.J. Johnson, William H. Macy and Bernard Erhard starred in the original production as three thugs plotting to steal a coin collection. Mamet waited two years for his Pulitzer. *American Buffalo* brought national acclaim to the Chicago theater scene.

October 24

1911 Mayor Carter Harrison Junior shut down the most lavish brothel in the nation. Ada and Minnie Everleigh's club was famous for opulent parlors and paying protection money to police and politicians. When the Everleigh sisters published an advertising brochure, Carter had seen enough. The sisters left with a million dollars and ended their days under assumed names in New York. The Hilliard Homes stands on the site today.

1913 Samuel Eberly Gross died in a Battle Creek sanatorium. Gross was a flamboyant real estate developer who built thousands of homes for working class buyers. Alta Vista Terrace is his one of his developments and he founded Grossdale, now Brookfield. But Gross is best remembered for claiming Edmund Rostand stole *Cyrano De Bergerac* from his *Merchant of Cornville*. Rostand said, "There are big noses everywhere."

1959 "Playboy's Penthouse" premiered. The first Playboy TV show was syndicated around the country from the studious of WBKB. The very first show featured an appearance by controversial comedian Lenny Bruce. "Playboy's Penthouse" ran for two seasons and returned briefly in

Chicago 365

1963. The show resembled a party at a bachelor pad with sophisticated guests, including beat poets and legendary jazz performers.

1964 The Southwest Expressway opened, a 15.5 mile highway connecting the Dan Ryan Expressway with U.S. 66 at the DuPage County line. On September 1, 1965, it was renamed in honor of former governor and U.N. ambassador Adlai Stevenson. In 1966, the highway was extended east from the Dan Ryan to Lakeshore Drive.

October 25

1674 James Marquette left from Green Bay to establish a mission in Illinois. On December 4, an ailing Marquette reached the frozen Chicago River. After traveling about four miles down the South Branch, the Jesuit missionary decided he could go no further until spring. Marquette and his two attendants moved into a fur trader's log cabin, the first structure erected by white men in Chicago.

1836 "Long John" Wentworth arrived in Chicago. Wentworth was six feet six inches tall and drank a pint of whiskey every day. He became publisher of the *Democrat*, served six terms in the U.S. House and two terms as mayor. One of his campaign speeches was succinct, "You damn fools...you can either vote for me or you can go to hell." Wentworth Avenue was named in his honor while "Long John" was still alive.

1995 A school bus was struck by an express commuter train in Fox River Grove. Seven children were killed and 30 were injured. Metra commuter train #624, traveling toward Chicago at about 50 MPH, plowed into the rear of the bus carrying students to Cary Grove High School. The accident happened at a marked train crossing at the intersection of U.S. Route 14 and Algonquin Road.

October 26

1921 Chicago's most revered movie palace opened at 175 North State Street. George Rapp called the Chicago Theater a "celestial city." The opening night program included *The Sign in the Door*, starring Norma Talmadge, a stage show with Buster Keaton and with Jesse Crawford on the Wurlitzer organ. The faded landmark narrowly escaped demolition in the 1970's. The restored theater re-opened on September 10, 1986.

Chicago 365

1946 Pat Sajak was born in Chicago. Pat started out as a guest teen D.J. on the Dick Biondi show on WLS. In 1969-70 he worked on AFVN Saigon, yelling "Good Morning, Vietnam!" He worked as at a series of small stations and as a hotel desk clerk before becoming a weatherman in Los Angeles. Merv Griffin hired him to replace Chuck Woolery as the host of "Wheel of Fortune" in 1981.

1947 Hillary Diane Rodham was born. She grew up in Park Ridge and met Bill Clinton while attending law school at Yale. They were married in 1975. She was blasted for keeping her maiden name during his first term as governor of Arkansas. As First Lady, she faced the Whitewater investigation and stuck by her husband during the Monica Lewinsky scandal. In 2000, she was elected as the U.S. Senator from New York.

1984 Michael Jordan played in his first game for the Chicago Bulls. He scored 16 points and the Bulls beat the Washington Bullets on opening night 109-93. During his first season, Jordan averaged 28.2 points per game and won the Rookie of the Year honors, leading the Bulls to the playoffs for the first time in four years.

October 27

1813 Joseph Glidden was born in New Hampshire. In 1873, the DeKalb farmer twisted two strands of wire around a short piece, or barb, to make fencing. He sold his patent for $60,000 and a 25-cent royalty of every 100 pounds sold. His invention changed the west forever and made him a rich man. Glidden donated the land for a new state normal school, which later became Northern Illinois University.

1884 Wilbur F. Storey died. The "Father of Yellow Journalism" came to Chicago 1861 and bought the foundering *Times*. Declaring that a newspaper's duty is to "print the news and raise hell," he told his war correspondents to "telegraph fully all news and when there is no news send rumors." Storey believed that municipal services, including schools, should be turned over to private contractors.

1941 The *Tribune* printed an editorial that said there was little chance of war with Japan. It included the line, "She cannot attack us. That is a military impossibility. Even our base at Hawaii is beyond the effective striking power of her fleet."

1961   Professional basketball returned to Chicago after an eleven year absence. Jack Brickhouse and Lou Boudreau had the call on WGN-TV as the Chicago Packers lost to the St. Louis Hawks, 117-106. The team was renamed the Zephyrs in 1962. In 1963, the team moved to Baltimore and became the Bullets, later the Washington Bullets.

October 28

1871   The *Tribune* called on the unemployed of New York to come to Chicago. The article said there was plenty of work at up to $5 per day for tradesmen willing to work through a Chicago winter. William Bross, part owner of the *Tribune* and a Lieutenant Governor, went on a lecture tour to lure workers. He may have wanted to help his city, or the anti-union Bross may have hoped to flood the market and keep wages down.

1893   Mayor Carter Harrison addressed a group of mayors in town for the final day of the Columbian Exposition. Harrison said he expected to live another 50 years to see Chicago approach London in importance. The city's first five-term mayor returned to his mansion at Ashland Avenue and Jackson Boulevard, where a servant let in a man demanding to see him. Patrick Eugene Prendergast was a lunatic, who believed Harrison owed him a cabinet position. He pulled out a six-shooter, fired three times, and Harrison fell mortally wounded. His son, Carter Harrison II, would also serve five terms as mayor.

1911   President William Howard Taft dedicated the Great Lakes Naval Training Center. The original 39 buildings took six years to construct, and the first recruits had arrived on July 3. Today, 50,000 recruits pass through Great Lakes RTC annually with an estimated 15,000 recruits at the installation at one time. The base now consists of 1,153 buildings on 1,628 acres. It is the U.S. Navy's third largest base.

1944   Dennis Franz Schlacta was born in Maywood. Franz worked on the Chicago theater circuit after serving in Vietnam. His movie debut came in 1978's *A Wedding.* In 1983, Steven Bochco offered him the part of Norman Buntz in "Hill Street Blues." He starred briefly in the spin-off "Beverly Hills Buntz" before winning the role of Andy Sipowitz on "N.Y.P.D. Blue" in 1993.

Chicago 365

1929 "Black Tuesday" brought the Roaring 20's to a halt. Two days later, the *Tribune* declared that the stock market scare was over. Over 750,000 people were out of work in Chicago by 1932. The 160,000 families receiving aid overwhelmed public and private agencies. Even Al Capone set up a soup kitchen. Just 51 of the city's 228 banks remained open and thousands camped out at the "Hoover Hotel," Lower Wacker Drive.

1954 It was reminiscent of the night John Dillinger was gunned down outside the Biograph Theater. Gus Amadeo had murdered officer Charles Annerino. Lieutenant Frank Pape, who had killed at least nine bad guys, forced a woman Amadeo had dated to lure him into the deadly ambush at Clark and Berwyn. Pape was known as "The Fearless Man," and inspired Lee Marvin's character on the TV show "M-Squad."

1955 Mayor Richard J. Daley inaugurated regular passenger service at the site once known as Orchard Place Airport. (Which is why your baggage tags still read "ORD" today) It was home to a C-54 factory during World War Two and was named in honor of air ace Edward O'Hare in 1946. Midway was overcrowded by then, but passenger service at O'Hare couldn't start until a new terminal was built.

1979 A nine-block long section of State Street, from Wacker Drive to the Congress Expressway, was dedicated as a "transit way." The $17 million project converted the street into a pedestrian mall, with a road for buses. In 1996, it took $24.5 million to put it all back and allow automobile traffic again. The project included Art Deco designs for the subway stations and vintage lamppost designs.

October 30

1936 Lorado Taft died in Chicago. He was an influential sculptor and educator known for monumental works. The *Fountain of Time*, located at the west end of the Midway Plaisance at Washington Park, is his masterpiece. The 110-foot long sculpture took 14 years to construct. It includes 100 figures, including a self-portrait of Taft, passing a figure representing Time across the water.

1939   Grace Wing, better known as Grace Slick, was born in Evanston. She started out as a model, before joining the group the Great Society in 1965. In October 1966, she replaced Signe Anderson in the pioneer psychedelic group the Jefferson Airplane. Slick became known for her drug use and sexual escapades. She formed Jefferson Starship in 1974. The group scored more hits in the 80's under the name Starship.

1972   During the morning rush, a bi-level Illinois Central Gulf commuter train equipped with a new type of brake system overshot the 27th Street Station and began to back up. A fast moving single level train slammed into it from behind. The accident killed 45 people and injured over 300. The engineer who overshot the station was new to the route and both engineers apparently didn't follow or didn't understand procedures.

October 31

1893   The "White City" fell silent as the World's Columbian Exposition closed. Out of the more than 200 buildings in Jackson Park that made up the exposition, only one remains. The Palace of Fine Arts was originally built out of plaster of Paris. It was rebuilt with stone in the late 1920's and is now the Museum of Science and Industry. The world's first Ferris Wheel was moved to 2643 North Clark Street in 1895. But an amusement park there failed, and it was moved to St. Louis for the Louisiana Purchase Exposition of 1904. The wheel was dynamited and sold for scrap in 1906.

1926   Harry Houdini died of appendicitis after being punched in the stomach. At age 19, he performed with his brother at the Columbian Exposition. On another visit, a Chicago Police Sergeant tricked Houdini. He jammed the handcuff locks so they could not be opened. After that, the magician always carefully inspected his cuffs. On another visit, Houdini exposed several so-called mind readers and mediums as frauds.

1934   The Century of Progress Exposition closed for good. The exposition was originally intended to run from May until November of 1933. It was extended to pay off the debts. Over 38 million people visited the fair. Balbo's Column, across from Soldier Field, is the only structure still standing on the original site. It came from the ruins of a Roman temple and honors fascist General Italo Balbo's trans-Atlantic flight to Chicago in 1933.

Chicago 365

1988 Sears announced a major restructuring. The company would sell the Sears Tower and buy back 40 million shares of stock at a cost of $1.6 billion. That added up to about ten percent of the total stock. The Sears tower was the company's most visible asset, but it had turned into an expensive white elephant.

Chicago 365

NOVEMBER

November 1

1945 John H. Johnson published the first issue of *Ebony* magazine. The former manager of the DuSable High School student newspaper founded *Negro Digest* in 1942. That magazine grew into *Ebony*, a "picture magazine for blacks." On November 1, 1951, Johnson published the first issue of *Jet*, a pocket sized magazine.

1950 The first expressway in the Chicago area opened. The Calumet Expressway and Tri-State Highway ran five miles between 159th Street and the Indiana State line. The highway is now part of the Bishop Ford and Kingery Expressways. Bishop Ford was the long time pastor of St. Paul's Church. Robert Kingery was the director of the Illinois Public Works Department.

1983 Australian media baron Rupert Murdoch bought the *Sun-Times*. After 34 years, columnist Mike Royko left the paper and moved to the *Tribune*, saying that no self-respecting fish would be wrapped in a paper owned by "The Alien." In 1986, Murdoch bought Channel 32 and a federal law against owning a newspaper and TV station in the same market forced him to sell the paper.

1999 Bears Hall of Fame running back Walter Payton died at his home in Barrington at the age of 45. The leading rusher in NFL history died of bile duct cancer, discovered while he was being treated for a rare liver disease. A few days after "Sweetness" died, 20,000 fans filled Soldier Field for a memorial service. The Bears would rename the Halas Hall indoor facility in his honor.

November 2

1896 The *Tribune* reported that Mrs. Harold Peck of Chicago had requested a portrait of her daughter painted by James McNeil Whistler be sent from London. Whistler said, "Allow my masterpiece to go to such a place as Chicago? Never! And my reputation and dignity of the artistic production? Never!" The painting stayed in London.

1914 The University of Chicago trustees voted to change the name of

Chicago 365

Marshall Field to Stagg Field. Amos Alonzo Stagg helped develop the modern game of football at the University and would remain an active football coach until he was 98. On December 2, 1942, a group of scientists achieved the first controlled release of nuclear energy in a squash court underneath the west stands at Stagg Field.

1925   The morality of today's youth was a hot topic in Chicago. Mrs. Charles E. Merriam, President of the Film Councils of America said, "Films are breaking down the standards of civilization and have become a serious threat to the moral standard of our youths." A few days earlier, evangelist Billy Sunday blamed the "looseness" on the automobile. Sunday said, "We've put the red light district on wheels."

1948   Harry S Truman upset Thomas Dewey in the presidential election. The pollsters gave Truman no chance and the *Tribune* had called him a "nincompoop." A printer's strike forced the *Tribune* to go to press before all the results were in, and the first edition headline blared "DEWEY DEFEATS TRUMAN." When Truman's train pulled in to St. Louis, someone handed him copy. He beamed and held it up for the photographers.

November 3

1908   Bronislav Nagurski was born in Rainy River, Ontario. "Bronco" played for the Bears from 1930 until 1937 and became the symbol of power football. He quit to become a pro wrestler when the team refused to pay him $6,500 for the 1938 season. Bronco returned to the Bears briefly in 1943 and scored the touchdown that clinched the NFL title. Nagurski was named a charter member of the Hall of Fame in 1963.

1929   Jack L. Cooper became the first African-American radio personality. His "The All Negro Hour" aired on WSBC until 1935. Cooper later began playing records over the air, using a home phonograph. He may have been the very first disc jockey. He certainly was the first African-American D.J. His ten shows a week reportedly reached half of all the blacks in Chicago.

1942   The Congress of Racial Equality, or CORE, was organized in Chicago. White University of Chicago student George Houser and black student James Farmer originally served as co-leaders of the group, which advocated nonviolent action. The CORE "sit-in" at Stoner's Restaurant in The Loop was the first protest of its kind in the U.S. CORE was at the forefront of the civil rights protests in the 1960's.

1992 Carol Moseley-Braun became the first African American woman elected to the U.S. Senate. The graduate of Chicago public schools and University of Chicago once worked as a prosecutor in the Office of the U.S. Attorney. She served in the Illinois House from 1978 to 1988 and became Cook County Recorder of Deeds. Moseley-Braun lost her bid for re-election to the Senate in 1998 and ran for president in 2004.

November 4

1813 William Bross was born in Sussex County, New Jersey. Bross was editor of the *Democratic Press*, which merged with the *Tribune* in 1858. He raised a regiment during the Civil War and exposed the Confederate plot to release the prisoners of Camp Douglas and burn the city. He also became Lieutenant Governor of Illinois. But Bross is best remembered for his work to promote the city, especially after the Great Fire.

1929 The Civic Opera House opened with a performance of *Aida*. Utility magnate Samuel Insull built the opera house. He combined the theater with offices on the upper floors, in order to make the opera company self-sufficient. The opera house resembles a throne, and is built facing west. Reportedly the architect had been rejected in New York and wanted the building to face away from the Big Apple.

1939 There was something new at the 40th National Automotive show in Chicago. Packard displayed the first automobile in history to be equipped with factory air conditioning as an option. The cooling coil took up the entire trunk and the price put it out of the reach of most car owners. Nash introduced the "Weather Eye," the first mass-market auto air conditioner, in 1954.

1960 Chicago owned the Most Valuable Player Awards in both leagues. Ernie Banks won his second consecutive National League MVP. Nellie Fox of the pennant winning White Sox edged out teammates Luis Aparicio and Early Wynn for the AL honor.

Chicago 365

November 5

1855 Northwestern University opened in a three-story framed building at Hinman and Davis Streets. The charter prohibited the sale of liquor within four miles of the university. That policy would remain in effect until 1971. Four students were awarded degrees at the first commencement.

1855 Eugene Debs was born in Terre Haute, Indiana. Debs spent a lifetime fighting for the rights of the working class, blacks, women and children. He was a five time Socialist candidate for president. Debs founded the American Railway Union, which refused to handle Pullman cars during the 1894 strike. Debs was jailed for obstructing the mails. He also spent three years in jail for speaking out against the war in 1918.

1960 The entire 16-mile, $237 million Northwest Expressway opened. The first section of the link between the Congress Expressway (later the Eisenhower) and O'Hare Airport had opened in 1958. The highway featured reversible lanes, which could be switched to accommodate inbound traffic during the morning rush and outbound during the evening. It was renamed in honor of John F. Kennedy on November 30, 1963.

1968 The Chicago Eight became the Chicago Seven. Judge Julius Hoffman ordered a separate trial for Bobby Seale, one of the defendants charged with inciting the 1968 riots. Seale continually disrupted the trial by demanding to choose his own attorney. At first, Hoffman ordered Seale bound and gagged in the courtroom. Seale would be sentenced to four years in prison for contempt, but the conviction was later thrown out.

November 6

1849 The County Board created a 36 square mile township bounded by today's Western, North, Harlem Avenues and Pershing Road. In 1857, it was named for Roman statesman Marcus Tullius Cicero. Chicago annexed ½ of the town in 1889. Berwyn and Oak Park were also formed from Cicero. Cicero was home to Al Capone, Ernest Hemingway and the huge Western Electric Hawthorne Works.

1955 The future first lady of California was born in Chicago. Maria Shriver is the daughter of Sargent Shriver and Eunice Kennedy Shriver, sister of John and Robert Kennedy. She began her career at KYW in Philadelphia in 1977. In 1983, she became a reporter for CBS and co-anchor of the "CBS Morning News." Shriver came to NBC in 1986. She married Arnold Schwarzenegger in May 1986.

1960   The "Ed Sullivan Show" came to Chicago. The show featured Charlton Heston from Northwestern University, reciting the Carl Sandburg poem *Chicago*. Chicago natives Mahalia Jackson, Benny Goodman, and Bob Newhart all performed, along with Edgar Bergen and Charlie McCarthy. The show also featured footage of sites such as O'Hare Airport, Hull House and the Stock Yards.

1993   The Bulls played their first game in the United Center, losing to the Miami Heat, 95-71. B.J. Armstrong scored the first Bull basket in the new building. Jerry Reinsdorf, owner of the Bulls, and William Wirtz, owner of the Blackhawks, formed a partnership in 1988 to build the arena to replace Chicago Stadium.

November 7

1833   Chicago adopted its first municipal code. The code specified that "every owner of any hog, sow or pig, found running at large" would be fined $2. It made it illegal to "run any horse, mare, gelding, mule or ass" through the streets. Miscreants who removed planks or lumber for the bridges faced a fine of $5. An "indecent exhibition of any stallion" also resulted in a fine.

1864   The Rebels planned to free 8,000 prisoners at Camp Douglas, burn the city, rob the banks, send the prisoners to stuff the ballot boxes to defeat Abraham Lincoln and set up a Northwestern Confederacy. But the Copperheads didn't know one of their own was a double agent. John T. Shanks exposed the plot, and the leaders were rounded up that morning. The election went on, with federal troops guarding the polls.

1890   America's most famous conductor announced he would leave the New York Philharmonic for the new Chicago Symphony Orchestra. Theodore Thomas arrived amid much fanfare but complained about the acoustics in the Auditorium. He wouldn't perform lighter fare for the masses and quit as musical director of the Columbian Exposition because audiences preferred the Midway instead of his highbrow concerts.

Chicago 365

1965 The Pillsbury Dough Boy made his debut, popping out of a can in a commercial for crescent rolls. Rudy Perz, a copywriter for the Leo Burnett Advertising Agency of Chicago came up with the idea for "Poppin' Fresh." Perz first planned to animate the doughboy. But he saw stop-action photography used for the credits of "The Dinah Shore Show" and changed his mind.

November 8

1897 The Illinois Supreme Court ruled in a case brought by Montgomery Ward, and ordered the lakefront cleared of structures except for the Art Institute. In 1836, the land was designated as "Public ground - a common to remain forever open, clear, and free of any buildings, or other obstruction, whatever." Ward said he fought to keep the land "for the poor people of Chicago, not for the millionaires."

1900 The first book by a Chicago newspaperman was condemned for its grim realism. Theodore Drieser's *Sister Carrie* told the tale of Carrie Meeber, a working girl who became a success because of an affair, instead of being punished for her sins. Doubleday Publishing tried to squelch the book and it sold just 500 copies initially. But *Sister Carrie* would inspire H.L. Mencken, Upton Sinclair, Saul Bellow and many others.

1921 Soprano Mary Garden uttered the first words heard on Chicago radio, "My God it's dark in here." The director of the Chicago Grand Opera Association was taking part in the inaugural broadcast of KYW. Westinghouse built the station to present only opera broadcasts and sell more radios. It worked. When the broadcasts began, there were about 1,300 radios here. There were over 20,000 when the season ended ten weeks later.

1939 Edward O'Hare was shot to death in his car at 2601 West Ogden. O'Hare was an attorney and ran dog tracks for Al Capone. He turned informant, hoping to get his son Butch into the Naval Academy. Butch would save the carrier *Lexington* and earn the Medal of Honor in 1942, shooting down five Japanese bombers. On September 18, 1949 a little used airport named Orchard Depot was re-named in Butch's honor.

1960 John F. Kennedy was elected president over Richard M. Nixon by just .02%. Some mysterious last minute votes provided by the Chicago

Democratic machine and Sam Giancana helped Kennedy win. Voter turnout in Chicago was an amazing 89%, compared to 62.8% nationally. JFK and Giancana were both involved with Judith Campbell Exner, who carried messages between the two concerning a plot to kill Castro.

November 9

1712   Writing from the mission at Kaskaskia, Jesuit Father Pierre-Gabriel Marest first referred to "Lake Michigan." The word is said to have come from the Ojibway (Chippewa) for "large lake." The French missionaries had referred to it as "Lac Pouans," after the Winnebago Indians. They later used "Lac des Illeeaouers" and "Lac des Illinioues," after the Illinois Indians. The Fox Indians called it "Marchihiganing."

1897   Alderman Nathan Plotke announced he would introduce a measure banning football playing within the city limits of Chicago. A few days later, The *Tribune* reported that Plotke had "looked on in horror" as Wisconsin played the University of Chicago. His bill was defeated.

1927   At the Commonwealth Hotel, three of "Machine Gun" Jack McGurn's goons beat comedian Joe E. Lewis into unconsciousness, slashed his throat and left him for dead. A few weeks earlier, Lewis had left McGurn's Green Mill Café to work at another club. Lewis made a comeback as a comedian, but he was through as a singer. Frank Sinatra played Lewis in the movie *The Joker is Wild*.

1999   Sotheby's auctioned off roughly half of the 313 bovines from Chicago's "Cows on Parade" exhibit. The two auctions, one of which was held at the Chicago Theater, raised nearly $4 million for charity. "Handsome Cow," covered with children's fingerprints, went for $110,000. Oprah Winfrey bought "Cowbeille De Fruits," for $36,000. Each of the buyers donated the purchase price to a charity of their choice.

November 10

1879   Poet Vachel Lindsay was born in Springfield, Illinois. He came to Chicago in 1901 and began writing poetry while working at Marshall Field's. Lindsay hit the road in 1912, reciting poetry in return for lodging or a meal. His works incorporated the rhythms of jazz and influenced the

Chicago 365

Beat Poets of the 1950's. Facing financial problems, Lindsay committed suicide by drinking a bottle of Lysol in December 1931.

1902   Captain George Wellington Streeter made his vaudeville debut at the Metropolitan Theater. He appeared in "Capt. Streeter's Discovery of the District of Lake Michigan." In 1886, he ran his boat aground and stood by while sand and landfill created 100 acres of land around it. For 30 years, he defended his self-declared independent district with a shotgun. "Streeterville" is now some of the most valuable land in the world.

1924   Mike "The Devil" Genna walked into the flower shop owned by Al Capone's rival Dion O'Banion at 738 North State. Genna grabbed O'Banion's outstretched hand as his companions John Scalise and Albert Anselmi opened fire. Over 5,000 people viewed O'Banion's body as it lay in a $10,000 silver coffin. Three bands and 24 vehicles hauling flowers led the nearly two-mile long cortege to Mount Carmel Cemetery.

1996   Traffic began moving on the new northbound lanes of Lake Shore Drive, relocated to the west side of Soldier Field and the Field Museum. The project completed Daniel Burnham's 1909 vision for a continuous lake front park. It created a campus linking the Field Museum, the Shedd Aquarium and the Adler Planetarium.

November 11

1887   Albert Parsons, August Spies, George Engle and Adolph Fischer were hanged on "Black Friday" at the Cook County Jail. They were convicted of inspiring the bombing during a labor rally at the Haymarket in May 4, 1886. But none of the men threw the bomb. On the gallows, Spies is reported to have said, "The time will come when our silence will be more powerful than the voices you strangle today."

1918   The *Daily News* reported that "Every conceivable sort of noisemaking device—dishpans, horns, revolvers, whistles, the whole category of ear-splitting paraphernalia—appeared as by magic," upon news of the Armistice. The celebrations continued into the night. Crowds lit bonfires and held mock funeral processions for Kaiser Wilhelm II, Germany's defeated emperor.

1929   Laverne Baker was born in Chicago. She began singing in church at age 12 and was headlining at the Club DeLisa in her early teens. After signing with Atlantic Records in 1953, she became a major R and B star, with hits such as "Tweedle Dee" and "Jim Dandy." During the '60s, she toured and directed shows for the USO in Vietnam. Baker was inducted into the Rock and Roll Hall of Fame in 1991.

1920   The cornerstone was laid for the Wrigley Building. The building is patterned after the Seville Cathedral's Giralda Tower and decorated in an adaptation of the French Renaissance Style. Charles Beersman was the chief designer. He covered the towers with over 250,000 gleaming glazed terra cotta tiles. The south tower was completed in April 1921 and the north tower was finished in May 1924.

November 12

1915   Anna Bollinger of Chicago gave birth to a baby with severe physical malformities. Doctor Harry Haiselden convinced her to allow the child to die three days later. Haiselden ignited a controversy over what he called "eugenic euthanasia," allowing "defective" infants in his care to die. Haiselden played himself in the 1916 movie *The Black Stork,* which dramatized his views.

1946   The first drive-up banking window in the nation opened in Chicago. The Exchange National Bank branch at 130 South LaSalle featured ten drive-up or "autobanking" teller windows with slide out drawers. An ad boasted that customers could drive into a special section and complete all their banking transactions from inside the car.

1968   Samuel Peralta Sosa was born in San Pedro de Macoris, Dominican Republic. Sammy shined shoes and sold orange juice to help the family make ends meet. He couldn't afford a glove, so he fashioned one out of a milk carton and never used a real bat until he was 14. He signed a minor league contract with the Texas Rangers at the age of 16 and made his Major League debut in 1989.

November 13

1833   The first items ever printed in Chicago came off the press of John Calhoun. He printed a batch of business cards for a Mr. Ingersoll. A few days later, Calhoun would publish the *Democrat,* the first newspaper in the city. On May 9, 1834, he printed the papers formally incorporating the city. By then Calhoun's paper boasted over 700 subscribers.

1911 Buck O'Neil was born in Carrabelle, Florida. After a legendary career as a player and manager for the Kansas City Monarchs of the Negro League, he moved on to Major League Baseball in 1956 as a scout for the Cubs. The Cubs made him the Major's first black coach in 1962. O'Neil is credited with discovering Ernie Banks and Lou Brock.

1963 Frank Sinatra recorded "My Kind of Town." Sammy Cahn and Jimmy Van Huesen wrote the song about Chicago that made its debut in the movie *Robin and the Seven Hoods*. The movie about 1920's gangsters also starred Dean Martin, Sammy Davis Junior and Bing Crosby. It was while on the set of this movie that Sinatra learned President Kennedy had been assassinated.

November 14

1942 A jury convicted six people from Chicago on charges of treason. Herbert Haupt was among a group of Nazis executed in August 1942, after their sabotage mission was discovered. Haupt's father and mother, aunt and uncle and two friends were convicted for helping him. Herbert's father argued that he was just taking care of his son as any father would. But U.S. Supreme Court upheld the conviction in 1947.

1996 Archbishop Joseph Cardinal Bernardin died of pancreatic cancer at the age of 68. The senior Roman Catholic prelate in the U.S. had told the public that his cancer was inoperable in August 1996. In September, he traveled to the White House, where President Bill Clinton presented him with the Medal of Freedom for his dedication to justice, racial equality and arms control.

1996 The new version of 1975 Broadway musical *Chicago* opened at the Richard Rodgers Theater in New York City. Bebe Neuwirth, Ann Reinking and Joel Grey starred in the revival, which won seven Tony Awards in 1997, including best actress honors for Neuwirth. The play was adapted for a motion picture in 2002.

November 15

1836 Publisher Richard Robert Donnelly was born in Hamilton, Ontario. R.R. Donnelly was one of the first commercial printers in Chicago and his firm became one of the largest in the Midwest. Donnelly lost it all in the Great Fire, but rebuilt his empire. The firm printed the Sears and Montgomery Ward catalogs. A subsidiary was a great success publishing dime novels, launching a paperback revolution.

1895 Cap Anson of Chicago became the first baseball player to receive star billing in a play. He was still playing at age 44 when he appeared in *A Runaway Colt*. The Chicago NL team was known as the Colts at the time. The show would play on Broadway for about a month beginning in December. Anson forgot a few of his lines on opening night.

1940 The community of Niles Center changed its name to Skokie. The change was necessary to end confusion with the neighboring Village of Niles. A poll to find a new name ended with Oakton and Ridgeview as the top choices. But the trustees wanted something more ethnic. So they chose the Potawatomi name for the area, which meant "Big Swamp."

1996 The cars returned to State Street. A $24.5 million dollar project did away with the old State Street "transit way." Since 1979, only buses and pedestrians had been allowed on the nine-block stretch between Wacker and the Congress Parkway. The renovation brought the street back to some resemblance of the glory days of the 1920's, when State and Madison was "The world's busiest street corner."

November 16

1939 Al Capone was released from federal custody. Agents secretly drove him to Gettysburg, Pennsylvania and turned him over to the family and his doctors at a crossroads outside of town. Ravaged by syphilis, Capone returned to his estate at Palm Island, Florida. He died on January 25, 1947.

1969 Brian Piccolo took himself out of the game as the Bears played in Atlanta. Piccolo said he was having trouble breathing. The 26-year-old running back had never asked to be taken out of a game. A few days later, Piccolo learned he had a rare form of cancer. On November 28, he underwent surgery and doctors were optimistic. But the cancer returned and Piccolo died on June 16, 1970.

1975   Walter Payton of the Bears rushed for 105 yards in a game against the San Francisco 49ers. It was the first time Payton had rushed for more than 100 yards. He would rush for at least 100 yards over 50 times in his career. Payton even rushed for over 200 yards in two games.

1991   The motion picture *Home Alone* was released. The movie from a screenplay by John Hughes starred Macaulay Culkin as a child left home alone in the Chicago suburbs when his family rushed off to vacation in Paris. Joe Pesci and Daniel Stern played a pair of bumbling burglars thwarted by elaborate booby traps. The house featured in the movie is at 671 Lincoln Avenue in Winnetka.

November 17

1878   Grace Abbott was born in Grand Island, Nebraska. Grace was one of the women of Hull House. She was a leader in helping immigrant families and fought against the unscrupulous employment agencies in the Canal Street area known as the "slave market." As head of the United States Children's Bureau, she was instrumental in passing important child labor laws.

1925   Rock Hudson was born Roy Scherer in Winnetka. The New Trier High School grad's first film role came in 1948's *Fighter Squadron*. It took him 38 takes to remember one line. He made several very successful films with Doris Day and starred in "McMillan and Wife" on TV from 1971 to 1978. Hudson was the first major celebrity to announce he had AIDS, which raised awareness of the disease. He died in 1985.

1926   The Blackhawks played their first game. A crowd of 9,000 was on hand at the Coliseum as the Hawks beat the Toronto St. Pats 4-1. The Hawks finished third in the American Division for their first season but were eliminated in the first round of the playoffs, prompting the firing of coach Pete Muldoon. Muldoon put a "curse" on the team.

1984   Michael Jordan unveiled his line of Nike sneakers. He wore the first Air Jordans in a game against the Philadelphia 76ers. Nike paid Jordan a then unheard of $250,000 annually for five years, plus incentives and royalties. But his endorsements sparked major growth for Nike.

November 18

1904   John William "Billy" Bate became the first person from Chicago to be "taken for a ride." He was a chauffeur who picked up a male passenger at the Auditorium Theater and was never seen alive again. For a time, police thought Bate might have been murdered by one of his many jilted lovers posing as a man. Police found five love letters in the dead man's pocket. The case was never solved.

1960   McCormick Place opened. Built on the Century of Progress Exposition site, the center was the dream of *Tribune* publisher Robert McCormick. A fire on January 16, 1967 destroyed the hall. The structure now known as the East Building opened in 1971. The North Building opened in 1986 and the South Building was added in 1996. McCormick Place West is set to open in 2008.

1986   Drug dealer Flukey Stokes was gunned down. Thousands of people turned out as Stokes was buried in a $9,000 casket with a white telephone in his hand. The funeral of his son "Willie the Wimp" in 1984 was even more remarkable. Willie was buried in a casket made to look like a Cadillac and had $1,000 bills stuffed in his hands. Stevie Ray Vaughn recorded a song called "Willie the Wimp and his Cadillac Coffin."

1990   The newspapers reported that fabled burglar Joseph "Pops" Panczko was going legit after serving time for his 200th arrest at age 72. He started out at age 12, stealing coats from his grade school, and worked with his brothers Paul "Peanuts" Panczko and Edward "Butch" Panckzo for a time. Pops was arrested again for passing a phony $20 bill in 1994. He died in December 2002.

November 19

1862   William Ashley, better known as Billy Sunday, was born in Ames, Iowa. He played for the White Sox from 1883 to 1891 and became an evangelist in 1896. His fire and brimstone revivals filled with denunciations of liquor, evolution and liberalism gained a massive following. Billy Sunday

Chicago 365

preached until he died of a heart attack in Chicago in 1935.

1863 Abraham Lincoln made a speech at the dedication of the National Cemetery on the battleground at Gettysburg, Pennsylvania. The next day, the *Tribune* was one of the few newspapers to praise the speech, correctly predicting that it would "live among the annals of men." But the review in the *Times* called it "silly, flat and dishwatery."

1941 Publisher Sillman Evans announced that Marshall Field III's new paper would be known as the *Sun*. The paper would sell 900,000 copies on the first day. Field also published "Parade," a Sunday pictorial supplement that can still be found in Sunday papers across the country. After purchasing control of the *Chicago Daily Times* in 1947, he merged them to form the *Sun-Times*.

November 20

1848 Chicago began its development into the largest railroad center in the world. Dignitaries and reporters took a trip from Dearborn Street to the Des Plaines River along the Galena & Chicago Union Railroad aboard *The Pioneer*. Legend says they passed a farmer on the return trip and convinced him to load his grain aboard, the first shipment of freight by rail to Chicago.

1900 Chester Gould was born in Pawnee, Oklahoma. He came to the *American* in 1924 but dreamed of having his work syndicated by the *Tribune*. He peppered Joseph Medill Patterson with comic strip ideas for years until Patterson bought Gould's strip about a detective called "Plainclothes Tracy." Patterson changed the name to "Dick Tracy" and the hardboiled detective made his debut on October 4, 1931.

1907 Fran Allison was born in La Porte City, Iowa. "The First Lady of Chicago Broadcasting" was a former schoolteacher who rose to fame as Aunt Fanny on "Don McNeil's Breakfast Club." In 1947, she accepted a job at WBKB, working on puppeteer Burr Tillstrom's new show. She didn't even ask how much it paid. Kukla, Fran and Ollie made their debut on October 13, 1947.

1988 The Blackhawks honored their two greatest goaltenders. The number one worn by Glenn Hall and Tony Esposito's number 35 were retired. Hall was a three-time Vezina Trophy winner as the best goalie.

Tony Esposito won the Vezina in 1970, and shared the trophy with teammate Gary Smith in 1972 and with Bernie Parent of the Flyers in 1974.

November 21

1875 Bishop Foley dedicated the new Cathedral of the Holy Name. The Great Fire destroyed the original cathedral and the replacement was hastily constructed. Within a few years, the building designed by Brooklyn architect Patrick Charles Keely was sagging on the Superior Street side, and the first of several renovations began in 1888. The interior was modernized in 1969.

1916 Sid Luckman was born in Brooklyn, New York. George Halas developed Luckman into the first T-formation quarterback. Luckman would lead the Bears to five conference titles and four world championships between 1940 and 1950. On November 14, 1943 he passed for a record tying seven touchdowns. Sid was elected to the Hall of Fame in 1965.

1944 Harold Ramis was born in Chicago. In 1969, Ramis started out with the Second City improvisational. Rejected as too "ethnic" for "Saturday Night Live," he helped found "Second City TV" in 1976. Two years later, Ramis co-wrote *Animal House*. He also wrote *Meatballs, Stripes, Ghostbusters,* and *Ghostbusters II*. He directed films such as *Caddyshack, Groundhog Day, Multiplicity, Analyze This,* and *Bedazzled*

1986 The first grand jury indictments were returned in a major FBI corruption sting. "Operation Incubator," resulted in 14 officials being charged with taking bribes from Michael Burnett, alias Michael Raymond. The convicted swindler pretended to represent a New York businessman seeking big collection contracts from City Hall.

November 22

1905 Department store heir Marshall Field Jr. was found at his Prairie Avenue mansion with a fatal gun shot wound. Rumors flew that he was shot at the Everleigh Club brothel, and brought home to die by the Everleigh sisters. A former worker even tried to blackmail the sisters.

Chicago 365

They hired a private detective who found Field shot himself accidentally.

1912   The *Rouse Simmons* went down in a blizzard off Two Rivers, Wisconsin. Seventeen men died. The schooner was famous as "The Christmas Tree Ship," bringing a load of trees every year around Thanksgiving for sale in Chicago. Captain Herman Schuenemann, known as "Captain Santa," went down with the ship. His daughters would sell Christmas trees in Chicago for many more years.

1924   The first football game was played at Soldier Field. A sell-out crowd was on hand as Notre Dame beat Northwestern, 13-6. At the time, the field was known as Municipal Grant Park Stadium. The largest crowd for any event at Soldier Field gathered on September 8, 1954. Over 260,000 people attended the religious Marian Year Tribute.

1963   The big local news that morning was that Judge Cecil Corbett Smith had been barred from hearing cases pending an investigation into his relationship with a murdered hoodlum who kept a "little red book" listing his contacts. 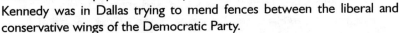 The papers also reported that President Kennedy was in Dallas trying to mend fences between the liberal and conservative wings of the Democratic Party.

> Listeners of WGN were tuned into the Country Fair program when Orion Samuelson broke in with a bulletin that President Kennedy had been shot in Dallas. Crowds stood around loudspeakers hastily strung outside stores in The Loop and huddled around TV sets in restaurants, bars and department stores. Mayor Daley burst into tears when he was told the president was dead.

November 23

1903   Chicago's most modern theater opened its doors at 24-28 West Randolph. The Iroquois Theater was billed as "absolutely fireproof." The city gave developers Harry J. Powers and William J. Davis permission to open early, despite many safety violations. The theater was not equipped with sprinklers or an alarm system. On December 30, disaster struck during a sold out performance of the musical *Bluebeard Junior.*

1897   "Chicago's Sweetheart" was born in Nebraska. Ruth Etting was headlining at the Marigold Gardens when she became involved with

Chicago gangster Martin "Moe the Gimp" Snyder. Her stunning looks and magnificent voice made her a superstar. She divorced Moe in 1937. In 1938, Moe shot Ruth's boyfriend and the publicity ruined her career. Doris Day played Etting in the 1955 film *Love Me or Leave Me*.

1927 The Savoy Ballroom at 4733 S. Parkway (now Martin Luther King Drive) opened. The Savoy could accommodate 4,000 people in its lavish ballroom and quickly became a hot spot for jazz. The Savoy even had its own basketball team, the Savoy Five. The team would be renamed the Harlem Globetrotters. The ballroom was demolished in the 1970's and the 47th Street Cultural Center stands on the site.

1936 Robert Johnson became the first artist to record "Sweet Home Chicago." No one is sure who wrote the song. Woody Payne is credited with writing it, but it is more likely that he just claimed the rights. The version by the Blues Brothers may be the best known, but dozens of artists ranging from Foghat to the Rolling Stones have recorded it.

November 24

1887 The very first softball game was played at the Farragut Boat Club gymnasium. George Hancock, a reporter for the Chicago Board of Trade, came up with the idea of an indoor version of baseball while a group of alumnae were waiting for the score of the Harvard-Yale football game. He tied the laces of a boxing glove together to use as a ball. The two groups divided up and played to a score of 41-40.

1958 Officer Leonard Baldy gave Chicago's first airborne traffic report over WGN. Just one week after the first "Flying Officer" began his broadcasts, Baldy covered the Our Lady of Angles School fire from the air and directed emergency vehicles through the crowded streets.

1963 Governor Kerner declared that November 25 would be an official day of mourning for President Kennedy. State offices were to be closed and the governor urged all businesses to follow suit. Meanwhile, it was reported that the gun used by Lee Harvey Oswald to kill the president had been purchased by mail order from Klein Sporting Goods, 4540 Madison Street.

Chicago 365

November 25

1912   John Sengstacke was born in Savannah, Georgia. In 1934, he became publisher of the *Chicago Defender*, a newspaper founded by his uncle in 1905. In 1940, Sengstacke founded the Negro Newspaper Publisher Association, now known as the National Newspaper Publishers Association. In 1956, he changed the *Defender* from a weekly to a daily paper. He served as publisher until his death in 1997.

1984   The Bears beat the Vikings 34-3 at Minneapolis to clinch their first Central Division crown. The Bears would beat Washington on December 30 for their first playoff win since 1963. But they lost the NFC Championship game to the eventual Super Bowl Champion San Francisco 49ers.

1987   Mayor Harold Washington must have been pleased on that day. He was seven months into his second term. After the bitter Council Wars, he finally had a majority on his side. At 1:36 pm., Washington died of a heart attack at his desk in City Hall. Black and white, rich and poor, they would come by the thousands to pay their respects. In 1991, the new central Chicago library was named in Washington's honor.

November 26

1833   John Calhoun founded the first newspaper in Chicago. The first issue of the *Democrat* reported that construction had started on 150 buildings in the past year. The paper started out as a four-page weekly and a subscription cost $2.50 per year. In 1836, Calhoun sold the paper to "Long John" Wentworth, a future mayor of Chicago. The *Democrat* published until 1861.

1897   A massive clock was installed outside Marshall Field's at the corner of Washington and State Streets. The cast bronze clock rises 17.5 feet above the sidewalk and weighs 7.75 tons. A Norman Rockwell painting made the clock even more famous. Tourists and natives still say "Meet me under the clock" today. The street was renamed Honorary Marshall Field Way in September 2002.

2002   The new Wacker Drive opened. Charles H. Wacker, chairman of

Chicago 365

the Chicago Plan Commission, pushed for the original bi-level roadway, envisioned by Daniel Burnham and Edward Bennett in 1909. It opened in 1926. The $200 million project reconstructed the oldest section, the east-west leg between Michigan Avenue and Randolph Street.

November 27

1926   Vice President Charles G. Dawes was on hand as ceremonies marked the dedication of Muncipal Grant Park Stadium as Soldier Field. Army played Navy to a 21-21 tie in the dedication game. The Gold Star Mothers urged the change to honor veterans.

1934   Lester Gillis, better known as "Baby Face" Nelson, shot it out with Agent Herman Hollis and Inspector Samuel Cowley on the Northwest Highway near Barrington. After crashing his car, Nelson sprayed machine gun bullets and cursed as he walked straight into the G-men's fire. Nelson killed them both and staggered back to the car with 17 bullets in him. His wife dumped the body in a ditch.

1969   Georg Solti began his 22-year-old tenure as music director of the Chicago Symphony. On May 7, 1973, Solti appeared on the cover of *Time* magazine with the declaration "The Fastest Baton in the West." *Time* declared that the Chicago Symphony was the top orchestra in America, "Sine qua non." Solti never lived in Chicago. When in town, he stayed in a suite at the Mayfair Regent.

1989   Twenty-one-month-old Alyssa Smith of Schertz, Texas became the first person in the U.S. to receive a liver transplanted from a living relative. Doctors at the University of Chicago's Wyler's Children's Hospital performed the 14-hour operation, transplanting a fist-sized piece of her mother Teri's liver.

November 28

1895   The first auto race in America took place on a snowy Thanksgiving. Only two out of six cars finished the 55-mile run from Jackson Park to Evanston and back. Frank Duryea won, averaging 7.5 m.p.h. The *Times-Herald* said those who scoffed at the horseless carriage "will be forced to recognize it as an admitted mechanical achievement, highly adapted to some of the most urgent needs of our civilization."

Chicago 365

1938   Young White Sox pitching star Monty Stratton lost his leg in a hunting accident near Greenville, Texas. In 1939, the team held a game to raise money for Stratton. He took the mound to show he could still pitch on his artificial leg. He went on to pitch in the minors, going 18-8 in the East Texas League in 1946. His story became a motion picture starring Jimmy Stewart and June Allyson in 1949.

1984   Over a decade after arriving at WGN from Dayton, Ohio, Phil Donahue moved his daily talk show from Chicago to New York. For the past four years, Donahue and his wife Marlo Thomas had commuted between the two cities. Donahue's show would go into nationally syndication and led the ratings until 1987. That's when another talk show host from Chicago, Oprah Winfrey, overtook him.

1994   Jeffrey Dahmer was killed in prison. Dahmer killed 17 people, mostly in Milwaukee. But two victims of his gruesome crimes came from Chicago. In 1991, he picked up Matt Turner at the Pride Parade, cutting off Turner's head and keeping some of his organs in the freezer. In June 1991, Dahmer lured Jeremiah Weinburger from Carol's Bar on Wells Street back to his apartment. His head was also in the refrigerator.

November 29

1934   The Bears beat Detroit 19-16 in the first NFL game to be broadcast nationally. The game also marked the start of the Thanksgiving Day football tradition. Graham McNamee and Don Wilson were behind the mike for the broadcast on NBC from Dinan Field at the University of Detroit.

1935   Halfback Jay Berwanger of the University of Chicago was named as the first winner of the New York Downtown Athletic Club Trophy for the best college football player east of the Mississippi. In 1936, the trophy was renamed after DAC Athletic Director John W. Heisman and awarded to the top player in the nation.

1948   "Kukla, Fran and Ollie" moved to WNBQ-TV, and the show was broadcast over a coaxial cable network to NBC stations across the Midwest. On January 12, 1949, "Kukla, Fran and Ollie" became the first

TV show to air over the entire NBC network. The puppet creations by Burr Tillstrom made their TV debut on WBKB back in 1942.

1963   At 12:37 p.m. almost one week to the minute from the time an assassin cut down President Kennedy in Dallas, the Chicago City Council voted unanimously to change the name of the Northwest Expressway. The *Tribune* said the John Fitzgerald Kennedy Expressway was "a fitting tribute to the late president who rode the route many times and called it one of the greatest highways in the U.S."

November 30

1866   Work began on the first underwater roadway tunnel in the U.S. Huge traffic jams had developed as the bridges over the Chicago River were raised much of the time to allow the passage of masted ships. The 1,605 feet long tunnel at Washington Street cost $512,000 and opened on January 1, 1869. It was used until 1953.

1947   David Mamet was born in Chicago. He first rose to fame with his plays *Sexual Perversity in Chicago* and *American Buffalo*. Mamet won a Pulitzer for *Glengarry Glen Ross* in 1984 and has penned several film scripts, including the Oscar nominated *The Verdict* and *Wag the Dog*. His work often is often riddled with profanity, reflecting his experiences working a variety of odd jobs in Chicago.

1952   Mandy Patinkin was born in Chicago. He has appeared in films such as *Yentl, Ragtime, Alien Nation, Dick Tracy* and most memorably as Inigo Montoya in *The Princess Bride*. He brought home a Tony for his 1980 Broadway debut as Che in Andrew Lloyd Weber's *Evita*. He won an Emmy for his role as Doctor Jeffrey Geiger on television's "Chicago Hope" and is also a successful singer.

1963   Police found the body of Irv Kupcinet's daughter, Karyn. Irv knew Jack Ruby in Chicago during the 1940's. Author W. Penn Jones claimed the *Sun-Times* columnist discovered Ruby was involved in a plot to kill Kennedy and told his daughter. Just days before the assassination, a long-distance operator reportedly heard her scream into the phone that the president was going to die. Her murder was never solved.

Chicago 365

DECEMBER

December 1

1915 A former West Side boxer named John Hertz founded the Yellow Cab Company. Hertz was a partner in an auto dealership, and started out using extra trade-in vehicles as taxis. He painted them yellow to distinguish his cabs from the competition. He started the Hertz Rental Car Company in Chicago in 1923.

1935 Louis Allen Rawls was born in Chicago. He began singing gospel at age seven and was a member of the Soul Stirrers and the Pilgrim Travelers, before heading to California. In 1958, while touring with Sam Cooke, he nearly died in a car accident. After appearing with Cooke on "Bring it on Home to Me," Lou began scoring solo hits. He went on to record 77 albums and a series of Budweiser commercials.

1953 Hugh Hefner's new publication made its debut. Hefner was a former employee of *Esquire*, who stayed behind when the magazine moved to New York. "Hef" didn't put a date on his first issue, because he wasn't sure there would be a second. But a nude calendar shot of Marilyn Monroe insured a sell-out of 72,000 copies of *Playboy*. By 1959, Hefner was able to afford a 70-room mansion at 1340 North State Parkway.

1958 Classes were about to be dismissed when smoke rose from a wastebasket at the bottom of a stairwell at Our Lady of the Angels School, at Iowa and Avers. Hot air and gasses built up until the flames suddenly shot into the second floor classrooms. There was only one fire escape, there were no sprinklers in the building and the alarm system was not linked to the fire department.
It was two minutes before the fire department was notified and three minutes before crews arrived on the scene to find children jumping from the upper floor. The fire was under control in an hour, but 92 students and three nuns were killed. In the wake of the tragedy, all school alarms were linked directly to the fire department and sprinkler systems were installed. The official cause has never been determined.

1968 The National Commission on the Causes and Prevention of Violence released its report on the chaos during the Democratic National Convention. The Walker report used the term "police riot" and said the police used force far in excess of what was required. Daniel Walker and his Chicago study team interviewed nearly 3,500 witnesses and took 20,000 pages of statements.

December 2

1942 The atomic age began in a squash court beneath the stands of Stagg Field at the University of Chicago. Enrico Fermi's team of 43 physicists achieved the first controlled nuclear reaction. The uranium was put between graphite bricks and surrounded by a wooden frame. Three physicists stood by, ready to pour a cadmium solution on the pile and run for it if the reaction went out of control!

1957 "You Send Me" by Sam Cooke hit number one. The son of a Chicago Reverend was originally a member of the popular gospel group the Soul Stirrers. He was fired after recording a pop record under a fake name. Tragedy marked Cooke's life. His wife died in a car accident and his youngest child drowned in the family pool. A hotel manager shot Cooke to death on December 10, 1964.

1987 After a long, turbulent night at City Hall, The City Council elected Eugene Sawyer as Mayor of Chicago at 4:01 a.m. The white aldermanic bloc pushed for the election of Sawyer to serve as interim mayor following the sudden death of Harold Washington. Sawyer was black, but most of the black community was for Alderman Timothy Evans. Sawyer lost a special election to Richard M. Daley in 1989.

2000 Smashing Pumpkins played their final concert at Metro, the same Chicago club where they started out over a decade earlier. The group originally consisted of singer/guitarist Billy Corgan, guitarist James Iha, D'arcy Wretzky-Brown on bass and Jimmy Chamberlain on drums. They scored big hits with "1979" and "Tonight, Tonight" Corgan formed a new group called Zwan in 2003.

December 3

1763 John Kinzie was born in Quebec City, Canada. The first white settler of Chicago was a silversmith and Indian trader who purchased the land originally owned by John Baptiste Point du Sable in 1804. Kinzie supplied food and liquor to the garrison at Fort Dearborn and served as the post banker. He also sold liquor to the Indians, which caused trouble for Kinzie and the soldiers.

1818 President Monroe signed the measure making Illinois the 21st state. Congress originally set the northern boundary of Illinois even with the line separating Indiana from the Michigan Territory. But the Illinois Territory representative, Nathaniel Pope, convinced lawmakers to move the line 41 miles north. If not for Pope, Chicago and Rockford would be in Wisconsin today.

1943 Ric Riccardo and his partner Ike Sewell planned to open a Mexican restaurant. But the food made Riccardo sick, so he suggested something he had tried while serving in Italy. Sewell thought pizza wasn't much of a meal. So the two men developed a pizza with thick crust and tons of cheese. The first Pizzeria Uno Restaurant opened on this date at Ohio and Wabash, and the Chicago Style pizza was born.

1967 The *20th Century Limited* made its last run from New York City to Chicago. The "Greatest Train in the World" made its debut on June 15, 1902. The phrase "red carpet treatment" originated when New York Central rolled out a red carpet to welcome *Limited* passengers. The Art Deco streamlined cars and bullet-nosed locomotives designed by Henry Dreyfuss in 1938 are still a stylistic influence today.

December 4

1941 The first edition of the *Sun* rolled off the presses. Inside, readers found an editorial warning "war is very near in the Pacific." Marshall Field III founded the paper to counter what he called an "un-American monopoly" of Colonel Robert McCormick's conservative *Tribune*. Field took over the *Times* in 1948 and merged it with the *Sun*.

1969 Officers stormed a battered flat at 2337 West Monroe, headquarters of the Black Panthers. Illinois Panther leader Fred Hampton and Peoria party leader Mark Clark were killed. Police fired nearly 100 shots, claiming the Panthers opened fire first. State's Attorney Edward Hanrahan and 13 law enforcement officials would be charged with obstruction of justice. They were cleared, but Hanrahan was finished.

Chicago 365

1977 The oldest house in Chicago was moved to a new location. All train service was stopped while the house, constructed in 1836 by Henry Clarke, was jacked up and moved across the "el" tracks. The Greek revival style home originally stood at 16th and Michigan. It was first moved around 1872 to 45th and Wabash. The home now stands at 1827 South Indiana, near its original location.

1997 Jerry Manuel became the first African-American hired to manage a big league team in Chicago history. He took over as manager of the White Sox. Larry Doby has served as interim manager of the White Sox for 87 games back in 1978. Manuel led the Sox to second place finishes in 1998 and 1999 and won Manager of the Year honors as the Sox won the division in 2000. But a September Sox swoon in 2003 cost him his job.

December 5

1894 Phillip Knight Wrigley was born in Chicago. He was an executive with his father's chewing gum company for 52 years and owned the Cubs from 1934 to 1977. He meticulously docked his chewing gum company pay for time he spent running the team. During World War Two, Wrigley organized the All-American Girls Professional Baseball League.

1901 Walt Disney was born at 2156 North Tripp. When Walt was four, his family moved to Marceline, Missouri. The Disneys returned to Chicago in 1917, and Walt drew for the paper at McKinley High School. Walt's first cartoon success came in 1923, with "Steamboat Willie." Walt provided the voice of the character, originally called "Mortimer Mouse." His wife, Lillian suggested the name "Mickey."

1933 Thousands waited as the clock ticked towards 4:32 p.m., and the 13 year dry spell was over. There were 27 arrests as the city celebrated the repeal of Prohibition, including a lawyer who punched out a waiter. Meatpacking magnate Oscar Mayer was the first person served when the bar re-opened at the Palmer House Hotel. The "Noble Experiment" was a failure, and allowed organized crime to flourish.

1962 Lenny Bruce was arrested on obscenity charges for his performances at the Gate of Horn in Chicago. He was tried in absentia and convicted on February 28, 1963. Bruce said the judge was guilty of

Chicago 365

"illegal, unconstitutional, and most fascistic...behavior." In July 1964, the Illinois Supreme Court overturned the conviction, citing Bruce's right to free speech.

1991 Richard Speck died of a heart attack. In prison, the man who killed eight nurses in 1966 had been taking female hormones and grew grotesque and bloated. In the 1980's, a videotape emerged showing Speck and other inmates taking drugs and having sex. On the tape, Speck was asked about killing the women. "It just wasn't their night," he shrugged. No one claimed his body, which was cremated.

December 6

1866 The first water supply tunnel in the U.S. opened. Designed by City Engineer Ellis Chesbrough, the two-mile long, five-feet in diameter tunnel was constructed under Lake Michigan to an intake crib. It allowed the water supply to be drawn away from the polluted shoreline, reducing the threat from cholera. The pumping station and tower still stand at Michigan Blvd and Chicago Ave.

1908 George "Baby Face" Nelson was born Lester M. Gillis at 944 North California. He turned to crime in his early teens and took the alias George Nelson after a fighter he admired. Nelson was fired by the Capone organization because he was too homicidal! He robbed banks with John Dillinger and killed an FBI agent in April 1934. He killed two more agents but was fatally wounded on November 27, 1934 near Barrington.

1909 James R. Mann of Illinois introduced a bill in the House that would bear his name. The numerous white slave rings in Chicago's Levee District inspired the Mann Act. Maurice Van Beever ran the biggest ring, which imported over 600 women from New York, St. Louis and Milwaukee. The Mann act made it illegal to bring a woman across state lanes for "immoral purposes."

1990 The signature of "Shoeless Joe" Jackson brought $23,100 at an auction in New York City, the highest price ever paid for an autograph from the 19th or 20th Century to that date. Jackson couldn't write, so he copied the shaky signature from one his wife wrote out. It was on a four by 1 ½ inch section cut from a document Joe signed in 1936.

December 7

1863   Richard Sears was born in Stewartville, Minnesota. The railroad worker got permission to sell an unclaimed shipment of watches in 1886. He made $5,000 and decided to go into the watch business in Minneapolis. Sears moved to Chicago in 1887 and placed an ad seeking another watchmaker. Alvah Roebuck answered. The first Sears, Roebuck and Company catalog came out in 1888, offering only a few watches.

1941   The Bears were playing the Cardinals at Soldier Field, when WGN broke into the broadcast with the news from Hawaii. Hundreds of fans left at half time to buy the latest newspapers. The Bears won the game 34-24. Mayor Kelly declared that the city police, health and fire departments were guarding transportation systems, utilities, communications, filtration plants and defense industries.
   Chicago was vital to the war effort. Work at the University of Chicago led to the development of the atomic bomb. The massive Dodge plant churned out B-29 engines. The Douglas plant at Orchard Field, the future site of O'Hare International Airport, built the C-54 Skymaster. Western Electric produced radar systems. The Stevens and the Congress Hotels housed 15,000 troops. Over 60,000 soldiers and 16,000 pilots trained at Navy Pier.

1949   Work began on a project envisioned by Daniel Burnham in his 1909 plan for Chicago. He urged the development of Congress Street into a great highway. Over 13,000 people were moved and about 450 commercial and industrial buildings up to 12 stories tall were leveled for the project. In 1964, the Congress Expressway was renamed in honor of Dwight D. Eisenhower.

1996   The body of mystery writer Eugene Izzi was found hanging from the 14th floor window of his North Michigan Avenue office. A rope ran from his neck to the leg of Izzi's desk. He was wearing a bulletproof vest, carrying brass knuckles and mace, and had a gun in the office. His death was a mystery, but police eventually ruled that no foul play was involved.

December 8

1940   George Halas and the "Monsters of the Midway" stunned the Redskins with their T-Formation and the man-in-motion in the NFL

Chicago 365

Championship Game. The Bears massacred Washington 73-0, in the most lopsided game in NFL history. It was also the first NFL Championship Game to be carried on network radio. Red Barber had the call from Washington on the 120 stations of the Mutual Broadcasting System.

1941 Over 2,000 men swamped the Army, Navy, Marine and Air Corps recruiting offices in Chicago. By mid-1944 each Chicago block had an average of seven men or women in the military. Cubs Owner William K. Wrigley donated lighting equipment purchased for Wrigley Field to the war effort. Chicago based Mrs. Japps Potato Chips would change the company name to Jay's Potato Chips.

1955 The 41-story Prudential Building was dedicated. The first major downtown skyscraper constructed since 1934 was the tallest building in Chicago until 1968. It boasted 30 automatic elevators traveling at 1,400 feet per minute. An observation deck and The Top of the Rock Restaurant originally occupied the top floor. The second Prudential Building was completed in 1990.

1972 United Airlines Flight 533 slammed into a Southwest Side neighborhood. The crash killed 43 people on the plane and two on the ground. One of the victims was E. Howard Hunt's wife, Dorothy. She died with $10,000 cash in her purse, which many presumed to be Watergate hush money. U.S. Representative George Collins also died in the crash. Investigators ruled out sabotage.

1979 "Babe" by Styx hit number one on the *Billboard* chart. Dennis DeYoung and Chuck and John Panozzo founded the Chicago group as The Tradewinds in 1963. They were known briefly as TW4, added guitarists James Young and John Curulewski and then changed the name to Styx. "Lady" became their first hit in 1975. Tommy Shaw replaced Curulewski and Styx became the Heartland's favorite rock band.

December 9

1889 The Chicago Auditorium opened with Madame Adeline Patti singing "Home, Sweet Home" to an audience that included President Benjamin Harrison. Dankmar Adler and Louis Sullivan designed the landmark. It boasted a first class 400-room hotel, offices, stores and a lavish auditorium that could seat 4,000. The completion of the Auditorium heralded Chicago's arrival as a cultured metropolis.

1924   The first Chicago pro basketball team made its debut. George Halas put up the money for the Chicago Bruins of the new American Basketball League. The ABL revolutionized basketball by eliminating the two handed dribble and disqualifying players who racked up more than five fouls per game. The league folded in 1931.

1934   In a contest that went down in history as "The Sneaker Game," the undefeated Bears lost the NFL Championship to the Giants 30-13 at the Polo Grounds. The Bears led 10-3 at the half as the temperature dropped to nine degrees and a sheet of ice covered the field. But the Giants changed into sneakers borrowed from nearby Manhattan College, and scored 27 points in the second half.

1953   John Malkovich was born in Benton, Illinois. He began his career on stage in Chicago, as a founding member of the Steppenwolf Theatre Company with Gary Sinise. Malkovich earned an Oscar nomination for Best Supporting actor in his very first film role, for *Places in the Heart*. He also garnered praise for *Dangerous Liasons*, and *In the Line of Fire*. He even played himself in 1999's *Being John Malkovich*.

December 10

1890   Grand Central Station at Harrison and Wells Streets opened. The Baltimore and Ohio Railroad owned the station. It also served the Pere Marquette, Soo Line, Chicago Great Western and the Chesapeake & Ohio. Grand Central, with its distinctive 242-feet tall square tower and six-ton bell, closed in 1969 and was torn down in 1971.

1931   The Nobel Peace Prize was awarded to Jane Addams of Hull House. She shared it with Nicholas Murray Butler. Butler was the promoter of the Briand-Kellogg Pact, which called for the renunciation of war as an instrument of national policy. Addams didn't receive the prize in person. She had been in poor health since a heart attack in 1926. Less than four years later, she was dead of cancer

1945   Frances Brown was stabbed to death in her apartment on Pine Grove Avenue. The killer scrawled on the wall in lipstick, "For heavens sake catch me before I kill more." Police said the "Lipstick Killer" was also responsible for the murder of Josephine Ross on June 3rd. In January, the dismembered body of seven-year-old Suzanne Degnan was found scattered in the sewers and William Heirens confessed to the crimes.

1988 Chicago's "Look Away" hit Number One on the *Billboard* chart. It was the group's third chart topper and one of three top ten hits from the *Chicago 19* album. The others were "I Don't Wanna Live Without Your Love "and "You're Not Alone." A whole new generation of fans discovered the band in the 1980's, even though writer and bass player Peter Cetera had left the group in 1985.

December 11

1874 James Lewis Kraft was born in Stevensville, Ohio. In 1903, he started selling cheese from the South Water Street Market to grocers around Chicago. In 1916, Kraft developed processed sterilized cheese, ensuring a long life when canned. Kraft continued to revolutionize the cheese industry with products such as Velveeta and Cheez Whiz.

1921 Just hours before he was to hang for killing four people, including a police officer, "Terrible" Tommy O'Connor escaped from the Cook County Jail. Because O'Connor was sentenced to hang, the gallows were kept in storage long after the state began electrocuting criminals. In 1977, officials finally decided Connor wasn't going to turn up, and donated the gallows to Donley's Wild West Town in Union, Illinois.

1964 Sam Cooke brought Lisa Boyer to the Hacienda, a $3 per night motel in Los Angeles. The exact details are unclear, but Boyer ran from the room half dressed and carrying most of Cooke's clothes. Hotel manager Bertha Franklin shot Cooke to death as he broke into the office in pursuit of Boyer. The death was ruled a case of justifiable homicide.

2000 A blizzard dumped a foot of snow across Chicago. Snow fell at the rate of one inch per hour in one of the biggest pre winter storms in city history. Two days later, another five inches fell. The total snowfall for December added up to 41.3 inches at Midway, the highest monthly total since 1928.

Chicago 365

December 12

1835   The first fire engine in Chicago went into service. The 3rd Volunteer Fire Kings was formed specifically to operate Fire Engine Number One. G.S. Hubbard ordered the engine at a cost of $894.38.

1933   The City renamed Crawford Avenue after Casimir Pulaski, launching a 20 year legal fight. Many felt it was a slight to Peter Crawford, an early Chicago pioneer. Pulaski, a Polish hero who aided the U.S. during the revolution, never sat foot in Chicago. The fight prompted the city to establish honorary street names, indicated by brown signs.

1996   McCormick Place South opened. The addition cost $675 million, took 3 ½ years to complete and added 840,000 square feet to the McCormick Place complexes. The 27 acres of new buildings are connected to the rest of the complex by pedestrian bridges over Lake Shore Drive. The International Housewares Show in January 1997 was the first regular event in the new section.

1997   The notorious "Bloody Maxwell" Street Police Station at 14th and Morgan closed. Constructed in 1889, the building was shown on the opening credits of "Hill Street Blues." During the 1920's most of the officers at the station were on the payroll of the bootlegging Genna Brothers. The station was also the scene of brutal interrogations. The old station was turned over to the University of Illinois.

December 13

1943   Ferguson Jenkins was born in Chatham, Ontario. Jenkins is the only pitcher to record 3,000 strikeouts with fewer than 1,000 walks and was the first Canadian born player named to the Baseball Hall of Fame. With the Cubs, he racked up six consecutive seasons with 20 wins or more. His 284 lifetime victories are the most ever by a pitcher who never appeared in post-season play.

1959   The Chicago Cardinals played their final game, a 35-20 loss to the Steelers in Pittsburgh. The team had dropped the last six in a row and finished with a record of 2-10. George Halas of the Bears had been trying for years to get the Big Red to move and the league took action when the upstart AFC threatened to place a franchise in St. Louis. The NFL voted to move the team to St. Louis on March 13, 1960.

1970   The Bears played their last game at Wrigley Field. Chicago beat the Green Bay Packers 35-17. The Bears headed moved to Soldier Field with a record of 221-89 and 22. That adds up to 332 games played at Wrigley, the most games ever played by a team in the same home stadium in NFL history.

December 14

1904   Theodore Thomas led the first concert at Orchestra Hall, the new home of the Chicago Symphony Orchestra. For the first 14 years of its existence, the orchestra had played at the Auditorium Theater and Thomas hated the acoustics. Tragically, he caught the flu during rehearsals for the dedicatory concert and died just three weeks after architect Daniel Burnham's beautiful building was dedicated.

1908   Morey Amsterdam was born in Chicago. He worked in a speakeasy owned by Al Capone, but a shootout at the club convinced him to find better gigs. In Hollywood, "The Human Joke Machine," wrote gags for Will Rogers, Jimmy Durante and others. He hosted "Broadway Open House" on NBC, a forerunner of the "Tonight Show." Of course he is best remembered as Buddy Sorell on the "Dick Van Dyke Show."

1963   Dinah Washington, The "Queen of the Blues," died of an accidental overdose of diet pills and alcohol in Detroit at the age of 39. Born Ruth Jones in Tuscaloosa Alabama, her family moved to the South Side of Chicago when she was a toddler. She began singing gospel at St. Luke's Baptist Church and took the stage name Dinah Washington after being discovered by Lionel Hampton's manager.

1980   More than 1,000 people gathered in Chicago to join in a worldwide moment of silence in honor of the murdered John Lennon. At the same time, a new type of music was emerging. "Groovy Ghost Show" by Casper (Terry Marshall) was the first recorded hip-hop music from Chicago. On the label, Marshall thanked radio personality Tom "Joiner" of WJPC.

Chicago 365

December 15

1908 Aldermen "Bathhouse John" Coughlin and Michael "Hinky Dink" Kenna threw their annual First Ward Ball. The bash opened with a parade of hookers and 20,000 drunken revelers packing the Coliseum. Kenna called the party a "lollapolooza" and proudly proclaimed Chicago "Ain't No Sissy Town."

1955 Cook County Board of Commissioners President Daniel Ryan dedicated a 4½ mile stretch of the Congress Street Expressway. Over 13,000 people were relocated, 3,000 graves and thousands of buildings were removed during construction.

1962 The Dan Ryan Expressway opened. Ryan was one of the men largely responsible for the expressway system in Chicago. One of the widest expressways in the world, the Ryan uses a "dual-dual" design. Seven lanes in each direction split into four lanes of high speed through traffic and three lanes that collect and distribute traffic. The rapid transit line in the median opened on September 28, 1969.

2003 Former Black Hawks star Keith Magnuson was killed in an auto accident in suburban Toronto. Magnuson was a passenger in a car driven by former Toronto Maple Leafs captain Rob Ramage. They were coming back from the funeral of former player Keith McCreary. Ramage was charged with impaired driving causing death. Magnuson played for the Hawks from 1969-80 and served as coach from 1980-82.

December 16

1892 Columbia Exposition officials approved a proposal from Pittsburgh bridge builder George Ferris for a wheel 250-feet in diameter to carry passengers. Two 140-foot tall steel towers would support it. Thirty-six wooden cars would hold up to 60 riders each. The wheel was dismantled in 1894 and re-used at the St. Louis Exposition in 1904.

1903 Police shut down a saloon on South State Street operated by Mickey Finn. Finn was a nasty little fellow who ran a school for pickpockets. He invented a drink called the "Mickey Finn Special," which the house girls gave to gentlemen. After the concoction knocked the men out, the girls robbed them, stripped them and tossed them into the alley. Thus was born the phrase "Slip him a Mickey."

1959   A group of University of Chicago students opened a cabaret in a converted laundry at 1842 North Wells. They named their new theater "The Second City." The troupe specialized in improvisation, taking suggestions from the audience. Second City would launch the careers of comedians such as Dan Akroyd, Alan Arkin, John Belushi, John Candy, Bill Murray, Gilda Radner and Joan Rivers.

1959   Roger "The Terrible" Touhy was shot to death. He had just been paroled after serving 25 years for a crime he didn't commit. In 1933, Al Capone framed his rival for the faked kidnapping of cosmetics magnate Max Factor. Touhy wrote a book called *The Stolen Years* and was sued for libel by Factor's brother, "Jake the Barber." As he lay dying, Touhy said, "I've been expecting it. The bastards never forget!"

December 17

1933   The Bears beat the New York Giants 23-21 at Wrigley Field in the first NFL Championship Game. Chicago trailed by five points with three minutes to play when Bronco Nagurski fired a pass to Bill Hewitt inside the 20-yard line. Hewitt tossed a lateral to Bill Karr, who scored the winning touchdown.

1926   Benny Goodman performed a clarinet solo for the first time with a group in a recording studio. The solo was part of the Ben Pollack and His Californian's recording of, "He's the Last Word." Goodman began learning music at Chicago's Kehelah Jacob Synagogue and he played in the Hull House Band. He made his professional debutat the Central Park Theater in Chicago 1921.

1936   Ventriloquist Edgar Bergen of Chicago and his wooden friend Charlie McCarthy made their debut on national radio. They performed on "The Rudy Vallee Royal Gelatin Hour" on NBC. Bergen began performing with his dummy in talent shows while attending Northwestern University. In 1937 they got they own show, sponsored by Chase and Sanborn. It was one of the highest rated in radio and ran until 1956.

1974   The third movie version of Ben Hecht and Charles MacArthur's

1928 play *The Front Page* was released. Walter Matthau starred as scheming Chicago newspaper editor Walter Burns and Jack Lemmon played reporter Hildy Johnson, who gets the scoop on escaped convict Earl Williams. Billy Wilder directed the film. The Front Page was remade for a fourth time in 1988 and called *Switching Channels*.

1938   Ground was broken for the State Street Subway. It took five years to construct. To cross the river, a 200-foot long tube of steel and concrete was built at a shipyard, floated to the site, and lowered into the riverbed. The State Street Subway opened on October 16, 1943.

1967   Chicago architect Barry Byrne died. The protege of Frank Lloyd Wright never finished the ninth grade. He established his own frim in 1915 and is best remembered for dramatic, ecclesiastical designs, including Immaculata School, St. Francis Xavier School in Wilmette, and the famous Church of Christ the King in Cork, Ireland.

December 18

1819   Wilbur F. Storey was born in Salisbury, Vermont. As editor of the *Chicago Times*, Storey was the father of Yellow Journalism. The paper was sensationalized, racist and filled with lies. At one time, Storey faced 21 libel suits. Burlesque performer Lydia Thompson horsewhipped him after Storey accused her of "capering lasciviously."

1898   Lieutenant Richard P. Hobson, who gained fame for sinking the *Merrimac* in Santiago Harbor, gave a lecture at the Auditorium. Afterwards, 163 Chicago women lined up to kiss the hero and set a new osculatory record. The record was shattered the next day in Kansas City, when 417 women lined up to kiss Hobson.

1913   Montgomery Ward died at the age of 69. After establishing the nation's first mail order business in 1872, Ward became an environmentalist and fought for the poor. His firm was the first to offer "satisfaction guaranteed or your money back." The company faded as America became more urbanized. The last "Wish Book" was published in 1985 and Montgomery Ward declared bankruptcy in December 2000.

1997   Chris Farley died in his Hancock Building apartment at the age of

Chicago 365

33. Just as his hero John Belushi, Farley died young of a drug overdose. Farley started out with the Second City Troupe. He is best remembered for his characters on "Saturday Night Live." Including Matt Foley, a motivational speaker who lived in a "van down by the river." Farley went on to star in movies such as *Black Sheep* and *Tommy Boy*.

December 19

1852   Albert Michelson was born in Prussia. Michelson was named as the first head of the physics department at the newly created University of Chicago in 1892 and served until 1929. He was the first to accurately measure the speed of light, work that would eventually lead to Einstein's theory of relativity. In 1907, Michelson became the first American scientist to receive the Nobel Prize in physics.

1898   Charles Yerkes lost his bid to keep control of the transit lines in Chicago. Yerkes went too far when he tried to extend his franchises for 50 years. He had obtained them through bribery. A few citizens dangled nooses over the railing to make sure aldermen got the message to vote against the extensions. Yerkes would move to London in 1900 and developed the famous Underground.

1929   The John G. Shedd Aquarium opened. Shedd was the second president and chairman of the Marshall Field Company. He donated $3 million to establish the aquarium, designed by Graham, Anderson, Probst and White. Over 200 exhibition tanks today hold over 5,000 specimens at the world's largest indoor aquarium.

1942   Maurice White was born in Memphis. He studied at the Chicago Conservatory of Music and was a well-known session drummer. With his brother Verdine, White formed a group to blend music with a multi-cultural experience. He named the group after the elements in his own astrological chart, but decided that Earth Wind and Fire sounded better than Earth, Air and Fire.

December 20

1951   In the midst of a blizzard, 88-year-old Colonel William G. Edens helped open the Expressway that bears his name. Edens was a Chicago banker and early advocate of good roads who sponsored the first state highway bond issue in 1918. Edens actually never owned a car and he never drove one.

1973 Gunmen killed Dick Cain. Cain lost his police job for spying on Mayor Daley's security chief. Sam Giancana then hired him to kill Castro and Cain trained pilots for the Bay of Pigs invasion. In 1962, he became Chief Investigator for the Cook County Sheriff's Police but was fired for corruption. After getting out of jail, Cain made the mistake of trying to take over organized crime in Chicago.

1976 Mayor Richard J. Daley sank a basket at a Park District event at a South Side basketball court. He complained of chest pains on the way back to City Hall and was taken to his doctor's office. A few minutes later, Daley was dead at the age of 74. Over 100,000 would view the casket at the Nativity of Our Lord Catholic Church in Bridgeport. Michael Bilandic was chosen as the new mayor.

1987 On "Walter Payton Day" at Soldier Field, Bears president Michael McCaskey officially retired Payton's number 34. In his final regular season game at home, Payton racked up 79 yards rushing and ran for a pair of touchdowns. Payton was named to the Hall of Fame in 1993.

December 21

1908 Mary Louise Gibson, daughter of the General Superintendent, lit the first blast furnace, and the massive U.S. Steel plant at Gary, Indiana opened. In less than three years, an instant city of 10,000 had replaced 12,000 acres of windswept sand dunes. The town was named after U.S. Steel Chairman Judge Elbert H. Gary.

1910 Montgomery Ward's battle to protect the lakefront ended when the Illinois Supreme Court ruled in his favor for a fourth time. Ward sued in 1890 to clear the area of buildings, except for the Art Institute. In 1836, the land had been designated as public ground to remain free of buildings. After the ruling, officials dropped plans to build the Field Museum in Grant Park. Buckingham Fountain now occupies the site.

1988 Speaking in Chicago, Jesse Jackson urged the use of the phrase

Chicago 365

"African American" to refer to blacks. He said, "It puts us in our historical context." He later added, "Every ethnic group in this country has reference to some land base, some historical cultural base. African Americans have hit that level of maturity."

December 22

1911   Thomas Jennings of Chicago became the first person in America to be convicted of murder on fingerprint evidence. Jennings left his fingerprints behind on the freshly painted porch of a man he killed. Edward Foster testified for the prosecution. Foster had implemented the system in Canada after learning about it from Scotland Yard detectives as the St. Louis World's Fair. Jennings was hanged.

1917   Frances Xavier Cabrini died of a heart attack at the hospital she founded in Chicago. She was 67. Cabrini established 75 hospitals, orphanages and schools across the United States, South America and Europe. She came to Chicago in 1899 and founded Columbus Hospital. Mother Cabrini became the first American saint in 1946.

1910   Twenty-one firefighters died when a brick wall collapsed during a fire at the Nelson Morris and Company Warehouse Number Seven in the Union Stockyards. The dead included the Fire Marshall, his Second Assistant, three Captains, four Lieutenants, eleven Pipemen and Truckmen and one Driver. It remained the greatest loss of firefighters during a single incident in U.S. history until 9/11.

1978   Police began removing bodies from beneath a home at 8213 West Summerdale Avenue in Norwood Park Township. Neighbors had complained about the smell for years. They were unaware that John Wayne Gacy, who once performed as a clown for kids, had buried the remains of 29 young men in the crawlspace. Four more victims were found in rivers. Gacy was put to death at Stateville in 1994.

December 23

1860   Harriet Monroe was born in Chicago. She first rose to prominence for her controversial poem commemorating the Columbian Exposition. The poem was rejected at first, but used anyway after Monroe insisted on being paid. Monroe is best remembered for creating *Poetry Magazine* in 1912. *Poetry* introduced such poets as Robert Frost and T.S. Eliot.

1914   Charles Pajeau was not happy when he couldn't drum up interest in the wooden construction toys he had invented. So he hired a group of midgets, dressed them up as elves and put them in a window at a Chicago department store to play with the toys during the Christmas season. The stunt helped make "Tinker Toys" a hit. By the following Christmas, Pajeau had sold over a million sets.

1933   Mayor Anton Cermak ordered Detective Sergeants Harry Lang and Harry Miller, to kill mobster Frank Nitti. They shot Nitti three times at his office in the LaSalle-Wacker Building, but "The Enforcer" survived. On February 15, 1933, Guisseppe Zangara shot Cermak while the mayor was with President Roosevelt in Miami.   The bullet may have been intended for Roosevelt, or it may have been payback by the mob.

1958   The final 45 miles of the original Tollway system opened. The original system consisted of about 187 miles of four lane highways with very few interchanges. The system was designed to move through traffic around the city. Since then, the tollways have become an integral part of the freeway system, used for local traffic as well.

December 24

1890   President Benjamin Harrison issued a proclamation inviting all the nations of the earth to "Take part in the commemoration of an event that is pre-eminent in human history and of lasting interest to mankind." The proclamation certified that Chicago had met all the requirements of legislation authorizing the Columbian Exposition.

1905   The first motion picture theater in the city opened. Operated by Aaron Jones, the 300-seat theater was located on State Street Near Adams. *The Great Train Robbery* was one of the first films shown. Admission was five cents. Jones would eventually own 36 theatres, including the McVicker and the Oriental.

1907   John Patrick Cody was born in St. Louis. Cody was appointed as

Chicago 365

the 6th Archbishop of Chicago on June 16, 1945. In June 1967, he became Chicago's 4th Cardinal. In September 1980, the US government began an investigation into the alleged diversion of church funds to Cody's life-long friend Helen Wilson. The investigation ended when Cody died of a heart attack at age 74 in April 1982.

1907 St. Vincent's College was officially chartered as DePaul University. At the time, there were fewer than 200 students. Today, DePaul is the largest Catholic university in the United States and the largest private institution in Chicago, with over 23,000 students. The school is named after St. Vincent de Paul, the 17th Century founder of the Vincentian Fathers.

1989 The 174-mile North-South Tollway opened, with drivers enjoying free tolls through Christmas. The tollway sends traffic around the congested surface streets leading to the area around O'Hare Airport. Designated as I-355, it extends from the Stevenson Expressway to the I-290 Extension.

December 25

1854 Pastor Patrick J. McLaughlin celebrated the first mass at Chicago's new $100,000 brick church. The Church of the Holy Name's 245 feet high steeple towered over State Street between Huron and Superior. The church served as the diocese cathedral until it was destroyed in the Great Fire. The new Holy Name Cathedral opened on November 21, 1875.

1865 The first cattle arrived at the Union Stock Yards. At one time employing 20% of Chicago's work force, the yards occupied nearly a square mile from 39th to 47th and from Halsted to Ashland. But Upton Sinclair exposed the darker side of the industry in his 1906 book *The Jungle* and stockyards began decentralizing in the 20's. The yards closed on July 30, 1971. An industrial park stands on the site today.

1935 Chicago direct mail salesman Duncan Hines had sent out a list of 167 restaurants he recommended as Christmas gifts. The response encouraged him to write *Adventures in Good Eating: a Guidebook to the Best Restaurants along America's Highways*, which sold five million copies. In 1950, he lent his name to a line of cake mix. Aurora Foods took over the Duncan Hines brand in 1997.

1939   Montgomery Ward was giving out copies of a new story to kids visiting the store Santa. Copywriter Robert Mays wrote the tale of a reindeer shunned for being different. May considered naming him "Rollo" or "Reginald" then decided on "Rudolph." In 1949, his brother-in-law Johnny Marks wrote a song based on the story of *Rudolph the Red-Nosed Reindeer*. Gene Autry recorded the Christmas classic in 1950.

1946   Shoppers at Marshall Field's saw a new character created by the Foote, Cone and Belding ad agency to compete with Montgomery Ward's Rudolph the Red Nosed Reindeer. "Uncle Mistletoe" and the other residents of Candy Cane Lane would star in a television program on WENR from 1948 to 1952 and later on ABC. Santa's ambassador returns each year, and tops the Great Tree in the Walnut Room.

December 26

1908   Jack Johnson became the first black heavyweight champion, defeating Tommy Burns. Johnson infuriated many whites with his proud manner and relationships with white women.   In 1913, Chicago authorities came after him on a trumped up charge of bringing a woman across state lines for "immoral purposes."   He served time at Leavenworth.

1921   Stephen Valentine Patrick William Allen was born in New York City. He was 18 months old when his father died, and his mother raised him in Chicago. Steve Allen is best remembered as the original host of the "Tonight Show."   But *The Guinness Book of World's Records* recognizes him as the most prolific composer of modern times. He composed over 8,500 songs.

1974   Jack Benny died of pancreatic cancer at the age of 80. A middle school in his hometown of Waukegan is named in his honor. The football team is named the 39ers, as a nod to Jack's repeated claims that he was 39 years old. In June 2002, the town dedicated a statue of Benny in a plaza across from the Genesee Theater, where he performed.

December 27

1944   President Franklin Roosevelt ordered the seizure of Montgomery

Chicago 365

Ward stores in several cities. Company President Sewell Avery had defied a War Labor Board order to renew a union contract and settle a strike. In April, troops had physically removed Avery from his Chicago office. The Army would run the stores until the end of the war.

1968   North Central Airlines Flight 458 from Minneapolis crashed into a hangar while landing at O'Hare Airport. The crash of the twin engine Convair 580 killed 27 people and injured 26 others. The National Transportation Safety Board found that the pilot became disoriented due to the glare of lights through the fog.

1976   The Chicago Civic Center was renamed the Richard J. Daley Center, Richard J. Daley Plaza in honor of the Mayor who died office on December 20 at the age of 84. Daley had originally dedicated the building on May 2, 1966. The plaza is home to the renowned Picasso sculpture. It is simply known as "The Picasso," because the sculptor never got around to naming it.

2002   The movie musical *Chicago* was released. Renée Zellweger, Catherine Zeta-Jones, Richard Gere, John C. Reilly, Christine Baranski, Dominic West, Mya, Queen Latifah, Taye Diggs and Lucy Liu starred in the film, based on the real-life cases of accused killers Belva Gaertner and Beulah Annan. *Tribune* reporter Maurine Watkins turned the story of their sensational trials into the original play.

December 28

1956   Teenaged sisters Barbara and Patricia Grimes left their Damen Avenue home to see *Love Me Tender* at the Brighton Theater. They were never seen alive again. Their nude bodies were found beside a road near Willow Springs on January 22, 1957. As in the 1955 murder of the Schuessler and Peterson boys, political infighting between the agencies involved compromised the investigation. The case remains unsolved.

1963   A. J. Liebling died in New York City at the age of 59. In 1949, he coined the term "Second City" to refer to Chicago in a book based on his somewhat derisive series of *New Yorker* articles. "Chicago is unique," Liebling wrote, "It is the only completely corrupt city in America." He also said that Chicago "seems a big city instead of merely a large place."

1998   The Bears fired coach Dick Wannstedt after the team finished 4-12 for a second straight season. The Bears would announce the hiring of Arizona defensive coordinator Dave McGinnis as the new coach before a contract was finalized. An irritated McGinnis withdrew his name from consideration and the team turned to Dick Jauron, Jacksonville defensive coordinator and former Packers assistant coach.

December 29

1905   Transit baron Charles Tyson Yerkes died in New York. Yerkes gained a virtual monopoly of the transit system in Chicago by bribing aldermen and built the "Loop" elevated railroad. He provided the money for the Yerkes Observatory and helped ensure that the Columbian Exposition would be held in Chicago. He went on to head the syndicate that built the London Underground.

1913   The first movie serial premiered in Chicago. Selig's Polyscope Company released *The Unwelcome Throne*, the first of 13 installments of the serial *The Adventures of Kathlyn*. Kathlyn Williams starred in the films. The *Tribune* co-produced the pictures and also printed "The Adventures of Kathlyn" in serial form.

1963   On a brutally cold day at Wrigley Field, The Bears intercepted New York Giants quarterback Y.A. Tittle five times and clinched their first NFL championship since 1946. The 14-10 win gave the Bears their seventh and last championship under "Papa Bear" George Halas. Mike Ditka was one of the Bears top receivers in the game and quarterback Bill Wade ran for two touchdowns.

1992   David and Sharon Schoo of St. Charles, Illinois were arrested as they stepped off a plane at O'Hare International Airport. They had left their nine and four-year-old daughters home alone for nine days while they went on vacation in Acapulco. As a result of the case, the legislature passed the "Home Alone" bill, which made it a criminal offense to abandon a child. The Schoos later gave their daughters up for adoption.

December 30

1847   John Peter Altgeld was born in Germany. Altgeld served as Governor of Illinois from 1893 to 1897 and is best remembered for his heroic pardon of the men wrongly convicted in connection with the Haymarket bombing. The pardons ruined his political career. Altgeld also spoke out against President Grover Cleveland's order sending federal troops to Chicago during the 1894 Pullman Strike.

1903 A standing room only crowd of 1,900 was enjoying a holiday matinee performance of *Blue Beard Junior* at the Iroquois Theater when a hot light sent flames licking up a drape. The star of the show, Eddie Floyd, tried to calm the audience. But the fire engulfed the stage. An asbestos fire curtain stuck before it could be fully lowered. Someone opened a stage door and the air swept in, fanning the flames over the heads of the terrified audience. They stampeded toward locked exits and bodies were soon piled ten feet high. In 15 minutes, at least 602 people lost their lives. Of those victims, 212 were children.

The disaster spurred adoption of fire safety laws for theatres, but no one was ever convicted in connection with the disaster. The building at 24-28 West Randolph re-opened less than a year later as the Colonial Theater. The Oriental theatre, now the Ford Center for the Performing Arts, now stands on the site.

1918 Alphonse Capone married Mary "Mae" Coughlin in New York. They had met at a dance, and Mae gave birth to a son on December 4, 1918. Not long after the wedding, Capone beat up an Irish gang leader who was insulting Italians. The Irish gang was seeking revenge, so Al took a position at a nightclub owned by his friend Johnny Torrio. The club was called the Four Deuces, and it was in Chicago.

December 31

1855 Officials announced all streets and buildings would be raised by up to 14 feet to bring Chicago out of the mucky marsh. A joke of the day told of a man on the street stuck in mud up to his head. "No thanks," he said to offers of help, "I have a horse under me." George Pullman raised buildings by using hundreds of men turning huge jackscrews. He used the fortune he made to begin building railroad sleeping cars.

1913 Charles Weeghman signed a lease for property at Clark and Addison formerly occupied by The Theological Seminary of the

Evangelical Lutheran Church. Weegham built a ballpark for his Federal League team on the site. The first game was played there on April 23, 1914, as the Federals beat Kansas City 9-1. Federals catcher Art Wilson hit the first home run in the stadium we now know as Wrigley Field.

1920 The $10 million Drake Hotel opened at Michigan and Lake Shore Drive with a gala New Year's Eve party. Self-taught architect Ben Marshall designed the 13-story hotel, which contains details copied from Italian palaces. Notables who have stayed there include Queen Elizabeth II, Prince Philip and Princess Diana, King Hussein, Winston Churchill, Eleanor Roosevelt, and Charles Lindbergh.

1978 Another 15 inches of snow paralyzed the city. A record 89.7 inches would fall that winter. Mayor Bilandic came under fire for the city's response and because Deputy Mayor Kenneth Sain had been paid $90,000 for a snow removal plan apparently copied from a Roosevelt University masters thesis. In February, disgusted voters turned against the Democratic machine and elected Jane Byrne as mayor.

Chicago 365

Selected Bibliography

Adams, Rosemary K., ed. *A Wild Kind of Boldness: The Chicago History Reader*. Chicago: Chicago Historical Society, 1998

Adrienne Drell, ed. *20th Century Chicago: 100 years, 100 voices*. Chicago Sun-Times, 2000

Ahrens, Art and Gold, Eddie. *Day by Day in Chicago Cubs History*. Chicago: Leisure Press, 1982.

Berke, Art and Paul Schmidt. *This Date in Chicago White Sox History*. New York, Stein and Day, 1982

Chicago Tribune. *Chicago Days: 150 Defining Moments in the Life of a Great City*. Chicago: Catigny First Division Foundation, 1997

Chicago Tribune: Various issues

Ciccone, F. Richard. *Chicago and the American Century*. Chicago: Contemporary Books, 1999

Furer, Howard B., ed. *Chicago: a Chronological and Documentary History: 1784-1970*. Dobbs Ferry, New York: Oceana Publications, 1974

Kirkland, Joseph. *The Story of Chicago*. Chicago: Bibble, 1892-1894

Lindberg, Richard. *Return to the Scene of the Crime: A Guide to Infamous Places in Chicago*. Nashville: Cumberland House Publishing, 1999

Lindberg, Richard with Williams, Biart. *The Armchair Companion to Chicago Sports*. Nashville: Cumberland House, 1997

Miller, Donald L. *City of the Century: The Epic of Chicago and the Making of America*. New York: Simon and Schuster, 1996

Sawyers, June Skinner. *Chicago Portraits: Biographies of 250 Famous Chicagoans*. Chicago: Loyola University 1991

Schoenberg, Robert J. *Mr. Capone: The Real and Complete Story of Al Capone*. New York: William Morrow and Company, 1992

Steele, Tim. *The Cubs Chronology*. St. Louis: Stellar Press, 2003

Selected Web Sites

www.baseballlibrary.com
www.bulls.com
www.chicagohs.com
www.state.il.us
www.richsamuels.com
www.wgnradio.com

www.brainyhistory.com
www.chicagoblackhawks.com
www.chipublib.org
www.prairieghosts.com
www.todayinsci.tripod.com
www.wlshistory.com

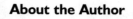

Chicago 365

About the Author

Joe Sonderman is a 1980 graduate of Hazelwood West High School who still lives in Hazelwood, Missouri with his wife Lorraine, and daughters Cathy and Kim. He has worked in St. Louis media for nearly 20 years, including stints as an air personality and music director for KHTR and KLOU. (103.3 FM) For nine years he worked as a traffic reporter, mainly on KMOX. He currently works at KMOX as a production assistant.

Joe is a passionate Route 66 historian and collector. His archive of postcards from "The Mother Road" is on line at www.greetingsfrom66.com. He spends his time in a home filled with Route 66 and St. Louis memorabilia, or driving Route 66 in his 1957 Chevrolet.